Forms and Substances
in the Arts

by Etienne Gilson

ETIENNE GILSON

Translated from the French by
SALVATOR ATTANASIO

Forms and Substances
in the Arts

Charles Scribner's Sons   New York

Printed in the United States of America
Library of Congress Catalog Card Number 66-24495

CONTENTS

"As a productive faculty of cognition, the imagination is endowed with the great power of creating another nature, as it were, out of the material that actual nature gives it."

IMMANUEL KANT:
Critique of Judgment #49

Introduction

THE OBJECT OF THIS BOOK is to test the validity of the general and abstract conclusions arrived at in *The Arts of the Beautiful*. The test will be made only with respect to what might be called the major arts, that is to say, those to which the other arts are ultimately reduced upon analysis and which are but combinations of the major arts. It is rare, moreover, to encounter a major art in its pure state, and when such an opportunity arises it is difficult to define the essence of an art of this kind in its absolute purity. Expressions such as pure poetry, pure painting, pure music, chiefly denote arenas in which the friends of the fine arts obviously find pleasure in taking each other's measure, but the philosopher's purpose is to separate into distinct concepts a real complex which rightly resists division into its components. Our only concern therefore is to prepare an intelligible frame into which all the particular kinds of beauty produced by each major art may find a place, including even those arts which are still the secret of the future.

This book should contain all the information necessary to make it intelligible to the reader, but it is only fair

1

to warn him in advance that he will often encounter expressions such as "the beautiful" and "beauty." Today such words suffice to discredit a philosophy in the minds of those who, by confusing the philosophy of art with metaphysics, imagine "the beautiful" as a sort of ideal category, a transcendent and immutable thing in itself, which the artist is duty-bound to imitate. Nothing of this sort is here in question. Beauty is a property inseparable from being, hence it is proper to every work of art; the function of art, moreover, is to produce, not to imitate. We shall never depart from concrete reality here save to extract from it those concepts which alone enable us to reflect upon reality. The task as such is difficult enough and subject to possible errors. Our hope is that none will be added to those which the book actually contains. For this hope to be fulfilled, all the reader has to do is to understand the book in terms of the concepts to which it refers, as we have set them forth. It should be possible to understand these concepts without necessarily being in agreement with them.

We shall cite some of the concepts which will be taken for granted here, if not approved, inasmuch as they have been studied individually elsewhere. It is only a matter of plainly stating some theoretical positions which shall be posited throughout this study.

The first is the distinction between calology, the philosophy of art, and esthetics. Calology is a part of metaphysics, whose subject-matter is the beautiful as a transcendental of being. Hence, it is a branch of ontology. Being, insofar as it partakes of the beautiful, goes far beyond the field of art. We do not propose to discuss being in this sense here. Esthetics is the apprehension of the beautiful as produced by the fine arts. I do not know whether or not this discipline is a science; in any case I have never been able to find access to it. The philosophy of art, if the arts of the beautiful are in question, has as its object human activity in the general order of *making*, whose proper end is to produce beautiful objects. These objects are commonly known as "works of art." Our assumption here is that both disciplines share a common concern with the work of art itself, but that they are in actuality distinct. They are connected disciplines, inasmuch as they have the work of art in common, but they are as distinct from each other as making is from knowing, the end of art being to produce a work, whereas esthetics presupposes its completion. Art terminates in a work of art, esthetic apprehension makes this terminus its point of departure. The two disciplines are as different as writing a symphony is from listening to one. Art alone will be under discussion here, considerations answerable to esthetics will figure in this study only as concrete experiences facilitating our understanding of art.

The book's very title implies acceptance of the classic distinction in philosophy between matter and form. At the outset the objection can be raised that this principle, by virtue of its applicability to everything, actually explains nothing. That is true, at least in the sense that by itself it does not suffice to explain anything.

Our principal intention has been to determine, as precisely as the subject matter allows, the structural elements of form not only in the arts of the beautiful but in each one of the major arts whose proper function is to fashion this form.

The word form does not suggest a very precise image to the mind. Among the twenty-five meanings or usages of the word in Littré's dictionary, none particularly applies to the work of art. André Lalande's authoritative *Vocabulaire* notes first of all that "this term is almost always opposed to matter" and follows it with an example illustrating its specific meaning: "A. Geometric figure consisting of the contours of an object. It is opposed to the matter of which this object is made. 'Wax takes the form of the seal.' " By broadening this notion to the limits of its generality and extending it to works of art, its meaning might also be described as that arrangement which makes the parts of a whole out of a plurality of elements and thereby structures the latter into a distinct object. This is one of the meanings that confirms the scholastic adage: *Forma dat esse*. Without pushing as far as the metaphysical ground of the formula, manifestly we speak of a being only when we can grasp a plurality in a principle of unity which is precisely its form. This can be the form of a concept, of a mode of reasoning, of a tree, of an animal, or of a man; it can also be that of a work of art. To say that a symphony, a poem or any book is "formless" is tantamount to denying its existence. This being settled, it remains for us to determine the nature of form in each particular work of art. Strictly speaking, form is proper to each art, and its discernment in the very process of perceiving it is what is called "understanding" a work of art. A critic has a hard job to determine whether a work lacks form or whether he fails to perceive it. Even an artist would find it equally difficult to discuss particular cases, for no two are alike, but we can try to distinguish the general types of forms proper to some of the fine arts. We shall not aim further.

This attempt, moreover, will lead us directly to the concept of matter, itself viewed as the kind of plurality which all artistry knows how to submit to the unity of form. All material substances are given in nature or made from natural products. Hence any art involves the use of substances of this type, but what we shall have to say about it presupposes the recognition of a truth which might be called Focillon's law: *the material substances of nature*

establish a new order upon becoming the material sub-
stances of art. This is a truth of major importance in the
philosophy of art, but seemingly it is a hopeless task to try
to convince those who have not been convinced by direct
evidence or by reading Focillon's *The Life of Forms in
Art.*[1] In this respect nothing can replace the third chapter
of this book in which Focillon formulates two principles
that complement each other. The first principle states that
"all different kinds of matter are subject to a certain destiny, or at all events, to a certain formal vocation"; the
second that the materials an artist uses for his proper ends
establish a new order "even when they are bound together
by the strictest formal propriety." The material substances
of nature and those of art constitute two distinct realms
"even if technical devices and manufacturers are not introduced." Indeed, all the *physical qualities* of a material
substance enter into the work of art only on the strength
of their *plastic qualities.* They no longer are only constitutive elements of being in the work of art but, more accurately, of being informed with beauty.

We shall come upon these notions again in a more
concrete context, but I thought it would be useful to in-
scribe them as an exergue, so to speak, at the beginning
of this work. Whatever the reader may think of this book,
I suspect that he will inevitably interrupt his reading to
make some reservation, to add a finer nuance, or merely to
deny an assertion. I did this so often while writing the
book and trying to keep it within its proper frame that I
fail to see how others can avoid doing likewise. The fact
is that in matters of art, more than elsewhere, it is hardly
possible to avoid seeming to confuse what one has not distinguished, or to separate what one does distinguish. Every-

1. Trs. by Charles Beecher Hogan and George Kubler, Yale
University Press, New Haven, 1942.

thing is given as a whole and the philosopher perforce must distinguish what art itself might try to render all at once. That is his trade. The friends of art do not need the philosopher to tell them that one can create beauty out of almost nothing, or lay before her an enormous amount of the most opulent materials and that, at times, the same artist does both successively, or dreams of doing so. There is not a single art which does not use other arts as materials without the least concern for the purity of essence which the philosopher must strive to extract because "quiddity" is the primary if not the ultimate object of his concern. The artist is free; no one is authorized to prescribe rules for him, nor impose upon him limits. The artist alone knows what *he wants to do,* and although the work almost always falls short of the desired end, partial success or failure are the only conceivable sanctions of his work. They come too late to affect it, and they are so uncertain that it is very difficult to say something intelligible about them. Be that as it may, I hope I have not provided any pretext for condemning or despising any particular work of art; I would like to be able to love them all, and I certainly have no intention of spoiling the pleasure others derive from some works of art which my own limitations often prevent me from enjoying. I merely wanted to put my own ideas into some kind of order; I hope too that I have avoided the spirit of controversy that flares up so easily over these matters; if on occasion I have taken the positions of others into consideration, it was only for the purpose of establishing my own more solidly. There are always several possible orders; it is hard enough to pursue one and altogether impossible to pursue several of them simultaneously.

Above all, I hope I shall not be taken unduly to task for having adopted a point of view toward art that may be

considered too narrow. Actually I had to take great pains
to keep it within its proper limits. Only a powerful metaphysical genius can attempt the synthesis of all aspects of
art, including the artist and the lover of art. Hegel was
such a genius. He was well aware of the inadequacy of the
term esthetics as a designation for the object of his study.
Rightly, Hegel saw the cause of this in the German school
of Christian Wolff, in which art was considered from the
point of view of the impression it produces on the beholder. He accepted the term, however, reserving to himself the right to determine exactly its different possible
meanings in the course of his work: "These lectures are
devoted to esthetics. Their subject is the broad realm of
the beautiful, in particular the field of art and more precisely the fine arts." Thus esthetics, calology and the philosophy of art are posited as a whole. We might prefer
another attitude with regard to the problems of art, but
since Hegel did exactly what he wanted to do, what right
do we have to pick a quarrel with him? Moreover, a great
mind always finds something interesting to say, whatever
the point of view. Thus Hegel deems the beauty of art to
be superior to that of nature, because it is the work of the
spirit. The assertion ties in too neatly with the requirements of his system not to be slightly disquieting, but it is
interesting. Is it true? I don't know too much about it and
I am not even sure that it does not compare two realities
that defy comparison, but what is beyond question is that
the presence of the mind is included in the apprehension
of a work of art, and Hegel forbids us to forget it. Furthermore, he defines the origin of art as "the rational impulse
man feels to raise his inner world and that of nature to
spiritual consciousness, to make of it an object in which he
recognizes himself." The definition is somewhat too broad
for what is being defined. Personally, what impresses me in

a work of art is the work itself and not myself. But can we say that Hegel is mistaken? His definition is loose, but it is not erroneous. But why should we prolong the discussion further in the course of which all truth would disappear?

No work on esthetics will ever match the brevity of Benedetto Croce's article, published separately under the title of "Esthetics in a Nutshell": *Aesthetics in nuce*. What a virtuoso! We sense that these pages literally flowed off the tip of his pen and that he felt no need to ponder over them. Yet nothing is missing, despite its brevity. In fifty-eight pages, we learn what art or poetry is and what it is not; the article contains a definition of "the science of art or esthetics," intuition and expression, expression and communication, "the theory of the particular arts and natural beauty," literary and artistic genres, esthetic categories, rhetoric, the grammar and the philosophy of language, classicism and romanticism, artistic-literary criticism and historiography. Even the history of esthetics is not forgotten and a relevant bibliography is added for good measure. Who would make himself ridiculous by complaining? If this panoramic view makes one dizzy, each one is free to choose a vantage point therein that especially suits him. Discoursing on the philosophy of art, one can even bestow upon himself the originality of making art the center of his philosophical reflections.

It would even be more fruitless to kindle a controversy here on the nature of art itself. In his excellent essay on *The Life and Work of Ravaisson,* Henri Bergson attributes the following formula to Ravaisson, although it is hard to say whether it actually originated with him or with Bergson: "It is the same intuition, differently utilized, which makes the profound philosopher or the great artist." This formula gives me the great satisfaction of stating exactly the opposite of what I believe to be true. If it were used as a point of departure, there would no longer be agreement on anything; there is no point in discussing it, but it is useful to bear it in mind, for if they are not the "same intuition," these two intuitions perhaps share a resemblance in their respective depths. In distinguishing characteristics, let us remember not always to set them in opposition.

Similar remarks would have a bearing on the opinions that we can entertain of philosophies of art with which we do not agree when the latter are formulated in the name of a general philosophy to which one lays claim. Philosophies of art have been derived from the doctrine of Saint Thomas of Aquinas. They should be ascribed to Thomism rather than be derived from it. As far as I know, Saint Thomas said almost nothing about the arts of the beautiful as such. His writings contain neither a philosophy of art nor an esthetic. All we find in them are the elements of a calology which might have been suggested to him by a reading of the Neo-Platonist Dionysius the Areopagite, but the metaphysics of the beautiful is part of the ontology; it goes beyond art in every respect. We also find in Saint Thomas's writings a definition of art which has wrought great havoc, even though it was not intended to define art as such, and even less the art of the beautiful, but rather to distinguish it from ethics. This is clearly seen in the stereotyped character of the formula, for it speaks of making (*facere*) only to distinguish it from acting in general (*agere*), and Saint Thomas is obviously more interested in the latter than in the former. Unquestionably art for him is an intellectual virtue. Moral prudence is also a virtue, but of another order: *"ars est recta ratio factibilium; prudentia vero est recta ratio agibilium"* (S.T., 1-II, 57, 4 Resp.). And that is true, for can we conceive of any human activity which is not presided over by a virtue, or of a human operation which is not finally conducted, judged and regulated by the intellect? The intellect digests, according to Albert Magnus. This is a useful admonition to those who would array art against reason, or even separate them. But Saint Thomas was not interested in art as factivity; his primary concern was to avoid confusion between the role of reason in art and in ethics. He said nothing about the art of the beautiful as factivity. As a theologian there was no reason for him to discuss it; let us not reproach him therefore for his silence on this matter.

It is legitimate to talk about it when making use of Thomas's name, but in that case it is more prudent to refer to a concept of art formulated by a philosopher who was really concerned with art and to whose authority Saint Thomas himself appeals everywhere, namely Aristotle. Reason is not absent in his concept, but it occupies its proper place in it, art being viewed as a *virtus factiva cum ratione* or *exis poietika meta logou,* which is very different, for it is the *poietique* or productive essence of art which imparts its meaning to the definition. By failing to go back to Aristotle from Saint Thomas, great minds have created an esthetics *ex nihilo Thomism* which they have placed under his authority. This is proof that Thomism lives on, or more simply, that thought never dies. But we have seen artists, naively trusting in the competence of philosophers, who perplexedly compare their personal experience of art with what the rationalist theories of this type say about it, and become troubled because they have not recognized in them the face of art.

There is some substance here. Like all sculptors, Eric Gall was a workman. Modelling was not enough for him, he wanted to be a stone-carver not by imparting form to the block but by extracting it from within the stone itself. In any case, for him the hand was no doubt the pre-

eminent tool and in his view art should make use of it.
Imagine his surprise when he came upon the assertion
"manual dexterity does not belong to art" written by
philosophers whom he admired, trusted and whose views
he hoped to share. He must have thought he was dreaming.
For after all, if manual dexterity has nothing to do with
art, what does the art of sculpture, of painting, or that of
playing any musical instrument consist of? We can easily
recognize in this lofty contempt for the hand that eight-
eenth-century rationalism which, though it bore the mark
of greatness and was beneficent in some respects, was no
less maleficent in others. Behind excesses of this kind there
generally lies more "jeandesainthomisme" than genuine
Thomism. Jean de Saint Thomas perhaps thought that it
was necessary merely to remove what was of excess in a
block of stone in order to obtain the statue. There is no
doubt that he did think, inasmuch as he wrote it, that the
work of learning to play the guitar—to acquire "fingers"—
does not bring a new art into being, but merely eliminates
the obstacle to its exercise. Let us grant that finger-
dexterity in playing the piano is not an art different from
that of playing the piano; it is an improvement of the same
art, but how are we to conclude therefrom that this art
does not essentially involve manual dexterity? By the same
token, all we would have to do in order to be able to play
Chopin's *Préludes* is to understand thoroughly Alfred
Cortot's instructions on how to play them. Unfortunately,
Cortot also prescribes finger exercises appropriate to each
prelude. As is the case with Debussy's *Les tierces alternées,*
the ability to play them calls for more than being intelligent.

"Art stands wholly on the side of the mind." All we
can do in the presence of such absolute certainty is to turn
to account the light that such a statement sheds on so

many real aspects of art which otherwise we would risk missing, or losing sight of. When reality has reached this degree of complexity, no particular aspect of truth suffices. If one excludes the body from the essence of art, the reason may be to spare us from making the mistake of excluding the mind from it. There is nothing more intelligent than the fingers of a pianist except, perhaps, the body of a dancer. Art, nevertheless, does not stand wholly on the side of the mind. The role played by the mind depends more or less upon the art involved, playing a greater role in architecture and poetry, and a lesser one in sculpture and in the execution of musical compositions, but *making,* which is the very essence of art, is brought to bear in the body and through it. But, again, what would be the point of kindling useless controversy? Even notions with which we do not wholly agree challenge us to do our utmost to avoid running the risk of losing sight of the least possible glimmer of truth.

After *Painting and Reality* (1958) and *The Arts of the Beautiful* (1963), this makes the third book that I have devoted to the philosophy of art. It will also be the last one, for even though I have been happy to have had the time to expound what others do not seem to have expounded sufficiently, I know that I have nothing useful to add. Further elaborations would be endless and all of us can make our own contributions. I have been saying but one thing, the art of the artist and what we say about it do not belong to the same order. I would like to add the order of art, which is neither to know nor to act but to make, to the Pascalian doctrine of the specificity of "orders." I am under no illusion that I am making a world-shaking revelation with this platitude, but I do want to invite those concerned with the arts to take it into consideration. Personally, it is above all a question of

paying a debt of gratitude. Some artists have become
rich, which is very good. Others were born rich, which
is even better. Up to now no one has given proper attention to the specific characteristics of the literature produced by *rentiers*. However, by far the majority of artists
have lived in uncertainty, in doubt, in travail, surrounded
by the indifference of a society which, without really being
at fault, condemns them to a kind of solitude. Indeed,
artists do not work for society. Their sights are set
higher, but it is for each one of us they toil. I was
prompted to write on art out of a deep, indeed passionate
feeling of gratitude toward artists, known and unknown,
whose works have enriched and enhanced life for me.
Often, they have even justified it in my own eyes. Upon
reading a beautiful line of verse, viewing or listening to
a beautiful work, how many times have I said to myself,
"After one has done something like this, one can die with
the certitude that living was worthwhile!" We know this,
but the artist himself is rarely altogether sure of it.
Hence we owe him this avowal. The artist is irreplaceable
in the exercise of his beneficent function. And the philosopher must be excused for having wanted to express his
thanks to him with the cumbersomeness that is inseparable from his own function.

I hope no one will find any cause for controversy in
the following pages. Originally, I had planned to answer
some objections in a special chapter at the end of the
work, but I concluded that any effort to dispel misunderstandings would only create additional ones. Some critics
have been offended by some of the positions I have taken.
I think they have misunderstood me. I said that criticism
has no bearing on art, but rather on the apprehension of
the work of art. The object which the critic sets out to
describe cannot be the work produced by the artist, but

what he thinks of it. The critic does not produce art but criticism, and the object of his activity does not pertain to art but to esthetics. This is the reason, moreover, why critics and estheticians most often refuse to distinguish between the two orders, inasmuch as their only chance to remain within the order of art is by blurring the lines of demarcation. But I think that they misapprehend the nature of the merit that is uniquely theirs and the meaning of what I say about it.

I have steeped myself in Sainte-Beuve. For me his substantial *Literary Comedy* has been what Montaigne's *Essays* have been for so many others. Sainte-Beuve suffered enough over the fact that he was not one of his own heroes so that we should not add to his suffering by attributing a confusion of this kind to him. How often we see him prepare a modest but honored place in his criticism for those demi-poets or demi-novelists among whom he hoped he would be accorded a rank some day! But at bottom he knew very well that Hugo was the poet, not Joseph Delorme. The excellent Charles du Bos, a more subtle critic, would have liked to persuade himself that to understand is to make equal. Therefore, he looked for elysium of the spirit in a kind of general spirituality in which elect critics, writers of genius and some inspired great men in all the arts would find a common homeland. He was laboring under a delusion. The artist really is interested only in what he is making, and in others only in their capacity as makers. They alone are his real family. The others are not strictly in his class, as it were, and count for little in his eyes. Who understood Delacroix better than Baudelaire? Who honored him more nobly? Who served him more intelligently? Yet there is scarcely any evidence of the slightest expression of gratitude on the part of the painter toward his eminent critic. Perhaps this widespread indifference translates into facts a profound truth, namely that of the radical distinction between orders that face each other. We will never be able to produce the least of La Fontaine's fables with all of the writings of Sainte-Beuve, Francesco de Sanctis and Charles du Bos taken together. It is not a question here of measuring degrees but, simply, of discerning orders.

There remains the large family of professors of philosophy, to which I belong, and of the professors of esthetics, to which I do not flatter myself I belong. I realize that any philosophy treating of art must expect to receive special attention from them. Some professors of esthetics have attributed to me absurdities so manifest, without, moreover, citing any supporting evidence, that these absurdities would merit being taken as subjects for study in themselves. One possible explanation for these inventions, perhaps, is that one always disturbs a philosopher by thinking differently from him. In the presence of a thought different from his own, a *reductio ad absurdum* suffices to liberate him from his disquietude. This catharsis may be useful, but hardly necessary. To suggest a certain philosophical interpretation of the arts of the beautiful does not imply disapproval of other interpretations. Hence no one should be disturbed by what I have to say. In my efforts to order my own ideas and to submit them to the judgment of others, I expressly accord the same freedom to them.

O N E

The Distinction Between the Arts of the Beautiful

PARADOXICALLY, ONE OF Alain's primary concerns in his work entitled *Systems of the Fine Arts* was to ascertain that the fine arts as such do not constitute a system.[1]

1. Alain's book is an excellent example of a book that one delights in reading and with whose author one likes to engage in a secret dialogue, but which it would be futile to discuss; for if its thesis is granted, everything is justifiable, and if it is not granted disagreement is inevitable on much of the detail. As far as I understand, Alain intends to take the arts of the beautiful as they are brought to bear in fact in the complexity of their concrete works. This provides him with ample material in which to display his taste for reflection and exercise his style. It is exactly the opposite of *venatio essentiae*. The two enterprises seem legitimate to me, but we would waste our time judging one from the point of view of the other. As has already been done in connection with another book, I simply permit myself to point out how far off the mark is the attempt to make Alain into a kind of modern Socrates. Socrates did not write anything. Moreover, ancient testimonies are agreed in attributing to him one major concern exemplified in his response each time to a question: "What are we talking about?" or, "What do you mean by this word?" Alain perhaps is wise to show reserve on this point, for he is not sure that all things are definable, but

They are not deducible from some general notion, first posited by the mind, which would furnish its own subdivisions. Assuredly, the poietic or productive activity from which they derive is one in its origin as in its general effects, but it varies in its particular effects according to the material substances on which it is brought to bear. These materials cannot be ordered into a system; they are simply what they are, and given the organs of cognition and movement at man's disposal he can utilize them to produce beauty.

It is the intellect's love of order therefore that tempts philosophers to organize the fine arts into some system in which the necessity of the whole would confer a kind of *a priori* justification upon each one of the arts. This same love of order invites them to attempt a classification of the arts of the beautiful, for classification is possible only on the basis of an ordering principle of some kind. But logical order exists only between ideas or between things which can be treated as ideas by reducing them, directly or indirectly, to an idea among others. It will be seen that such is not the case with the fine arts. *Homo artifex,* who is but a remarkable variety of *Homo faber,* is hardly less ancient than *Homo sapiens* and *Homo loquens.* He is the selfsame man, and he has left us evidence of his poietic creativity in the order of the beautiful which antedates by far those which enable us to attribute an articulated language to him. History begins with writing, but man sculpted and painted long before he wrote, and he began very early to make plastic objects with the usable materials at hand. Cave art includes sculptured, engraved objects decorated with line drawings of a formal perfection at times surprising, as well as broad painted wall surfaces

I have often observed how difficult it was to catch him red-handed making definitions in the matter of the arts.

where a concern with composition is revealed in the arrangement of the figures. The manner in which these are ordered in the space that nature placed at the artist's disposal clearly shows that so-called "pre-historic" man was already pretty much like ourselves; placed in front of a bare wall, he felt the urge to cover it with figures in his own fashion according to the possibilities offered by the free space and the available means for decorating it. It will be objected that he had ends in view other than those of creating "art," and that is no doubt true, but whether the ends he had in mind were of a magical, religious or practical character, the artist of Altamira certainly intended to pursue such ends through painting. This is what makes him essentially a kinsman of modern painters.

No serious hypothesis can be advanced regarding the possible character of the arts of language or of sound at the time when man was decorating the walls of his cave-dwellings. Even less probable is the conjecture that these remote ancestors already exercised their voices, as infants in the cradle still do today. Besides, the history of the fine arts is alien to our present purpose. We wish merely to note that the arts have their origins in an ensemble of empirically given possibilities which, on the one hand, are determined by the organs of the human body proper to cognition and movement, and, on the other, by the physical properties of certain material substances. Man invents as many fine arts as he finds in the nature of the different material substances suitable for being worked on through the natural means at his disposal. Before long he will supplement these natural means by tools appropriate to the materials that are to be worked on and by the invention of new materials which, if need be, will be manufactured with art and art's end in view. New arts are possibly yet to be born. If so, this will be effected in a wholly empirical manner and in keeping with the development of art itself, or of industry. What is striking, in any case, is the fact that some major arts have been practiced since the beginnings of the historical age and that no new major art has been invented since the Greeks.

In default of systemizing the arts, we can try to classify them. Classification is absolutely necessary if the arts are to be discussed in an orderly way. The problem, moreover, offers philosophers a prime occasion to be at variance not only over the manner of classifying the arts but, first of all, over those works which it is opportune to classify. What are works of art and how many kinds are there? Disagreement sets in from the start of the discussion. The reasons for this are multiple, but one of the principal ones seems to be the confusion that exists, intentional or not, between the meaning of the word "art" in the expression "fine-arts" and the meaning ascribed to it when it is used as an equivalent of "technique." Perhaps there is no need to talk about confusion here, for the word art, in French and English, is a continuation of the Latin *ars* whose meaning is tantamount to that of the Greek word which we have made *technique*. Any technique is an art and, when it is understood in this sense, the word inevitably brings to mind the definition of art so dear to the scholastics: *recta ratio factibilium*. The formula suggests the notion of a rule for making something well. Obviously every art of the beautiful involves rules of this kind; there is a technique, or more simply a "know-how," in each of the arts whose end is to produce objects. Only those whose purpose is to produce objects desired for their beauty alone have a right to the title of fine arts, but it happens in fact that some techniques employed for ends other than the production of the beautiful surreptitiously creep into the general tableau of the fine arts. Hence the confusions which, perhaps, are not all avoidable.

So many are the bonds connecting these two orders of operations, in which one contains the other as genus does the species, that an exact demarcation is difficult. Such a demarcation, perhaps, is not even desirable. Yet philosophical reflection must apply itself to it and can do this only by distinguishing the fine arts from the other techniques in general terms of the proper ends which they pursue. All techniques are operating rules, each one of which determines a way of making something well, whereas the fine arts are ways of setting about properly for making something beautiful. Now any work that is well done has its own beauty inasmuch as it is well done, its beauty being the resultant of the perfect adaptation of the means to the end. We call it a "beautiful piece of work." Saint Augustine's lost treatise *De pulchro et apto* may have had something to say about this genre of beauty. Be it as it may, this distinction clearly implies that a fine art, to the extent that it presupposes a technique, includes a knowledge of the operating rules in default of which a successful execution would be difficult or impossible. Tricks of the trade and the knack of doing something well are never enough, but they are everywhere necessary. The most exceptional natural gifts, the loftiest genius, cannot dispense with "know-how" and dexterity in any art.

The inclusion of the techniques of good workmanship in the arts of the beautiful is no warrant for confusing them. Hence we should be wary of the tendency to classify among the fine arts mere perfection in the application of any technique and in the results it obtains, for in such a case the result is always beautiful, but it does not necessarily follow that the art which produces it is one of the fine arts. It was a mistake, I think, to have wanted to include ballroom dancing, horsemanship and fencing, acrobatics, and even military parades in a system of the fine arts. Indeed, there are elements of the beautiful in the movements of a good dancer, in the way a good horseman holds himself in the saddle or simply in the way he puts his mount through the paces, just as there are in the precision and grace of a well-executed military parade or in a gymnastic feat performed with ease. There is no less beauty, moreover, in the movements of the carpenter, the blacksmith, the laborer and the sower. Generally speaking, we cannot remain insensitive to the artistry involved in the practice of all sports which impose on the body the discipline and rhythm required for the proper execution of movements. Yet, even though the result is beautiful, beauty is not the end on which this discipline sets its sights. To dance well, to play well, to bear oneself well in society are the arts of gracious living whose aim is the perfection of what one is. A good military parade is a beautiful parade but its ends are always discipline, the assertion of order, the repeated drilling of the troops; in short, the primary concern is the command of armies. They are not the operations of an art whose end is beauty.

A second cause of confusion is due to the fact that these kinds of beauty, albeit of a different order, have in common the attribute of being kinds of beauty that are desirable as such and capable of being grasped at the same time in a single and self-same experience. Taken together they are perceived as a single beauty. This explains why in the work of art we do not distinguish clearly between the pleasure we derive from the natural beauty of the model, and that produced in us by the art of the sculptor or the painter. A fine horseman resembles his statue, a beautiful portrait makes us believe that we are beholding the natural beauty of the model, with the result that each individual beauty nourishes the other to produce the greatest visual pleasure. The same observation applies to the utilitarian arts. Perfection in the adaptation of ends to means with a practical end of any kind in view is accompanied by a beauty of its own which is, so to speak, the natural beauty of the products of factivity. This industrial beauty is even closer to that of nature than is the beauty of the fine arts. Advertising experts know how to exploit this kinship between the natural beauty of machines and that of the human body. The figure of a graceful young woman standing beside a luxurious motor car, or on the bridge of a ship, or in front of a sleek airliner offers a visual image of harmony to which few remain unresponsive. The quality common to all these kinds of beauty is their gratuitousness. On the other hand, it is difficult to combine felicitously the beauties of nature or of industry with those of the arts whose proper end is beauty itself. The beauty of a machine is in some way natural to it, like that which accompanies the right proportions of a human body, but it is always hazardous to confuse an effort that is accessory to beautification with one aiming at good workmanship. The incongruous mixture which results therefrom is rarely a pleasing sight. All too many embellishments work their way into the products of industry on behalf of this miscellany of heterogeneous intentions; in the view of people of taste, these machines which are made to look pretty generally produce an effect that is both distressing and ludicrous. True enough, the taste of the public for whom the industrialist works is often different. Because of his refusal to harmonize with the different ends pursued by other techniques, his error at least aids the observer to perceive the specific character of the technique of the arts of the beautiful.

The situation is not altogether the same with respect to the commonly accepted distinction between the
decorative arts and the fine arts. The decorative arts have
an unchallengeable right to be counted among the company of the fine arts because their end also is the creation
of beauty. But they are in a special class because the
beauty which the decorator intends to produce is of an
accessory character and subordinated to that of a major
work whose end he must serve. Hence it is not possible to
lay down a general rule here. Very few architects are
happy with the embellishments that sculpture presumably
adds to their work. Yet, it is possible to conceive a
collective work in which each decorator would exactly
follow the intention of the master-workman, and would
integrate the product of his art seamlessly with the ensemble of the project so that the work as a whole would
enjoy a perfect unity of style and a genre of beauty. Such
successes are unfortunately rare. Beautiful statues and
beautiful paintings often spoil beautiful churches; nor is
there a lack of frescoes which actually disfigure walls.
Decorative art abjures itself if it practices self-restraint; on
the other hand, if it boldly asserts itself it betrays its function as a decorative art. A choice must be made. Does not,
perhaps, the profusion of gesticulating statues typical of
some forms of Baroque architecture reveal a secret desire,
as it were, in their creators to see a hesitant architecture
come to a decision and turn resolutely toward sculpture
or architecture rather than remain in a state of bastardy
between the two? Be it as it may, decorative art at its
worst is displaced art; often it is an undesirable art, without it necessarily being the architect's fault, for left to
itself the work is pathetically powerless and nothing pro-
tects it against the uses that are made of it. At rare times,
decoration is so perfectly integrated with the main work

that both become as one. But to effect this perfect fusion, the beauty of the decoration must not be so striking as to obscure the beauty of the whole. If it fulfills its function properly, it is somewhat like the violinist of a quartette who forbids himself to play as a soloist. Thus, as a participant in the beauty of the whole which it adorns, decorative art merits its place among the fine arts.

Some may consider these distinctions useless subtleties. More precisely, they will censure them as evidence of a regrettable tendency to think abstractly in matters where concrete result is paramount. According to them, no object of beauty exists which does not serve some useful purpose, hence why would not a useful object be a work of art, as long as it is beautiful? It is that and also many other things at the same time, but inasmuch as it serves ends other than beauty it does not belong to the fine arts. The *Descent from the Cross,* on view in the Cathedral of Anvers, is first and foremost a painting; in addition, it has become a decorative work serving as ornamentation to a work of architecture; further, it is a work of religious art, a means of teaching sacred history, a tourist attraction because it has a three-star recommendation in the Belgian travel-guides, with all the financial consequences that this privilege entails for the church which contains the painting, the city in which it is found, and for the travel agencies and the hotels catering to tourists. The picture which the artist paints is already in itself the object of an inevitable utilitarian calculation, for the artist lives from art as the priest lives from the altar, indeed much more so, as a general rule. But those who remind the philosopher of these facts only set before him once again the complexity of the real which is the point of departure of his own attempt to analyze and order it. At the beginning of these facts lies the act, bearing no relation to them, with which Rubens long ago executed this celebrated composition. He made his living from his art, and a very good living too. But he had deliberately chosen to live from it as have so many others who, though living in poverty as painters, would have preferred death to any other style of life. Let us recall Van Gogh and Gauguin, among others. It would not be an exaggeration to say that all those who deal with art live from art, except the artists. Art historians and biographers, estheticians, curators of museums, art dealers, in short all those engaged in the more or less profitable exploitation of the artist's work merely exploit the fruits of his genius to their profit. One can earn money from Van Gogh's misery simply by writing a book about it. The function of philosophical analysis remains no less that of extracting from the matrix the essence of the art of the beautiful imprisoned therein. It is found in the act of painting, hence all the rest must be brought into relation with it.

A final cause of the reigning confusion in the classification of the fine arts, which indeed has almost become a rule, is that which considers the philosophy of art and esthetics as identical disciplines. They are, however, two different disciplines. True enough, the work of art is at the center of both, but the philosophy of art considers the work in its relation to the artist who produces it, whereas esthetics considers it in its relation to the spectator, the listener or the reader who perceives it. Two distinct orders are involved here, for the artist is never the spectator of his work while he is working on it, the views that he takes of his work in progress being so many integrating elements of the act of producing them, and the spectator of the work is never its author since the experience that he acquires of it presupposes that the work is fully wrought. When the painter becomes the passive viewer of his picture, it is a sign that it is finished. The work to be done, which is the core of the artist's concern, is specifically different from the work wrought by another on which the reflection of the spectator and of the critic is brought to bear. The object of esthetics is the work of art given in the experience of the person who perceives it; this object can have become wholly different from what it was when it emerged from the artist's hands, and the esthetician has no less a right to take it as it is and to analyze it in terms of his experience of it. On the other hand, what is not given to him is the art which fashioned the work, for he does not possess it and even if he did he too would be as incapable as the artist to repeat the singular, unique act through which the work was produced in the first place. Artistic creation is a freedom structured of freedoms which do not lend themselves to enumeration, for though they are multiple they form but one whose history cannot be told by anybody, not even by the artist, because we know the outcome only after the event, whereas it is of the essence of the creative act that when it is happening the person who lives it is himself ignorant of its end.

The confusion between the philosophy of art and esthetics is ineradicable because it allows the commentators on art the illusion of really participating in the productive efficacy of the artist. Thus they feel themselves on the same side as the artist, like those who sit in the grandstands believe they are sportsmen because they like to watch those who actually engage in them. This is the source of countless difficulties, one of which specifically affects the problem of the classification of the arts, because the philosopher, who tries to distinguish them, naturally substitutes the point of view of the consumer for that of the producer, which he is not. Therefore the resultant classifications are answerable directly to esthetics rather than to the philosophy of art.

Kant's influence was crucial in this respect. *The Critique of Pure Reason* begins with an "esthetic" whose purpose is not to define the experience of the work of art, but rather to determine the conditions of sensible experience in general. These are the two *a priori* forms of the sensibility, space and time. It was inevitable, therefore, that some "estheticians" should decide to distinguish the arts of space from the arts of time by ordering them from the point of view of their apprehension by the subject, to whom the arts are given as objects. Sculpture and painting would be examples of the former, music and poetry would represent the others. But one should have been wary of this all too facile expedient, for in connection with these two forms, Kant himself pointed out that the form of time finally includes that of space. In fact, all apprehension being an act of cognition, even space must accommodate itself to the conditions of the act in which any object is cognized. Hence it is impossible to speak of an art which would pertain to space alone, for everything given in space is simultaneously in time. Indeed, the converse is true, it requires time to visit a monument or to look at a painting, but the listener and the music which he hears are always somewhere in space. It is therefore *a priori* impossible to make a distinction in the fine arts between the arts of space and the arts of time from the point of view of their esthetic apprehension.

Nor would we be any more successful by posing the problem from the point of view of art itself. In fact, works of art, as human creations, are subject to the burden of the human condition, which is to endure. Whether it is a question of architecture, music or poetry,

time is as involved in the operations required for the production of works of art as it is in their apprehension by the
consumer. Time is needed, sometimes years and, in the
case of collective works, even centuries in order to bring
some enterprises to completion, such as the construction of
temples or of palaces whose completion exceeds the limits
of a life or a generation. In one sense, such works are
never really finished, for no matter how long the time that
was required to bring them into being there is practically
no end to the time that will be needed to prevent their
destruction or demise. For their part, music and poetry
are always being produced somewhere and the written
symbols which preserve them fill books, which in turn rest
on the shelves of libraries, which with the passage of time
increasingly and ceaselessly take up more and more space.
And musicians follow the fate of music, for just as the
"monuments of antiquity" last in time, so does a symphony
orchestra, a quartette, a singer "occupy a place." In general,
these two great frames of sensible experience are also two
universal laws of material life, to which all works of art are
subject; hence they cannot be used as criteria for distinguishing them.

We might perhaps be more successful by substituting
for the esthetic point of view that of the philosophy of art.
The latter implies a metaphysics of art, that is to say an
ontology which considers the works in their substantial
structure and in their relation to their cause. Taken as
singular beings, actually existing works of art are essentially material objects which are given as sense data. Esthetics deals with our apprehension of them, but the
philosophy of art is rightfully concerned with the material
from which these works of art are wrought, and this consideration provides an objective means for distinguishing

them and, perhaps, even for drawing the broad outlines of a system for classifying them.

Furthermore, in trying this approach we must bear in mind that the prime matter of which philosophers speak cannot possibly be in question here. The artist does not work on a pure indeterminable substance which is not *nec quid, nec quale,* the possibility of whose actual existence, moreover, is at best doubtful. The respective material substances on which the different arts work do not enable us to distinguish them inasmuch as they themselves are distinct from each other. Every material is differentiated from the others by reason of the natural form which makes it stone, wood, color, musical sound or a written or spoken word. They are called materials, despite their forms, because the artist freely takes possession of them in order to make works of art out of them. In this sense, the natural forms themselves act as materials in relation to the form, specifically different in origin and in finality, which the artist imparts to them for the production of the works he has in mind. This is a rule of general import, the consequences of which are innumerable, because *everything* which the artist presses into service for the purpose of his art plays the role of matter in relation to the form of the work. On the other hand, since this matter is not the prime matter of the metaphysicians but rather some substance already determined by its form, the artist using it as a material is forced to take account of its natural formal determinations in the artistic use that he makes of it. The sculpture can choose to work in wood, stone or marble; he is totally free in this respect, but once his decision has been made his art must respect the conditions imposed by the natural form of the material on which he will have chosen to exercise his skill. This determination goes even further. Michelangelo was free to do everything it is possible to do with a given block of marble of this or that cut, form, grain and color. This is the source of the unceasing interaction between the material and the operations of the artist, who draws inspiration from both in order to invent the forms that will best suit him. The material, inasmuch as it is determined by its natural forms, itself brings a positive determining action to bear to which the artist cannot remain insensible. When the sculptor asks himself whether a block of marble shall be a god, a table or a basin, the marble has something to say about it. In its own way, in fact, it is the first to speak, announcing its vocation.

This manner of operation would be in keeping with the feeling expressed by many artists which can be summarized in the well-known words of Robert Schumann: "The esthetics of one art is the same as that of the others; only the material differs." It has often been quoted only as a reproach. Taken within the limits that Schumann had in mind, it is true. He did not claim that forms are of the same nature in all the arts, but rather that if they are different in music from what they are in architecture, in sculpture, or in painting, it is precisely because the mind, in creating them through an act that is always essentially the same, must adopt the forms to the exigencies or demands of the different materials on which the artist works. Thus the diversity that exists in the techniques of the arts really is attributable to the diversity of the materials on which they are brought to bear. Perhaps we do not always express ourselves properly when we speak of art as an effort to overcome the resistance of matter. This resistance is real, and this is why creativity is always an effort, but while the artist pits himself against it in order to conquer it he also bases himself upon it in order to surmount it. Far from being an enemy, the material of his art is an ally of the creator: an accomplice whose suggestions he gladly accepts and whose call he hears before he sets to work. For we must never forget the great image of the Greek philosopher: matter desires form as the female desires the male, and we can add vice-versa. From this point of view we can understand not only the great divisions of the arts in general, but also those within each of them which determine the different properties and possibilities of the materials which they use: in painting, for example, the types of paintings such as frescoes, oils or water colors; and alongside the different manners of painting, engraving and the different arts of the engraver, on wood, on stone, on copper, through the graving-tool or etching and so forth. In the presence of a given material the artist always asks himself: "What can be done with it?" He knows what he is talking about when he praises the "possibilities" of the stone or of the wood at hand, as well as those of the different techniques from which they are inseparable. This is why it is so difficult to distinguish the two notions of art and technique in reality, for the arts cannot be classified according to their materials without at the same time classifying them according to the techniques which are used to work them. Technique is the particular manner of imparting to a particular material the particular type of form that is proper to it.

If we take account of these precise distinctions, we will be more disposed than ever to give up the idea of ordering the arts of the beautiful into a synthesis in which each of them would find a place assigned to it on the basis of a general principle. Man produces works of art with the materials that he finds and in accordance with the means at his disposal. This is not a deduction but a confirmed fact.

In an altogether general way, works of art can be

classified in two major groups, according to whether their material is inorganic or organic. Within the first group, we shall distinguish the arts of extension and the arts of sound. Within the second group, composed almost exclusively of the arts whose material is man himself, we shall distinguish the arts of the human body and the arts of linguistic expression, spoken or written. In none of these groups, particularly the second, are we to expect clear and sharp distinctions, and, even less, contradistinctions. All arts by origin are arts of man, and all those for which man furnishes the material itself are connected with each other through the "human" qualities of the materials used. A dance movement is executed by a human body, a song is produced by a human voice, an intelligible word rightfully belongs to the human language. Everything here connects and communes in a natural identity, but there is diversity in the unity.

Such will be the order that we here intend to sketch along broad lines, basing ourselves on these general notions.

Among the arts of extension, we shall distinguish the arts of volume, principally architecture and sculpture, and the arts of surface,[2] principally drawing, painting and those arts derived from, or associated with, them.

2. It would take a long time to discuss the opposite thesis, but it will be found forcefully expounded by M. Charles Lapicque who combines the double authority of the painter and the philosopher. See his *Essais sur l'espace, l'art et la destinée,* preface by Jean Wahl (Paris: Grasset, 1958), notably pp. 16–20 and 183–185. I refer the reader to it and draw his attention to the difference of the two points of view. I speak of the work of art itself, whereas Lapicque speaks above all of its apprehension by the spectator. From the point of view of this work, it is without importance that it involves only one center of perspective (as in that of the Italian Renaissance, known as Albert's perspective) or several as in all other kinds of

Among the arts of sound, which include all forms of music, we shall distinguish musical instruments and types of vocal music; the voice being a living sound, the latter constitutes a transition, a kind of bridge between the arts of inorganic matter and the arts of man.

In turn, the arts of man will be distinguished in three principal groups: those of which the human body furnishes the material, such as the dance; those whose material is language, namely different forms of spoken or written poetry; and finally those of which, for lack of a term that is more directly significative, we shall say that human life itself is the material, whether it involves imitation or a free re-creation, such as the arts of pantomime and the theatre. The creations of these latter arts require almost the totality of appearances given in experience, including man himself in his body, his gesture, in the intonations of his voice, in the words that he utters taken in their very meaning, including what is most intimate and almost sacred in him, his personality.

If it is permissible to prefer other classifications which in fact might be desirable from other points of view, this

---

painting, ancient or modern. I don't know whether it is proper to call the latter a "dynamic perspective." In fact, all perspectives are such for the eye of the spectator and, on the other hand, the movement required for the perception of the picture affects only the spectator, not the work itself. The picture presents simultaneously the traces left on a surface through successive movements. It itself exists all at once. As we shall see more amply in connection with architecture, the conditions of the esthetic experience of the picture are affected by it: this is why it is totally present and one can transverse it from any end and even, if one wishes, from the back. We cannot read a poem backwards, or play a symphony backwards, or present a play without being concerned about the order of the scenes or of the verses. All the arts of time find themselves in this situation.

distinction of the arts of the beautiful is eminently legitimate in a study which considers them from the distinct
point of view of their materials and forms. A more general
objection would hold that such a distinction neglects some
very important arts, some of which occupy a first rank in
contemporary letters.

The novel is the most notable among the cases of this
kind. For various reasons, the novel occupies a more important place than poetry in contemporary literary production. On the other hand, it cannot be denied that many
novels are works of art. Who does not immediately think
of *Madame Bovary?* Flaubert nearly died in order to give
birth to this masterpiece which he willed for the pure
beauty of its form, as he himself never ceased to repeat.
Flaubert's letters to Louise Collet are an irreplaceable
document on the creative travail of a writer whose ultimate
end is beauty alone. It was inevitable that the passage from
his letter of January 16, 1852, would be frequently quoted:
"What seems beautiful to me, what I would like to write
is a book about nothing, a book dependent upon nothing
external which would sustain itself by the inner strength
of its style, as the earth is suspended in space; a book that
would have almost no subject or in which the subject
would be almost invisible, if such a thing is possible." Such
a thing is possible, of course, but on the condition that it
not be a novel. *Madame Bovary* has a subject, as every
novel must have. Flaubert might well have chosen his as
the most mediocre subject possible so that the novel would
owe nothing of its beauty to it, but it is there nevertheless,
with all the onerous limitations it entails. To choose the
novel in order to write a literary work without any subject-
matter or end other than its own beauty was a form of self-
deception regarding the nature of that literary genre.
Flaubert keenly felt the contradiction inherent in the

project that he had set for himself when he had to write "a coarse and gross dialogue" between a woman and "a parish priest" because the subject required it. How write a dialogue of this kind which would ring true and possess a style at one and the same time? "I reached the conclusion sometimes," he himself says, "that it is impossible to write." Yet, while discussing this very *Madame Bovary*, Albert Thibaudet made a point of insisting on the reality of the characters created by Flaubert in this masterpiece,[3] about which the author repeated twenty times that the subject in no way suited him. Perhaps Flaubert was mistaken about himself? See how masterfully he prepares his "great scene of the agricultural meetings," this "rustico-municipal feast"! Does not this art of inventing the real also have its beauty? Flaubert asked himself this question. He knew that others responded affirmatively, and he did not try to deny the question, but he had his doubts: "They say it's also art, and everything is art. But by dint of seeing so

3. If I am mistaken here, only Albert Thibaudet would be able to correct me but, unfortunately, he is no longer among us. See his pages on Flaubert in *Histoire de la littérature française de 1789 à nos jours* (Paris: Stock, 1936), pp. 336–338, and above all in *Gustave Flaubert, sa vie, ses romans, son style* (Paris: 1922), the inexhaustible comparison between the pair Corneille-Balzac and Racine-Flaubert. Finally there is always Flaubert himself. We can hear him in the texts collected under the title, *Extraits de la correspondance ou Préface à la vie d'écrivain,* presentation and selection by Geneviève Bollème (Paris: Editions du Seuil, 1963). The *Presentation* in fact includes precisely the following utterance, which is so true, from the *Education sentimentale,* first version (Paris: Conrad, 1910), p. 259: "Every work of art has its special poetics in virtue of which it is fashioned and subsists . . ." If *Madame Bovary* did not exist to recall this truth to the philosopher as well as to the critic, I would be grateful to this unsurpassed novel for arousing in me a doubt which I feel that I have not altogether succeeded in removing.

much art, I ask where are the fine arts?" The philosophy of art will never surpass the profundity that Flaubert's reflection arrived at by itself.

Flaubert criticizes Balzac for having remained too alien to the concern of art, yet Balzac, though less an artist than Flaubert, is by far the better novelist. It is impossible to discuss novels without bringing up Balzac, but it is equally impossible to avoid asking oneself: to what order of literary creation does his work belong? In the preface of 1842 to the *Comédie humaine,* Balzac presented himself as an observer of what he called "social nature." [4] This is what he purposed to observe and learn about before all else, so as to portray it later in his work and thus compete with all the data of civic life. Taine called the *Comédie humaine* "the largest warehouse of documents that we have on human nature along with Shakespeare and Saint Simon." If this is true, Balzac's work set knowledge rather than beauty as its end. No doubt, his work has a beauty of its own. It is enough to re-read the short story "Colonel Chabert" to sense its greatness, but it is the greatness of a biologist whose imagination creates objects by virtue of the passionately objective way with which he describes them. There is no perspective, everything in the story is on the same plane and has a right to the exact same treatment: the solicitor as much as Colonel Chabert, the clerks and the errand-boy as much as the solicitor, the office as much as

4. The preface of 1842 to *La Comédie humaine* is clearer than any commentary could be. Even if it contains an element of imagination, Balzac's scientific ideal is sincere and is lucidly expressed. "Hence there have existed, and hence there will always exist in all times, social species just as there are zoological species. If Buffon has wrought a magnificent work in trying to represent the ensemble of zoology in one book, was there not a need to fashion a work of this kind for society?" *Balzac,* vol. I (Paris: *Pléiade*), p. 4. If this is not the Balzacian novel *in toto,* at least it is an essential trait of it.

the clerks, and in the office the cardboard boxes, the dos-
siers, that old pouch inherited from Chatelet, in short
everything that is describable in detail. It overwhelms the
reader with a simulated truth, and at times it is a trifle
tiresome; many find Balzac unreadable, but they are artists
of style. The novel, as Balzac understood it, is an art, even a
great art, but it is not an art of the beautiful.

This is not said to diminish the novel, not even as a
work of art. Our concern here is not to pass judgments but
to classify objects by defining the notions we have about
them. Many arts, rich in beauties of all kinds, are not
essentially arts of the beautiful. History is not an art of
the beautiful, even if a Michelet is the historian. Neither
is eloquence one of the fine arts, even though the oratorical
art merits the name. But eloquence employs the beautiful
for the ends of persuasion which are its proper end. It
would have made Bossuet indignant to be told that he
preached sermons for the love of art: the end religious eloquence sets itself is religion. The history of literature, which
Francis Bacon conceived and described long before it existed, is not to be included among the fine arts. Nor are
works of literary criticism, even when their authors are
De Sanctis, Sainte-Beuve and Charles du Bos. Indeed, the
more they attain the perfection of their respective types,
the more do these literary genres differ from the fine arts.
There is an art of the beautiful in literature each time that
the end of a word is its own beauty, independently of its
truth. This is why poetry, finally, is the supreme form of
the arts of language, for it is understood in advance that
multa mentiuntur poetae, and no one holds them to strict
account.

This homeland of the arts which, though rich in
beauty, are not fine arts, is immense and populated by
servants of the mind, themselves artists but not primarily

the servants of the beautiful. Balzac included among them Colonel Chabert: "If he pursued his military fame, his fortune, himself, perhaps it was in order to obey that inexplicable feeling, an embryo in the heart of all men, and to which we owe the researches of the alchemists, the passion for glory, the discoveries of astronomy, of physics, of all that which impels man to make himself more important by increasing his stature by deeds or ideas." All these men have a right to our respect and sympathy, but none of their "deeds," to use Balzac's language, surpasses in gratuitousness the work of the servants of the beautiful, loved and served for its own sake. Their model is Stéphane Mallarmé whose volume *Vers et Prose* sold at the average rate of 250 copies a year for almost sixty years.[5] The poet publishing his slender volume of verse has been compared to the traveller who leans over the edge of the Grand Canyon in Colorado to drop a feather and then cocks an ear to catch the sound its fall will make upon hitting bottom. Philosophy is perhaps the only discipline that can render this ultimate service to the arts of the beautiful, and can recognize them for what they really are. By insisting upon the transcendental specificity of the beautiful as a good of the sensibility, and consequently upon that of the arts of the beautiful as being essentially dedicated to its service, it can at least protect them against the last danger besetting them: annihilation as the result of being confused with those arts which, by usurping the title of the arts of the beautiful, occupy their place in thought as if it were not enough to have taken their place in reality.

5. Henri Mondor, *Autres précisions sur Mallarmé et inédits* (Paris: Gallimard, 1961), p. 114.

TWO

Architecture

ACCORDING TO THE USUAL meaning of the word, architecture is the art of constructing, ordering and ornamenting buildings in conformity with plans drawn up beforehand. The architect lays out the plan of all construction of this kind and directs its execution. There is no reason to dispute this usage, only it must be exactly circumscribed and determined if we wish to speak of architecture as one of the fine arts. One of these arts, to be sure, answers to the name of architecture, but all architecture is not necessarily one of the fine arts. Architecture can be included in this category only if the architect's principal purpose is to create the kind of beauty proper to the building constructed according to his plans.

A fairly wide-spread view of the problem would dispense with the need to pose it at all, for it is traditional to consider architecture as the mother of all the fine arts, that is to say of all those which, according to the usual dictionary definition, have as their object "the representation of the beautiful." First of all, we can ask ourselves whether architecture's purpose is to "represent" anything at all. Secondly, architecture has obviously provided practitioners of

39

other arts with opportunities to bring their skills to bear: buildings to be ornamented with statues, walls, ceilings or vaults to be adorned with decorative paintings, wood-panellings and iron-work to be executed, and so forth. Yet very ancient statuettes such as the Aurignacian Venus, the mural paintings like those in the Lascaux caverns and other prehistoric sites seem to antedate the construction of proper buildings. Once integrated with architecture, these arts have regularly made efforts to break away from it. Whether this was a step in the right direction or an error on their part is another question, but the fact is they did. Hence it is not clear that architecture is one of the fine arts inasmuch as it is the source or the mother of other arts of the beautiful.

Taken in this broad, usual and therefore legitimate sense, architecture presents a character that is wholly un-expected from an art of the beautiful: of all the arts, it is the only one most obviously related to a practical need. Man builds habitations to shelter himself against cold, heat, wind and rain. To build a shelter with materials of any kind is a purely technical problem that can be solved in many ways according to the materials available, the con-venience with which they can be found or produced and, finally, according to the kind of order and arrangement ultimately imparted to them to give them the form of a human shelter. Any form of this kind is necessarily in-vented; the simplest general plan calls for a roof supported by walls which afford an opening called a door through which one can come and go. Simpler constructions also exist but it seems that ever since the human habitation assumed this form it has not undergone any change down to our day. The most impressive temples, the most magni-ficent palaces, the most complex modern structures, fac-tories that look like miniature cities—which moreover are

better planned than the latter—all finally follow this same
model: walls, roofs, openings for lighting and ventilation.
The art of constructing edifices of this kind is a genuine
art but it is essentially a utilitarian art. Like all the products of factivity, buildings can have a beauty of their own,
but it is a beauty that is itself utilitarian, at least in the
sense that it is born of the perfect adaptation of the means
to the end. The master-builder, or architect in the broader
sense of the term, does not seek beauty for its own sake.
If he chances upon it even to the extent that he might have
willed it into being, this beauty, even though very real, is
of a kind properly suited to an architecture that is essentially functional. The beauty proper to factivity does not
belong to the order of the arts of the beautiful any more
than does natural beauty; inasmuch as it aims to achieve
the beauty proper to factivity, architecture cannot be considered as one of the fine arts.

Many will be surprised by such a simple remark.
They will object that functional architecture, on the contrary, is the only architecture which is truly beautiful and
should unquestionably be ranked among the fine arts.
Architects themselves betray an obvious tendency to ex-
tend their sphere of competence, which would constitute
a real authority. The pursuit of the beautiful always finds
a place in this sphere but it is no longer the principal goal;
indeed, at times it is rather hard to locate it at all.

Some confuse architecture with the body of town-
planning, itself a confused notion. Aristotle, no doubt,
would admit that town-planning is architectonic in relation
to architecture proper, but its problems are concerned with
providing a setting and as favorable a habitat as possible for
the full and harmonious development of human life. Controversy abounds over what this setting and habitat ought
to be, surrounding every conceivable subject, including

sociology, ethics and even metaphysics, but no mention is ever made of the pursuit of beauty constructed in space for its own sake.

The conception underlying the construction of housing poses problems which, though less lofty, are just as complex. First of all, housing is conceived in terms of utility rather than of beauty. This has been known since time immemorial, and whenever an architect has forgotten it the budget-director of the project has taken it upon himself to remind him of it. In 1750, after studying the plans for the future École Militaire which Ange-Jacques Gabriel was to build, minister Paris-Duvernay wrote to the architect: "It is less a question of erecting a monument to the glory of His Majesty than of building one that would be useful to the State. There is no point in trying to strike a balance between beauty and usefulness when the two cannot be realized." [1] What are considered as utilitarian re-

1. Quoted in Ch.-M. Widor, *Notice sur la vie et les oeuvres de Charles Girault (1851–1932)* (Paris: Firmin-Didot), p. 9. Read at the annual meeting of the Académie des Beaux-Arts, December 2, 1933. I ask the indulgence of architects, who are all too familiar with this kind of documentation, if I mention the following data taken from an article in the *U.S. News & World Report*, May 6, 1963, p. 54, for the enlightenment of philosophers for whom the fine arts above all are an object of reflection: The most recent trend in housing construction: buyers are above all demanding more spacious houses with more bedrooms, more rooms as such. In the new houses that have been built, 50 per cent have two or more bathrooms as compared with 32 per cent in the older houses. More than four out of five of the new houses have a car-port or a garage, as compared with three out of four in the older houses. The trend favors construction on ground-level without basements. Less than 30 per cent of the new houses have a whole or a partial basement as compared with 41 per cent in the older houses. Moreover, more than 88 per cent of the new houses are one-storey structures as compared with 88 per cent of the older houses. Naturally these ratios vary according

quirements today by far exceed anything which the eighteenth century could imagine. The necessity of making place for the useful inevitably limits the builder's formal freedom.

This is so true that nowadays an architect is merely the head of a collective enterprise in which the engineer plays a role as important as his own. Often, indeed, the engineer replaces him. Famous contemporary architects, in Europe and America, take pride in the fact that they never set foot in a school of Fine Arts; "functional" architecture, they say, is the only architecture *that satisfies* the mind, and in this way attains beauty.

True enough, the pursuit of utility does not exclude the pursuit of beauty. It is also true that it should be possible to obtain from the edifice built for utilitarian purposes effects that would translate its very utility into beautiful forms. In such a case, if success is complete, the beautiful forms are not only accommodated to the function but express it.[2] Such is the case with "industrial beauty" in

to regions, the percentage of two-storey houses and basements being higher in the colder regions. Not a word is said about style nor, of course, about beauty. What happens first of all is that the buyer "often demands a fourth bedroom, a central air-conditioning system, a modern kitchen with equipment included in the construction, and a common family room." This does not mean that the concern with art plays no role but it does mean that if the architect wants to build houses, these are the demands that he had to expect from his clients in 1963 in the United States. Beauty, if it comes, will be given into the bargain.

2. Ath. Sfaellos Charalambos, *Le fonctionalisme dans l'architecture contemporaine* (Paris: Vincent-Fréal, 1952). Notably: "Functionalism in contemporary architecture tries to express: 1. Function through an esthetically satisfying form; 2. Formal perfection through working and functional elements. Its final result in that case is the fusion of these two apparently contradictory tendencies." Cf. Robert Auzelle, "Le fonctionalisme dans l'architecture," *Bulletin men-*

general. Utility has its own perfection, attained by the perfect adaptation of means to ends. When this adaptation is successful the useful is endowed with the beauty proper to it as exemplified by a beautiful ship, a beautiful automobile or a beautiful machine. Like the beauty of nature, the beauty of the machine is given into the bargain, and the beauty of a building is similar. Just as one makes nature look ridiculous by embellishing her, and a machine becomes a ludicrous object if it is adorned with statues or anything else reminiscent of one of the fine arts, so does the architect who thinks he is improving the looks of a building by adding columns that serve no purpose or capitals without a definite function expose himself to the kind of sarcastic comments that so many of his colleagues have directed against the canons of architecture and of "styles" which survive in some institutes of Fine Arts. Such protests are justified, but it remains no less true that utilitarian beauty is not what the fine arts directly intend to attain. If they also have a unique functionalism it can be said to consist in the creation of the beautiful for its own sake, independently of any utilitarian considerations. In this respect, one of the paradoxes of architecture as an art is that the beautiful is never its sole and exclusive end. A painting answers no other purpose save that of being seen, music that of being heard, poetry that of being read, but the most beautiful of doors serves to let people pass through it, any window serves to let in light, and even the breathtaking solid walls of the Doge's Palace, an unending delight to behold, had the function of enclosing meeting rooms—something we are quite surprised to learn upon

suel d'information de la Société des architectes diplomés par le gouvernement, 116 (1963), pp. 622–630. This study is of the greatest importance to the philosopher for its concrete discussion of architecture's real task.

visiting the interior. Thus to speak of architecture exclusively as an art of the beautiful requires us first of all to
make an effort at abstraction, after which we must bear in
mind that this was our point of departure.

This paradoxical nature of architecture is clearly expressed in the remark of a modern architect who was happy
over the fact that for once in his life he had been lucky
enough to receive a commission to construct a building
that would "be useless." Indeed even the pedestals of
statues and triumphal arches, in principle, serve some
purpose. As for city halls, post offices, railway stations,
schools, hospitals, barracks, prisons, banks, large depart-
ment stores and other similar edifices, the interior arrangement of their space determines their exterior structure,
and obviously the whole is made to serve utility. The construction of a totally useless building is therefore a rare
event, but at times the useful is of such a nature that it
does not necessarily determine any particular structure.
The less the structure of an edifice is determined by its
purpose, the more directly it is answerable to architecture
in the strict sense of the word that makes it one of the
fine arts. This is why, in all times and perhaps most obviously in our day, religious edifices, whether temples or
churches, have directly belonged to this relatively untram-
melled architecture which can attain its particular utilitarian end while committing itself to the creation of beauty as
an artistic end. Essentially, a Greek temple or a Christian
church is nothing else but an altar protected from the elements by a roof and surrounded by walls. What is involved
in this case is a functional purpose of a kind that practically
imposes no conditions in terms of dimension, form, or particular ornamentation on the edifice in question. This or
that religion can even exclude this or that form of figure
ornamentation, or actually forbid it altogether, it matters

little; as long as the edifice subsists as a place of worship, of prayer, or even simply of veneration, it is strictly a temple. The architect is free to conceive of it as a pure object of beauty, that is, as if its very beauty constituted the essence of the offering made by man to the divinity. This is why the church is the only object of beauty in so many villages. The other achievements of any urban civilization partake of beauty to the measure in which their architect, in order to produce them, was free to make use of the variable measure of freedom that his "specifications" left him. What is left is utilitarian beauty, which is real beauty but not our concern when we try to understand architecture as one of the fine arts.

The creation of architectural beauty presupposes the void that architecture requires. The architect works in space empty of all solids as the musician works in the silence which is the void that sound requires. Strictly speaking, music can base itself on noise but not on sound, unless it assimilates it. In the same way architecture can base itself on natural forms; indeed it always does this inasmuch as being fixed in place it must always accommodate itself to a site. It does this by utilizing the site, but it cannot accommodate itself to another architecture if it is to be truly creative. Construction is preceded by the work of demolition or levelling, or at least the architect must start out from a space that nature has left free of obstacles and that, by virtue of this very fact, can be occupied by structures imagined by an architect. Obviously, the overall design can even utilize the particular configuration of a terrain in order to obtain the best architectural advantage from it, but this very decision is part of the work to be wrought, constituting its first free moment of creativity. Some architects insist that a building should be integrated as completely as possible with the site; for example, they will not build a structure on the top of a hill, but against it so that the hill can serve as a backdrop. No doubt this is sound reasoning, but it would make Mont St. Michel impossible. On the other hand, other architects strive for effects that the first group considers wrong and undesirable; their idea is that the building should contrast with the environment, and cut itself sharply off from it. But certain low dwellings, rooted directly in the ground, which look like other undulations in the terrain, also have their peculiar charm. These are the different questions that an architect must wrestle with. But whatever his decision, he must first of all clear the terrain for the new structure. This is why architects themselves are such dreadful destroyers of architecture: their work can arise finally only upon an empty space.

This work is the building. As with all works of man, the first cause of a building is its final cause. But there are several kinds of final causes. One of them is the perpetuation of some great collective remembrance by endowing it with an important meaning: a hero, a victory, an exploit, an event of joy or sorrow or anything else of a commemorative nature. In that case it is a simple monument. Its purpose determines its structure. Since a monument has no definite practical purpose, it has no interior, or practically none. While building it, the architect does not have to worry about what it will look like inside. In the first place, a monument cannot have an interior at all as in the case of a commemorative stele; secondly, the only purpose of the hollow of the structure is to make it possible for one to move around in it and ensure easier upkeep or easier access to the summit. Such are towers, lantern-turrets in burial grounds, and trophies of all kinds. Some types of monuments belong to both orders, but mainly to the first, because they can contain chambers which do not serve any architectural purpose, as is the case with the pyramids of Egypt. Constructions of this kind are solids, or the solid dominates the empty space to such a degree that we can consider them as simple solids. The purpose of these architectural works, therefore, directly affects their construction.

The one feature shared in common by all these monuments is that they are willed and built to last. This is not necessary—what is necessary in the free country of art?—and we can amuse ourselves by erecting a flower-bedecked triumphal arch designed to last but a day, in order to honor a champion cyclist in our time, or a poet in days of yore, but monumental architecture requires a more solid material, especially as its purpose is to perpetuate the memory of the man or the event it recalls. An open-air altar is a monument of this kind; only a lasting monument is fitting to celebrate the Eternal. Dolmens and mennins defy the ravages of time, and they were willed into being for an unlimited duration; the triumphal arches, which serve only to be passed under or merely to recall the glory of those who were the first to pass triumphantly under them, the columns of Trajan, the column in the Place Vendôme, or others. Monumental tombs and cenotaphs of all kinds do not contain any interior space arranged for the purpose of being seen; once they are completed, all that is expected of them is to last, and they often do.

The second possible purpose of a building is to shelter human beings (a house), animals (the stables of Chantilly or of Strà), or objects (a museum). This creates new problems. The latter have an exterior like the buildings belonging to the first order; they occupy a part of the space which contains them while implanting their forms within it. But at the same time they create an interior space; they are not contained in this space but they contain, determine and shape it. Often, monuments of this kind are also associated with a commemorative or glorifying function, but this is neither their exclusive nor proper end. This time it is the durability of a utilitarian function that is counted upon to ensure memory. A simple habitation, however, has no other purpose save that of being habitable; so negligible is its commemorative function that when the house is finished, death enters. In any case, hollow solids of this kind pose problems of arrangement and communication in terms of the interior space, such as the rooms of a palace with their corridors, their staircases (often themselves a monument within a monument), their landings, and their exit-doors. The same is true of temples or churches, whether their enclosed space delights the beholder with the sudden impact of its unity, or whether it charms him by the adroit arrangement of naves, aisles, transepts, chapels, apses and small apses which break up the unity through many artifices, principally the pillars.

The material of architecture is the solid, or solids, used to delimit the portion of empty space to be occupied or enclosed. This material can be natural, like wood or stone, or artificial like brick, cement, steel, glass, or any other industrial product of this kind. In any case, the building material chosen is not only solid but relatively durable. The work of the architect, like the building material he uses, is a tri-dimensional volume. This volume, inevitably colored by the natural color of the materials used, by the color which it acquires with the passage of time, sometimes even by the color which is added to it, is essentially immovable in space and, in its substance, wholly alien to movement. Any edifice which "moves," that is to say, one whose horizontal stones, elevations or elements begin to shift in relation to others, is on the road to ruin. This is why the building materials must be inorganic, or if they are organic they must have ceased to live, like those oaken beams which acquire the hardness of stone. Whether it is introduced into the building from within, or from without, organic matter threatens it with destruction.

Solid, situated in space and inert, the work of the architect is given all at once. It is simultaneous as though by definition. Obvious as this may be, it is nevertheless contested in the name of a principle that is equally obvious, only the two principles are not applicable to the same fact. Some people, especially in architectural circles, forcefully insist on what they call the dynamic of space which, furthermore, they hold to be a constitutive element of architectural beauty. That may be, but it is a dynamic of the immovable. Such assertions once again confuse the esthetic point of view, which is that of the spectator, with that of art itself. It takes a lot of movement to erect a building, and even more to ensure that it will remain standing up after having been built. Movements likewise are required on the part of the spectator. The fatigue that comes over visitors to a palace or a cathedral is sufficient evidence of the muscular exertion it takes to know such structures, even superficially, in all their principal aspects. Thus, it is rightfully contended that it is impossible to apprehend a building as a whole, that is to say in the totality of its form, without making a tour of it, without perceiving from the outside its principal parts in their reciprocal relations and in the ever changing perspectives which a visitor's own moving about from place to place offers to his view. The same holds true for the interior, with the monumental entrances of palaces, their formal staircases, their enormous rooms and the surprises which they hold in store for the visitor, such as the unexpected small apartments which he suddenly comes upon by way of narrow galleries cut off from charming vestibules whose forms, proportions, and whose very order of succession are a constant source of delight to the eye. When we visit one of these palaces, we should make a tour of the interior, but once inside we should also survey the outside of the structure from the vantage point of the windows and now and then from the balconies, from where we can pick out in the distance a public square of the city and the architecture of other monuments, or a garden with its flower-beds and its fountains, or the mirror of a lake with an island whose church is etched against the mountainous backdrop of the landscape. True enough, all this was foreseen, calculated and finally brought into being through the art of the architect. He included in the plan of his work the movements which would be required to see the structure, and even if he may have failed to do so they are inseparable from his work, for without them man would not be able to avail himself of the services which the edifice must purvey, nor to perceive its beauty.

Nothing could be truer, and such remarks apply to the sequence of adventures that await the lover of beauty during the exploration of a cathedral whose perspectives, inside and outside the structure, ceaselessly change in accordance with shifts in the observer's position. Although the artist must provide for the esthetic apprehension of his work, such apprehension does not belong to it per se. The artist works on the material that must produce the esthetic experience of the beholder, not on the esthetic experience itself. A building is not composed of vistas, perspectives, or vantage points—no matter how adroitly they may have been included in the architect's calculations—but of stones, walls, pillars or columns arranged so as to provide precisely such perspectives and such vistas for the spectator. The spectator moves, but the building does not. By virtue of its material, it is, upon completion, rooted in existence simultaneously in the totality of its parts. The architect's work does not unfold in time like a poem or like a musical composition. Like all that persists, a building endures in time, but it is immobile in the flow of time in the primary sense that it is immovable in its very being, inasmuch as it is not in a process of becoming like a phrase that is being spoken or sung, but is something wholly evolved, wrought and perfect. That it requires time to become aware of this in no way implies that its proper being is composed of fragments succeeding each other in time.

The amazing development of the scientific study of art and of art criticism enables us to understand why the viewpoint of the consumer so often replaces that of the artist. A good collection of photographs of the cathedral of Chartres discloses many details which its master-builders, perhaps, never gazed upon. As for the aerial perspectives disclosed by vertical shots taken over ancient châteaux, ancient fortresses, public squares or cities, we can be absolutely certain that the architects of the twelfth and thirteenth centuries never saw such vistas as the helicopter and photography make possible to see today. The dynamism we attribute to them is that which we ourselves give them; the only dynamism these works of art actually possess is an energy of immobility.

Moreover, the analysis of esthetic experience would not exactly appear to confirm the opinion that architecture is an art of movement. The spectator feels perfectly that he has the movable experience of an immovable reality. What is involved here is not merely the awareness, at times overpowering, that such masses, like mountains, "cannot move"; rather, as the spectator moves from one place to another in order to see the different parts of the structure successively, he perceives those which he sees in relation to those which he no longer sees, or does not yet see, but which he knows and senses are there.

This awareness is expressed in the certainty, inseparable from the experience of architecture, that the experience is reversible. We cannot read a poem or listen to a symphony backwards, but we can begin our visit to a building from the wrong side. All we have to do is to make an about-face during our tour and we can start it all over again simultaneously in all respects. Since there are an infinite number of such directions, they could not have been exactly calculated by the architect nor, for that matter, did he have to foresee them in order to produce them; all he had to do was to create the possibility of our producing them by moving around on the outside or in the interior of the immovable mass. It is said that "architecture *is walked through,* traversed." [3] Architecture, in-

3. Le Corbusier, *Entretien avec les étudiants des écoles d'architecture* (Paris: Les Editions de Minuit, 1957), 4. Since it is an "art-book," this book is not paginated. The writing is dated October 17, 1942 (see its colophon). It goes without saying that the remark taken into consideration here is not, in Corbusier's thought, a definition of architecture. For him it states essentially what architecture is in reality: "regulation of the terrain and *built volume*" (in italics in text). Another definition, in artist style, which is simply quoted, is found not far from the beginning of the work: "Architecture is the sapient, correct and magnificent play of volumes assembled under light." This is tantamount to saying, a built volume. The now classic comparison between architecture and music has found its most seductive form in Paul Valéry, *Eupalinos ou l'architecte, Oeuvres,* vol. II, ed. Jean Hytier (Paris: Pléiade), pp. 103–105. Music and architecture both have this kinship with us of being "two arts which enclose man or, rather, which enclose being in his work . . ." It would be a pity if such pages had not been written, but it would be a greater pity still to remain insensible to the seductive views they set forth. However, reason must know how to defend itself even against the charm of Monsieur Teste. One is not necessarily *inside* architecture, for one can view it from without;

deed, is walked through, but architecture stands still. The
house, the palace or the church is walked through, not so,
however, with a symphony which runs its course; and this
time it is not we who provide the movement but the symphony which sweeps us along with it. Architecture is the
art of that which is to last as music is the art of that which
is to pass away. Happily for us, music dies only to be
reborn, but it is restored to life just as we knew it the
first time, in the inflexibility of the same order—the one
it imposes on us—and not the one which we impose at
leisure on the inert and at times slightly ludicrous mass
of the monument.

Thus the nature of its material particularizes architecture, but like any art it is the producer of beings determined by their forms. Essentially, it produces an edifice, a
volume occupying space whose exterior forms and interior
structure are pleasing to the eye through the order, proportion and arrangement of the parts. In this sense, it is

viewed from within, there one is in effect surrounded on all sides
but by the limits of a space, whereas if at times we feel ourselves
surrounded by music it is in that case time that surrounds us (p.
102). To call time "an intelligible and changing space" is a metaphor rather than a concept, and without rejecting it as such it
must not be permitted to create confusions. The acts commanded
by the mind of the architect produce an object which lasts by itself
in space, the acts of the executants commanded by the mind of the
musician produce impermanent sounds which succeed each other in
time and whose existence is linked to that of the successive acts
which produce them. It is our body which is in a structured space;
our duration is not even included in that of the symphony, it accompanies it. At the end of the first act of *Parsifal* we are all older
by an hour and forty-five minutes, from the orchestra conductor
to the musicians, the singers in the chorus and to the last of the
accessorists; the *Festspielhaus* in which we were actually enclosed
is still there, alas, for it is architecture, but *Parsifal* has ceased to
exist because it is music.

extension determined by visible forms. The dynamic of architectural spaces is reduced to that which they make possible, they themselves do not set it in motion.

Building material is not the proper material of architecture. The material of architecture, rather, is the building material already organized into elements, each one of which is a response to some prime construction problem. Such are, among others, the wall, the angle formed by the juncture of two walls, the openings made in the wall in the form of doors and windows, the roof or the vault, in short, those parts of an edifice required to define and isolate a closed portion of space. These formal elements are indispensable and independent of any consideration of beauty; their material can be different but the relationships between the materials of which they are composed are the same, or at least very similar, and this is the feature that confers a certain unity upon their group. An angle wall poses problems and presents similar features regardless of the material out of which it is built; the roofing constitutes another group of the same kind, but it is a real one because architects talk about it as a distinct unity: it is always through the roof, they say, that a building comes to a bad end.

We could perhaps discover the secret origin of architecture if we could watch the formal virtues of its building material come into being. Architect or not, the man whom necessity transforms into a builder will always proceed in the same way: a vertical wall, a horizontal roof. To construct a building whose parts are harmoniously integrated by employing the resources of modern technique, the builder will content himself with piling little houses on top of each other up to the height permitted by the terrain and building material used without endangering the solidity of the edifice. It is here that we can perhaps best

discern the formal vocation of the material and the influence that it brings to bear on the art, for walls can be
built with anything at hand, but the first way that was
devised for putting up lasting walls was to superpose
stones of manageable dimensions and of suitable form—or
which were made suitable by cutting—either by leaving
them in their plain state as is done to this day, or by
joining them together with some kind of mortar. "All the
solids of a construction," wrote the admirable Charles
Blanc, "are composed of props and of propped-up parts."
The wall is the pre-eminent prop. Pillars and columns are
only broken or open walls; the essential element of architecture is the wall.

Walls are of all kinds according to the materials of
which they are made—puddled clay, brick, concrete, glass
—and the choice of which are to be used depends on the
freedom of the entrepreneur limited only by considerations of convenience, local resources and, finally, cost. The
problem pertains to the order of building, which includes
the order of architecture but which, as we have said, is
not to be confused with it. Building is an art (*Baukunst*)
distinct from that of architecture (*Architektur*) and which
the latter presupposes. It is an art of industrial factivity,
or of manufacture which, as we have seen, has a beauty of
its own. A beautiful but badly built edifice might deceive
the eye of the general public, but no architect will be
able to stand the sight of it; without the art of building,
it is no longer architecture but decoration. An essential
feature of architecture, viewed as one of the fine arts, is that
it presupposes another art whose specific end is to ensure
the solidity of the edifice. Now, masonry pursues this end,
and when it makes this solidity visible it yields the beauty
proper to it, that of the beautiful wall integrated with
the beauty of the edifice as a formal unity. Here as

elsewhere the beauty of art flourishes on other kinds of beauty.

This can be better understood if we compare the mason's art to that of the carpenter. What is more beautiful than a flawless work of carpentry? Not too long ago a walker in the streets of Paris, or of any other large city, would stop in his tracks at the sight of one of those scaffoldings whose logical and harmonious structure gives the mind a sense of complete gratification. Logic and geometry are visibly materialized. This emotion is perhaps joined by another which we hardly dare mention since it so greatly risks being merely subjective, linked to the feeling of a kind of distant but real kinship between man, the living entity, and the wood, the residue of this other living entity, the tree. All wood is not useable for construction purposes, not even oak if oak is required. What is so particularly engaging and intimate about the wooden hut whose charm is desired even in palaces by means of costly woodwork? But let us not pursue these considerations which would be necessarily endless. What endows the carpenter's craft and creations with nobility is the fact that he works on elements susceptible to geometric forms which upon being conjoined are endowed with a formal unity that is pleasing to behold, even if the purpose is manifestly utilitarian.

The same holds true for the mason's artistry. Although it is more distant from man than wood since it is not a living entity, stone is no less a natural product. It is not found everywhere, we know where it comes from and we call it by its name. Like wood, indeed even better, it lends itself to division into units having a geometric form. Its chief virtue is solidity, mother of duration, and a wall is beautiful with the beauty proper to stone when, having been built for solidity, it expresses this quality. There is scarcely a man who, left to his own devices, would not learn the answer to this problem by his own reasoning. After man went beyond the stage in which materials were held together by virtue of their weight alone, he had recourse to cut stone. At the start, as if at the beginning of an infinity of possible variations, we find the elementary arrangement of the bed of stones, that is to say the regular super-position of the stones, parallel with their beds. In typical walling in its perfect form, the joints of a course are placed opposite, or nearly so, to the middle of the stone that is immediately higher or lower. This arrangement prevents the disjunctions from spreading from one bed of stones to the other. The solidity thus ensured is expressed by the formal unity of a visible geometric arrangement: the sight pleases us, it is a beautiful wall. Other courses can be created with stones of different forms, for example, by alternating respectively stones having long and narrow surfaces, or by laying the stones out in a wholly different manner, according to the materials available. The result is always a quality of beauty that is directly answerable to the building art. The art of the Romans was essentially the art of masonry. This is why they were so fond of partition walls, especially in all artifices that heightened the overall effect of the particular structure of each wall. The Greeks were, above all, architects. They did not fix attention upon the wall by devices like cut stone in series, or by motif-creating arrangements. Seeking, rather, the formal beauty of the edifice itself, they avoided stressing its structural elements.

Architecture, viewed under this aspect, utilizes for its proper ends a building material already organized into elements each one of which is a response to a construction problem. We have just discussed stone as a fundamental building material. Brick, glass and all the other materials used in modern construction would merit consideration from the same point of view, that is to say in relation to architecture properly so-called. Discussions of this kind could go on indefinitely, for it is impossible to decree *a priori,* in the name of any principle, that a particular building material ideally lends itself to plastic beauty or, conversely, that it is naturally hostile to it. All that philosophical reflection can do here is ask whether the duality of the art of building and of architecture may not be at the base of the difficulties which no disputation will ever resolve.

It is fashionable among modern builders to heap abuse on architects who cling to the classic style because of their inability to find a style proper to reinforced concrete, or even to plain concrete. The latter unhesitatingly acknowledge this shortcoming. One of them may be considered as their representative spokesman for having made this avowal: "We are beginning to construct in concrete but we continue to think in terms of stone." [4] It is easy to misuse an admission of this kind, but it would

4. A remark attributed to the architect Tournon in Le Corbusier, op. cit. about six pages before the end. Whether or not it is authentic the remark expresses a fact, but Le Corbusier somewhat over-hastily makes "an honest confession" of it. What this remark expresses is a fact. Its author refers to a "tenement building on Rue Nungesser-et-Coli, constructed of concrete and which proclaims precisely that here the architect *has thought* in concrete," but this is not the question. The question is to know whether this idea in concrete is a beautiful idea. Here, all objective criteria are lacking. We will never know whether what the contractor takes for architectural beauty is not simply the quite legitimate satisfaction that he experiences at the sight of his technical success. Since Roman times, builders have sought beauty in bigness which is precisely the criterion of technical success in the art of building. It is the beauty of the genre pyramid, which is real, but it behooves esthetics, not the philosophy of the fine arts, to define the beauty proper to it.

be more instructive to ferret out its meaning. If relatively few architects sincerely and persistently try "to think in terms of concrete," the reason may lie perhaps in the fact that concrete does not suggest any architectural idea to them. In other words, they do not love concrete; a building made out of concrete does not strike them as pleasing to behold. This material which lends itself to everything and does not impose on the architect any formal conditions proper to it, being grey, dull, monotonous and indifferent to the play of light, first of all inflicts a curious feeling of deception on the eye. A wonderful and highly appropriate material to use in public works which must be integrated with nature such as dams, dikes and other engineering facts of this kind which also have a beauty all their own, concrete is deceiving in architecture through a kind of absence of the building art. The architect experiences an insurmountable aversion when he does not perceive this art, pleasing in itself, in the finished work. It would be useless to object that concrete is also a building material because this is not a question here. What is at stake is to ascertain whether concrete is a kind of structure from which architecture can be created; if the architect's answer is negative, he scrutinizes the building and finds no architecture in it.

The problem is of a universal character in an age like ours in which industrial progress has super-abundantly increased the number of potential building materials and the techniques enabling their utilization. In its most general form, the question is whether any potential building material is susceptible to artistic form. In this respect the attitude of the contractor or of the engineer is quite different from that of the architect. In the presence of a new building material or of a new technique, the former will be very eager to use it. To what purpose? To do

everything that it is possible to do with it. It strikes him as
absurd not to utilize a means of production which, as the
achievement of our scientific and technological age, opens
up new perspectives to the builder. Those who hesitate,
or reject it, are denounced as reactionaries. At times this
is true but not always, nor necessarily. A sure way of
bringing ridicule upon oneself is to prophesy a case in
which this would not be true, yet it is not certain that any
new technique is bound to find a beauty proper to it, or at
least a beauty akin to that which we expect from an art
of the beautiful. Today in literature, in poetry, in painting, in the theatre, everywhere, we find new means of
expression in search of a beauty which would be their
unique creation. We never know how long the quest ought
to go on in order to ascertain whether the failure is the
fault of men or of things. For a very long time now we
have known one thing: stone is the pre-eminent building
material of the architect's art. The reason for this may lie
in the fact that stone introduces the minimum industrial
intervention between the artist's conception and his work.
All we see of the form wrought in stone is the form itself.
Be that as it may, and whatever the outcome may be, cur-
rent experience favors stone. And this experience goes back
a very long time. Since the time of the Romans, the
golden age of masonry, imitation has always been a one-
way process. Plaques of all kinds, the crudest replicas,
have always aimed at having what was not stone look like
stone, not vice-versa. On the ground of symbolic fact, let us
recall that in the first bridge in Paris built of concrete
cut stones were simulated to reassure the public. This
symbolic fact can serve for a host of others. Even when it
imitates wood, cement engenders a disturbed feeling in
the beholder. In the future, when cement fully prevails,
we may know of the architectural masterpieces for which

the arts of the beautiful can be indebted to it. Assuredly, it can serve other arts which have or can have their own beauty, and since all beauty is pleasing, none is negligible. But this is not in question here. We possess new building materials for which we do not yet have styles. It is simply a question of ascertaining whether some of these materials do not contain artistic forms that are proper to them. It is certainly possible. The philosopher is not qualified to answer the question as to whether this is a fact that can be ascertained or disproved. People deplore the ugliness of so many modern buildings. Perhaps this ugliness is inevitable, for there is no way to prohibit builders from utilizing any new materials and adopting all new techniques. And it is possible that among these new materials for which we have not yet found beautiful forms, there are some which do not contain them.[5]

Of all artists the architect is the one whose art is most encumbered with limitations. He does not choose the kind of building to be constructed; this is decided only by the client, whether he be a private person or a public body; the architect will build the city hall, the railroad station, the school, the low-cost housing project or private mansion which others need. Rarely is the location left to

5. The connection between the technique of construction and architecture is so close that if the former changes, an architect can have the impression of finding himself before a building that is a nullity. Here is a well-known architect who is not an enemy of new building materials: "Steel, concrete, glass, are magnificent building materials with magnificent possibilities!" But he takes his students to see Ronchamp and his reaction is wholly negative: "As a master builder, I think that Ronchamp is absolutely not a building." Why? "It denies all the laws of building." Paul Schmitthenner, "Tradition und Fortschritt in der Baukunst" in *Reden und Gedenkenwort (Orden Pour Le Mérite für Wissenschaften und Künste)*, 3, 1958/59, p. 57.

his choice. The building material, the interior arrangement and, for this very reason, its exterior aspect are in
part predetermined by the functions that the edifice must
serve and the financial resources available. There would
be no end to listing in detail the restrictions symbolized by
the "specifications"; the architect, in fact, is never sure
that he has seen the last of them. Yet the person with a
passion for building endures all in the hope of ultimately
realizing his dream: to create the new being, a structure
perfectly occupying its space, solidly implanted in the
ground and which although serving a useful purpose
will be a pleasing sight to behold. Before, there was only
an empty terrain, which perhaps even had to be cleared;
later, the building rises on this spot; the architect looks
upon it and thinks that, after all is said and done, it is
his work. If he has created an artistic work, this work will
resemble him and he has enriched the world with it,
and it is with pride that he is ready to sign his name to it.

What did he contribute that was peculiarly his own?
Form. But even here, he was not completely free. A style
can be forced upon him, models can be suggested to him,
in short he can be enslaved to tastes that are alien to him;
but if he is sure of his own taste it will be the architect
who finally decides what the building is to be. His
creation, the first act from which all the rest will ensue, the
act in relation to which the subsequent ones will be
arranged in keeping with their purpose, is an act of the
mind. More precisely, it is an act of the creative imagination which conceives the anticipated image of what the
edifice will be once it is built. Hence the architect's main
problem is to invent its general form. Any volume in space,
solid or not, has a form. Form is the arrangement and the
ordering of parts so that the eye may perceive the whole as
a unity. In relation to what is external to it, form consti-

tutes the volume into a distinct entity; by delimiting its
contours, it defines it. In relation to what is internal to it,
and which in consequence constitutes the volume, form is
that which makes of it a whole. The whole of a volume is
not the sum of its parts, but rather the ensemble of the
parts insofar as its form confers unity upon them. Leibniz
would add that it also confers being upon it inasmuch as
being and being one are the same thing. There is a form
for everything that exists, but in the case of an edifice
which is to be built, or is already built, it involves a form
given in space visible to the eye and conceived with the
aim of being pleasing to the beholder. To imagine such a
form of a possible edifice is to create it in the mind, while
waiting for it to assume the dimensions of being in reality.

Even if we do not go beyond this act of imagining,
the formal imagination of possible volumes does not start
out from a vacuum of images. We know nothing about the
beginnings of architectural invention, but archeology and
the history of art show that this invention unfolds in
that of general formal types called styles. The origin of
each style, the first acts that announce its advent, are also
shrouded in mystery and provide historians with subjects
for speculation which they find both irresistible and ultimately deceptive. We try to divine a future style in the
forms out of which it would not have emerged if it were
not in them, but from which it still had to emerge. In any
case, historians and architects are agreed upon recognizing
what they call the primacy of technique in the history of
styles. Speaking abstractly, and by using a very general
formula embracing all possible cases, we can say that an
architectural style appears at the moment when a technique of construction yields the formal beauty proper to it.

The concept of the "life of forms," which Focillon has

so forcefully and brilliantly formulated, assumes its full significance here. Architectural forms live because the architects, who create them, are living beings. Their discoveries and the formal experiences that time and circumstances permit each one of them accrue and are compounded until that moment when, in the imagination of some of them, the new technique reveals itself as rich in possibilities which up to then were still unknown in the order of beauty. Much time had to go by before the discovery of the resources latent in the semi-circular arch and in the semi-circular vault. These exceedingly simple forms permitted the unfolding of the Romanesque style with the naves in *Sainte-Foy de Conques* or *Saint-Etienne de Nevers,* and of apses such as those in *Notre-Dame-du-Port* at Clermont, or in *Santa Maria e Donato* at Murano, to cite only at random. Later the ogival, or pointed, arch was born within the same Romanesque style as an element of the new construction which, in the imagination of the architects of the Ile-de-France, in turn engendered the Gothic style. Today historians analyze monuments in terms of plan, structure, elevation and ornamentation, or in terms of other similar distinctions, but all this was born of the edifice itself and first of all from the projected image of it originally conceived by the architect. As an artist he thinks of construction through volumes; he becomes a surveyor, engineer and worker, if need be, only so that the image may become a reality.[6] From the moment the plan pre-

6. There is no architect who, as long as his age and vigor permit him, does not like to prove before his men that he can pitch in and do their work too. At any rate, it is certain that the invention of constructed forms presupposes that of new processes required in order to construct them. The architect who finds an extraordinarily efficient collaborator in his contractor may find

cedes the interior vision, the reign of pedantry begins and architecture enters into a state of decline.

The nature of the problem can easily be recognized in our time when concrete is still trying to determine whether it can create a style; or rather in the history of the other technological revolution heralded by the advent of the American skyscraper. Architect Frank Lloyd Wright often pointed out that the first buildings of this kind consisted merely of a pile of low houses superposed upon each other. One day his teacher showed him a photograph of a recently built skyscraper, simply saying, "Look, that's a tall building"; in other words, a building conceived in terms of tallness and not merely as a heap of low buildings, piled one upon the other up to the desired height. To do that it was necessary that an architect think about a new form which would make an organic whole out of the ensemble of the structural elements included in the edifice. The formal invention in that case consists in casting, so to speak, this multiplicity into a unique form created to receive it. Now that the problem has been solved at the building level, will it also be solved at the level of architecture? Up to now the skyscraper is the meeting-ground of all the ancient styles rather than the revelation of a new style, but it is too early to prophesy without running the grave risk of being mistaken.[7]

---

himself becoming one. Indeed, it is classic to hear the contractor who will confide to anyone who will listen that the building would not stand up without him, as if the architect alone had been involved in the project.

7. There are encouraging signs. It seems that it is no longer believed that a skyscraper has style if it terminates in a Florentine villa, in a Siamese tiara or in any specimen of a style already known. The most recent skyscrapers that have been built try to find their own roof. As regards the constructions of traditional dimensions, it is possible that they have already found their style, but that our eye

Philosophers do not easily take to the notion that the purpose of architecture is to produce buildings revealing only their beauty. In contrast to those who forget the beautiful in favor of the useful, metaphysicians betray beauty for the sake of truth. In an essay written in 1900 on the philosophy of Ravaisson, Emil Boutroux asked in the most natural way in the world: "Indeed, are not the arts themselves an effort of the mind to grasp and express that which is most perfect and essential in nature and in man?" Thus understood, the function of "works of genius" is to disclose a certain "conception of things." Reflection upon architecture helps to free us from this error. The anonymous creators of the Greek orders, those who were the first to experiment with the use of the semi-circular arch and then with the ogival arch, or those who were the first to return to the Greek modes which, actually, had never been forgotten, do not seem to have wanted to know or express existing reality, but rather to create. Their effort aimed at producing a being whose beauty would justify its existence, and which would be an addition to nature instead of an expression of it. It is significant that in his sermon on death, the classic Bossuet should have found a

---

is not yet accustomed to discerning it. Styles assert themselves with the greatest clarity at the very moment that they are on the wane. Finally, we can ask whether the characteristic of a new architectural style is not found elsewhere than in the presence of a formal new element. We already recognize a "modern" edifice at first sight. In trying to know why, we learn first of all that it is not classifiable in the ancient styles; in the second place that the novelty of forms is closely related to the use of some new materials; and finally that their use has the effect of enabling the adoption of lines which formerly were still impossible. Therein lies one of the principal difficulties. The desire to attempt everything that has become possible with the new building materials and new techniques does not guarantee that the result of the experiment will be beautiful.

key to the realm of art in the dogma of the creation of the world. God made the world like a huge machine of which man can make use and which he can further embellish by his art. And how could man do this if he did not bear within himself "some artistry derived from this primal artistry, some fecund ideas drawn from these original ideas, in a word, some likeness, some flow, some portion of this artisan spirit that has made the world?"

Can we determine exactly what is proper to the architectural form which this thought creates? It is all the more interesting to attempt it inasmuch as it is confirmed by reflection, as fluid and immaterial as the matter which it orders is solid. The contrast perceived between the immateriality of artisan thought and the weight of the mass that it orders seems to be included in the esthetic experience of architectural beauty. Indeed, there is a mysterious something in the event. It is really a thought which has become stone by mobilizing for this purpose the docile bodies of innumerable human beings freely acquiescing to serve it, or forcibly made to bend to its law. There is human blood in the mortar of any great monument and much human pain in the beauty of a cathedral. How many workers died on these immense crosses? Along with the poets, we prefer to think that all this was done by the waving of a magic wand, but the mystery remains. When Amphion, the son of Jupiter and of Antiope, built the walls of Thebes by the sound of his lyre, the stones, of their own volition, gently slid into the desired position in the walls. This beautiful myth has crossed the centuries but not without attracting the attention of some meditative persons born to understand it. Faithful to their vocation, the German Romantics formulated the meaning of this myth. Schelling translated it into a concept when he defined architecture as the "inorganic, artistic form of plastic music"; and Schlegel coined a felicitous phrase, which rightly enjoyed a great vogue, when he called it "a crystallized music." Such images draw attention to a very important point. Whatever building material it uses, architecture consists in imparting to it a form whose intelligibility is perceptible to the senses. This form is the work of the mind, and by virtue of this authority it bears its own justification within itself. The geometric relationships between the forms of volumes constructed in space contain their complete meaning within themselves; like the relationships between sounds that the musician creates, those established by the architect between lines, surfaces, and volumes obey mathematical laws and in neither of these two arts does the manner in which they are arranged aim at the reproduction, representation or imitation of any external object. The meaning of an edifice is in itself; the plastic structure realized by the architect is its own justification.

This autonomy of architecture is evident from the moment a choice is made regarding the elements to be used. If we look carefully, we can easily find in nature forms similar to those organized by the architect. The architect does not find ready-made straight lines in nature any more than the musician finds therein the musical sounds which he combines according to definite laws. Delacroix declared that nature abhors them and tries to destroy them—right angles, perfect arches and so forth. Assuredly, there are no forms the idea of which is not suggested by nature. The artist creates neither from a vacuum of matter nor from a vacuum of forms, but those forms which he uses are intermediaries between the perfect geometric forms which exist only in the mind and the rough outlines met with in nature. The ensemble of invented elements that architectural invention utilizes consists of straight lines, plane or curved surfaces whose forms are calculated and owe as little as possible to chance—in short, all the figures and solids that geometry conceptualizes and that stereotomy produces. As in music, everything in architecture is a work of art, even its material. Everything in it is creation.

Architecture does not speak, it is. It is enveloped in a great silence, but man, being a great talker, strains his ingenuity to make it talk. We must have recourse to ancient Greek temples, primitive Roman churches or Cistercian chapels to offer examples of pure architecture whose whole beauty is in the form. If architecture keeps silent, monuments are made to talk. They are sculpted, painted, they are made to tell the Bible story in a hundred ways, that of Amiens or any other. As long as the decoration is integrated with the edifice and does not alter its line, not only does it not act as a disturbing element but it varies the plays of light by catching it on the surfaces. Moreover, taken in itself, a sculptured or painted ornament can be a perfect masterpiece, but it is answerable to another art. The effort to ascertain the nature of architecture and to define it in itself does not commit us to isolate it from what it is not. There are Baroque churches which are nothing more than a pretext offered to the sculptor to display his virtuosity. This does not make sculpture into architecture, and the effect produced is a question of personal taste. Pure architecture, perhaps, would have only a handful of faithful followers if buildings offered themselves to view without an imagery designed to fix the attention of the beholders.

The formalism of architecture enables us to understand why the great philosophers and theologians of the Middle Ages, whenever they had occasion to talk about artists, usually cited only the architect. Saint Thomas, who inherited this idea from Aristotle, cites no other, and he does this only to compare the architect to the metaphysician. The First Philosophy, which is the supreme architectonic science, stands at the summit of the hierarchy of the sciences, since its proper object is the cognition of the principles upon which the whole edifice of knowledge depends. Thus, since Wisdom is architecture, architecture is like the wisdom of an ensemble of manual operations which it arranges and regulates with a same end in view.

This explains the favor enjoyed among scholastics by the famous definition of art as a good, reasoned method of production. For it quite fittingly applies to the architect who invents, projects, prescribes and superintends, but does nothing with his hands. Once more, he resembles the musician who composes the symphony but does not play it. This results from the fact that both handle only forms, although in different ways. In contrast to the musician, the architect needs neither an interpreter nor executants to carry out his plan; all he has are contractors and workers who do not confer existence upon the materials of the work in the way that executants create musical sounds, and who do not decide, as does the orchestra conductor, how the work will be realized. The architect disposes as he pleases of the assured materials, all he has to do is to choose them, and since he is ultimately responsible for the whole he wields authority over the whole operation, but he does not construct. The very nature of the operations to be carried out opposes this. The architect is shown holding a square-ruler, a compass, a simple ruler. A plumbline can be seen alongside him, but he is never pictured with a trowel in his hand. Like the composer, the architect is a white-collar worker. His work is done at an architect's table, on which the future volumes are schematically projected.

We are talking here about architecture proper, but

it is obvious that the completed edifice, house or monument, is not the work of architecture alone. Architecture,
being an art of space, attracts all the other arts of space
which obtrude to adorn it, but also to disfigure it, or in
any case live off it parasitically. The arts of eloquence
and music are the only arts which ally themselves with
architecture without harming it. Since they are not arts
of space, they can associate with it and exploit it without
harm. When Monteverdi's music used to be played on
Fridays in the festive hall of the palace in Mantua, the
architecture did not suffer from it. Ornamentation forms
part of the edifice, but the architect is not its author.[8] To

8. The history of art rightfully takes the edifice as it is, or was,
in the global unity of its form, its structure, and of its ornamentation. Its useful function even belongs to it. When a Gothic cathedral loses its altar, by becoming Protestant, it loses its intelligibility
and its beauty at the same time. Roman art is not pure architecture;
its ornamentation belongs to it only in the measure in which its
bands, capitals and statue-columns have been willed by an architect. If there is something excessive in this philosophic spirit of
abstraction, we will look for its antidote in John Ruskin. *The
Seven Lamps of Architecture* will provide the reader with the opposite of almost everything I have said here. In Ruskin's book architecture is illumined by the lamp of Truth, it imitates nature, and
the illustrations with which the author accompanies his text reproduce ornaments and decorations as though architecture consisted
essentially in that. Yet who would wish that Ruskin's book had
never been written? It is replete with beauties all its own, it abounds
in correct estimates of its objects, and if the author has chosen to
talk more about what he likes in the monuments of architecture
than about the very essence of the architect's art, was this not his
prerogative? Ruskin is reproached for his moralism, but who will
deny that there is a probity of art, and that it is essential to beauty?
It is a good thing that most of the possible points of view on the
same object are already taken, even if we can occupy ourselves
with them only one at a time in order to arrive at a clear view. If
we refer, for example, to Aphorism 22, which expresses a prudential

ordain whether or not there is to be ornamentation depends on special circumstances. In any case, it is remarkable that the great mural decorations, whether on walls or on vaulted ceilings, smoothly integrate with painted architecture, in camaïeu or in *trompe l'oeil,* as if to effect a harmony between the two arts of space which do not deal with it in the same spirit or in the same way. Some architecture calls for painting and statuary, some rejects them. The most favorable circumstance is that in which, as in Romanesque art at the time of its flowering, architecture secretes its own ornamentation. But these are problems outside the frame of architecture proper. Their solution depends on the taste of the artists. Moreover, we are thereby touching upon problems of esthetics, distinct from poietic activity which is the very substance of art.

There is only one point in which esthetic experience obviously affects art in its very poietic function. If the artist's general purpose is to produce the work, once this work is wrought the purpose of the finished work is to be seen. Therefore, the architect must construct the edifice such as it must be in order for it to be seen as it should be seen. Even as a simple optical instrument, the eye has its exigencies. Therefore, the architect must calculate the site, the dimensions and the proportions in terms of the way in which they will be seen. The Greek architects knew this. In the Parthenon the deliberate inward inclination of the columns, the thickness of the angle columns, the exact emplacement of those in the middle of the colonnade were so many devices to give the edifice the appearance that it has for us today. Relationships of a strictly mathematical, rather than an optical, character would spoil the impression that the artist wishes to produce. Likewise, in

mistrust of sculpture in architecture, we will see how different theoretical views can at times agree on the same reality.

a Gothic cathedral, in looking for the exact place for the two towers of the façade—a problem whose complexity is sufficiently revealed by the history of art—the architect runs into the difficulty of passing from the horizontality of the façade to the verticality of the spires. The so-called gallery of Kings solves the problem, provided that the simple small columns of the façade are of a height they must have to ensure the apparent dimensions which they ought to have. Some of these conditions of the esthetic experience are unfortunately beyond the architect's power. It is not so much the edifice that will change as, inevitably, the site around it. *Saint-Germain-des-Prés, Notre-Dame de Paris* and *Sainte-Chapelle* have become unrecognizable because the absence of style in the structures around them today makes them archeological remains denied by their environment with which they in turn contend. The architectural sites for which these edifices were originally built have ceased to exist for a long time. The architect loses exclusive control over his work even before it is finished. Restorers know very well that the appearance of a monument is almost always improved by restoring it to its original state. The architect is not able to foresee exactly how this edifice will age; the esthetic reality of his work escapes him to the degree of his ignorance on this point; he can only make the building as durable as possible, and nothing allows him to foresee exactly when or how it will eventually meet its demise.

THREE

Statuary

IT IS EASILY GRANTED that statuary progressively cut itself off from architecture during the transition from low-relief to high-relief to full-round. The hypothesis satisfied the imagination, but the continuity which it implies is not evident, for there exist prehistoric statuettes and nothing about them indicates that they are posterior to an evolution of this kind. Nevertheless, the ensemble of operations whose end is to create in space a hollow volume defining the contours of a habitable space differs specifically from that whose intention is to create solids the proportions of which are pleasing to the eye.

These solids (or objects giving the impression of being solid) are statues. From the earliest beginnings to our day, the art of statuary has been closely related to social activities alien to the arts of the beautiful. Religions, nations, families, at times individuals have had recourse to statuary to illustrate their beliefs, their feelings, their vanity, but actually this art is quite apart from all that. Connected so closely with collective or individual representations of this kind, it merely serves them by producing statues. And it makes these representations serve it as much as it serves them, for statuary has always lived on them, and it exists as an art of the beautiful only to the extent to which the sculptor, regardless of the feeling inspiring the "commission," seizes the opportunity to produce a work capable of pleasing the eye.

One is so far from limiting this plastic art to its proper object that the definitions made of it sometimes neglect to mention beauty as being among its ends. Sculpture, according to one definition, "is the art of expressing ideas, feelings or characteristics by the chosen and obvious imitation of living forms." Viewed thus, "sculpture is a powerful means of public education, because its creations perpetuate among men the presence of a higher beauty in the visible and tangible forms which are manifestations of the spirit." [1] But how many times has not the artist first made the statue for its own sake and then looked around for a label denoting that which the viewer might wish or imagine it to express. Even granting that statuary is an art of expression and of the expression of ideas, the fact remains that it conveys this expression through the medium of statues and that its proper end is to produce them. What, then, is a statue?

Inasmuch as it belongs to the arts of the beautiful, its first character is to appear to the beholder as a solid block, constituting a distinct whole in space, immovable as the inert material of which it is made and the sight of which is desirable in itself. What is here in question, therefore, is statuary in its perfect form, which is full-round, and of which it can truly be said that it produces distinct and isolated objects in space. Indeed, this is why the temptation to define it as an imitative art is almost irresistible, for it frequently imitates, and when it does it gives the impres-

1. Charles Blanc, *Grammaire des arts du dessin,* book II, ch. 1; op. cit., pp. 329 and 333.

sion of emulating nature, indeed almost of competing with it—and sometimes with a semblance of success. This feeling is aptly expressed in the myth of Pygmalion. We can say of a statue: all it lacks is the gift of speech. In this respect, neither painting, music nor literature is comparable to sculpture. The sculptor must find in this feeling a source of the joys proper to his art. The reason for this is that his work is a *thing* among others and that it preserves its ontological status even if its purpose happens to be imitation.

The statue, made of a solid of some kind, is as inert as the material substance used to make it. This is why statuary is an art of space, for it is of the essence of the statue that it be given all at once. Some last for millennia. "The bust outlives the city" says the poet, but statues last in the simultaneity of their parts, or of those which survive the ravages of time. The same controversy that revolves around the nature of architecture is repeated here. It is pointed out that it is impossible to see a statue without envisaging it in all its aspects, which cannot be done unless the spectator moves around it. True enough, but in this case it is the spectator who moves around to see it just as the sculptor moved around while making it, but the statue itself does not move. Kant has clearly established that the form of space is given in that of time. Before him, Aristotle had asserted that we think in time, but it does not follow therefrom that space is time. An art of movement is one in which the works themselves exist only successively in time, part after part, not an art which requires that the artist move in order to produce them, or that the spectator move in order to behold them. Whether they are heavy or light, statues are immovable solids, and it is precisely for this reason that the spectator must move when looking at them. Whereas music, the dance, or dramatic art, in order to exist, move before spectators fixed in their seats, sculpture's essential immobility requires the spectator himself to move around it so that he can view it as a whole. A statue, no doubt, can be set on a rotating platform, but in that case it would be necessary to immobilize it in order to see only one aspect of it all at once.[2] When statues are carried in a pageant, the spectacle can take on a hallucinatory beauty, which invariably produces a strange effect, like the Spanish statues that swing gently to and fro with an almost living grace when they are borne in religious processions.

Statuary is the art of making statues, whatever the process. Sculpture proper is the art of making statues by working directly on a block of wood, stone or marble, using a hammer and chisel, so that ultimately only the form of the statue subsists. This process, called direct carving, is distinguished from the statuary obtained through modelling. Sculpture works directly on hard material, whereas modelling is practiced on a substance that is soft and suitable to being moulded by the hands with the help, if necessary, of knives, chisels or other similar tools. Like sculpture, modelling produces statues, but it is a statuary of a different kind.

The basic material of sculpture is a natural product endowed with its own structure and with physical qualities that determine its formal vocation. Men have sculpted stone and wood, secondarily ivory and bone, since time immemorial. The initial choice of one of these materials predetermines in part the kind of statue that will be ob-

2. The rotational movement imparted to the statue produces a curious effect of unreality, for in that case all its aspects are presented successively in the same light, whereas the immobile statue offers different lights and shadows to the spectator who moves around it. The *real* statue does not move.

tained. The color will be necessarily different. The statue
has a skin. The more or less deep brown of wood can be
distinguished at first sight from the greys or reds of granite,
as the whitenesses of ivory differ from stone or marble. The
physical qualities of the materials chosen are infinitely
varied, so to speak. The wood chosen is often the heart of
oak, of ash, or beech, but this can also be a sap-wood that
has been left to age for a long time to gain the required
hardness. These woods differ among themselves and the
statues bear the marks of the differences, but they have in
common the quality of being structured matter, alive at
one time, and whose substance, henceforth inert, nevertheless remains that of an organized body. Its fibrous,
knotty structure, variegated by a thousand irregularities,
poses problems for the artist that often turn out to be suggestions. Sometimes the artist finds the form in the structure of the wood. To a lesser degree, perhaps, but no less
surely, stone and marble speak to the sculptor who is about
to subject them to his artistry. The anecdote about Michelangelo's repeated visits to a block of marble, as though to
consult with it from time to time on what it itself desired
to become, symbolizes a profound truth. Matter aspires to
the form potential in it. The more form dominates, the
less it need fear a dialogue with matter, and, at times, to
heed it. Hence, there can be an intelligible relation between
material form and artistic form; the form that art imparts
to matter does not come to it exclusively from without.

No doubt it is along this path that we must seek the
reason for the high esteem in which sculptors hold direct
carving, even when they do not practice it. The artist in
this case is in contact with the material, as though in
intimate communion with it, first through its direct and
almost personal resistance to him, then on a deeper level
through the ceaseless interrogation to which he submits the

material and to whose responses he hearkens. It is still true
to say that direct carving is superior to any other technique
of statuary because of the absolute mastery of the craft that
it requires; it has little tolerance for mistakes. But the real
reason for its eminent dignity is attributable to the fact
that no other technique strives so literally "to extract form
from the potency of matter," if we may use Aristotle's old
formula, or, in other terms, to actualize the form which
the material contained only as potency. Let us not conceal
the ambiguity surrounding these words; such is always the
case when we approach the region of principles, but we
should also be wary of taking them for mere verbiage! No
doubt, what Michelangelo saw in the block of marble
which he visited was not the future statue, for if it lay
within the marble only the marble knew it, but rather he
waited for silent counsel from the form of the block, from
the grain of the stone, and from the color of its skin, regarding the kind of a statue it had the vocation to become.
The path of execution is the true path of sculpture, along
which counsels of this kind multiply to such a degree that
the form of the matter and the form of the mind seem to
unite to guide the hand and the chisel. Perhaps there is no
other case in which artistry merges more completely with
the execution itself, and in the last analysis it is to this fact
that the technique of direct carving owes its eminent
dignity.

Philosophy has no special prerogatives except where
principles are concerned; only art itself can say what it is,
and this is why it is outside the philosopher's competence
to discuss practices and techniques in order to discern their
spirit except on the basis of what artists say about them
and of the works they produce. By questioning artists,[3] we

3. When asking questions of artists we must be wary not to
interpret what is only their personal manner of understanding and

soon learn that there is more than one way of practicing
direct carving, depending on whether it introduces more
or fewer intermediaries between the hand guided by the
mind and the material on which it works. Here again, it
appears that the sculpture which is more purely sculpture
is also recognized as its highest type. This is the sculpture
of those primitives whose works are so greatly admired by
many artists, to the dismay of persons of taste. "Negro" art
puts such persons in the presence of a technique, that of
pure sculpture, from which modern man is separated by
centuries, perhaps by millennia, from the history of art.
Specifically, it is that the technique in which the artist's imagination informs matter without any other intermediary
save the tool held in his hand. In other forms of sculpture,
a drawing stands between the sculptor and the statue.
During the Renaissance, sculptors worked from sketches,

---

practicing their art as a theory of the same. The demonstra-
tions, at times somewhat dramatic, that some "masters" give in
the ateliers which they direct are likewise subject to caution.
Finally, their trade is not that of the philosopher; we must not
always interpret as definition certain outbursts which at bottom
are only practical counsels given in a paradoxical form in order
to engrave them on the memory. "Sculpture, although this may
surprise you, is nothing else but drawing, don't expect more, it is
nothing else." Daniel Marquis-Sébie, *Une leçon de Antoine Bourdelle à la Grande Chaumière* (Paris: *Artisan du livre,* 1930), p. 17. Indeed, it is something else and Bourdelle knew it. Let us add that
at that time he was teaching students to model clay from a living
model, which is a special exercise. On the following page, he recalls the example of Ingres, but Delacroix would have protested.
Bourdelle adds: "All of you here must clearly understand that in
order to sculpt it is necessary to draw for the same reason that the
pianist forces himself to practice exercises." But piano exercises
are piano exercises, whereas drawings are not exercises in sculpture. One would take pleasure, however, in watching the mind of
an expert at work, pp. 18–19.

later from the live model, and even used the method, by far the worst and yet the most widely practiced of all times, of sculpturing statues from statues. The more intermediaries that come between the artist and the material of the work, the less is the artistry marked by vigor and freedom.

The second sovereign branch of statuary employs the technique of modelling. Until recently, the principal materials used for modelling have been clay, wax and plaster. The latter is suitable for all kinds of projects; clay is preferred for works of large dimensions, wax being used for works of smaller size, such as busts and even jewels of which the artist desires to make models before proceeding to the definitive execution.

Whatever material he may use, the modeller does not do the work of a sculptor, strictly speaking, but modelling has so generally replaced sculpture that it seems pedantic to insist on a distinction between these two arts. Those who faithfully visit the exhibition of the works executed for the *Prix de Rome* for Sculpture do not remember ever seeing there anything else but freshly modelled grey clays of potential statues, still to be executed. The success of modelling is easily understandable. The plastic material it utilizes is as malleable as stone is resistant; with clay nothing is ever definitive, any mistake can be corrected, none is fatal. Even without taking into account vulgar considerations, which are not without importance, such as the lowering of the cost price of the materials on which the artist pursues his experiments, modelling in itself offers such facilities of execution, it is not at all surprising that there are relatively few sculptors in stone today.

Its very facileness constitutes the danger to which modelling exposes the artist. By this, of course, we mean the facilities that it permits him, indeed to which it invites him. The sculptor can pursue only the realization of one and the same purpose on one and the same block. The statue, whose form he ferrets out in stone or marble, cannot make place for another in the course of the execution. Of course it changes under the artist's hand, but it is always the same work in different moments of its progress. The facilities enjoyed by the modeller are such that, while preserving all proper proportions, his work changes form under his fingers like the vase incessantly metamorphosized under the fingers of the potter. Even if the unity of form is maintained up to the end of the execution, the temptation remains to burden the work with details not required by this form and which in consequence obscure its recognizability. But the artist yields to the temptation to execute these details simply for the personal pleasure of exercising a skill at times bordering on virtuosity. Finally, the very malleability of clay and wax, or of modelling paste, excludes the collaboration of the material in the birth of all form which characterizes sculpture, imparting its proper perfection and approximating its works to those of nature. A plastic material which is wholly amorphous and strictly homogeneous has nothing to say to an artist who examines it; in the finished work we will never feel that substantial unity of matter and form which is proclaimed in those works whose very form owes its precise configuration to its matter.

The influence that the spread of modelling has had on statuary is appraised in different ways. As the name indicates, modelling means to work from a model. When the artist has passed from the model to the statue, he can make a cast of it from which other castings will be made. Castings can be obtained through different processes each of which utilizes a different material, different techniques which, consequently, lead to artistically different results. Bronze is the best known material. Nothing gives us a more vivid idea of the nature of the relation between art and technique with respect to the artist himself than the exciting account of the casting of *Perseus* in Benvenuto Cellini's memoirs. Whatever the details may be, the aim of an operation of this kind is to impart the form of a previously modelled statue to a metallic mass which is almost indefinitely durable. The process dispenses with the more complex work which consists in executing in stone the statue as it emerges from the modeller's hands. The casting of the statue marks the transition from art to industry, thereby granting us the benefit of the increasing infallibility of its techniques, but we draw further and further away from the characteristic act of the sculptor in which the mind, through hand and tool, engages personally in a dialogue with an individually determined material. Bronze is an avatar of the model; it has its characteristic beauty plus the paradoxical feature of preserving the maximum suppleness in the forms and in the relief of the metal. Donatello's charming and somewhat disquieting *David,* at the Barzello in Florence, whose back is hardly in the heroic mould, provides a useful contrast to the powerful *David* executed in marble by Michelangelo. The conception underlying the works is not here in question; rather what ought to hold our attention is the relationship between their conception and their execution, and the respective media employed. Who would deny that each of the works has a beauty proper to it? It would be impossible to place them mentally on a common scale to measure the degree of this beauty; their perfections are incommensurable and we should all feel free to follow our own preference, if we have any. The fact remains, however, that if we have formed a certain idea of statuary through reflection, and if we compare the notion of two arts rather than the success of two creations, we will inevitably be led to the conclusion that the casting of a model is several degrees removed from the act by which the sculptor directly carves the wood or the marble. Art always denies itself some perfections when it grants itself some facilities.

Historians of statuary seem to admit the progressive disappearance of sculpture proper as a second consequence of the spread of modelling. The modeller, having never served his apprenticeship, does not even have to forget what he has learned about sculpture. In order to transform his own model into a statue of stone or of marble he must call on specialists who perform this operation as a trade. Thus the artist has recourse to the "rougher-out" whose function consists in sculpting statues which he himself has not conceived. The operation is possible and the person who performs it is often a highly talented artisan. Indeed some of these artisans devote themselves to the art of statuary, as was the case with Pompon (although in his personal production this excellent animal sculptor always insisted on bringing his own models to completion himself).

Feasible as the operation is,[4] it cannot be reversed. It is by definition impossible to retrace one's steps over a path that one has never taken. The "rougher-cut" can never reconstitute from a modelling a sculpture that has never existed. Therefore he will never go beyond the point to which the modeller has brought his work, not because he does not know the art of stone-carving—after all, that's his

4. Alain goes very far in this direction. "It is not hard to imagine a machine for sculpting which would give the stone or the marble the exact hollows, reliefs and dimensions of the model." *Système des beaux-arts* (Paris: Pléiade), VII, 1 p. 366. Philosophers have a great facility for inventing these machines in their heads, but assuming such a machine has been invented, its work would still presuppose that of the sculptor; it would multiply his works without having the artist work at making them.

craft—but because he himself does not have to create a beautiful form by working on the stone directly in the manner of the sculptors of old. The statue-maker himself would not be able to transform into sculpture a model which he has not conceived by following the shape of the material and by being in intimate communion with it. Neither the "rougher-out" nor the statue-maker can fashion a sculpture out of something which was not sculptured in the first place.

One of the direct results of this situation is that the greater part of modern statues are in reality replicas, in stone or in marble, of original models in clay, wax or some kind of plastic material. The dimensions of the replica moreover can differ from those of the original; all that is required is the application of the mechanical processes of enlargement or reduction without the artist's personal intervention being necessary, something inconceivable in direct carving. Hence there are fewer and fewer true sculptures in existence. Likewise, there are fewer and fewer sculptors in the strict sense of the word. The philosopher is not qualified to make prophecies, but it seems reasonable to conjecture that the future of sculpture is bound up with the advent of artists whom technological progress has not yet cut off from the roots of their art. This is the meaning of the stir caused by so-called "Negro" art which disconcerted so many of our contemporaries. Primitive peoples will perhaps step into the breach. In our time, of course, primitive peoples do not remain primitive for long. We have seen Eskimo art decay in twenty years thanks to the enlightened care of a paternalistic administration. Let us hope that from time to time some artist will be found who is destined to rediscover an art whose pure form is as old as man. There need not be a large number of them, for only a few artists suffice to fashion the happiness of man-kind, provided they are truly great. Phidias and Praxiteles, Michelangelo and Verrocchio, Pierre Puget and their emulators have staked out a time-honored path on which we can assume others will more or less safely follow.

We change worlds when we proceed from architecture to statuary. Sculpture has no connection with architecture, neither in terms of its end nor of its techniques; we find nothing of the beginnings associated with the act of the sculptor in the act of constructing an edifice. Furthermore, we perceive no resemblance between an edifice and a statue; on the contrary, the differences are striking, the most obvious one being that architecture does not imitate anything. No house suggests that it is a model of something in nature, whereas it is impossible to utter the word "statue" without mentally forming the question: of what? The statue in which the sculptor actualizes the perfection of its essence is almost always the representation of a man, of a woman, of some animal, or of one of those beings conceived as the effigy of a god. Statues of things can be made, but this is a rare event and it is not even certain that the notion is a meaningful one. The sculptured or modelled representation of an inanimate object in no way differs essentially from this object itself. The statue of a marble chair is a marble chair, but the statue of a seated man is not a seated man.

This natural destination of statuary to represent living beings explains the predilection of sculptors for the human or animal form or, that is to say, for subjects each of which has a definite unity and is a whole isolatable in space and around which the beholder can walk. In short, sculpture burdens philosophical reflection with the problem of the relation of art to imitation, for what is at stake this time is not merely to ascertain whether statuary is possible without imitation, but rather whether statuary is not imitation by birth and in essence.

It is imitation at least in one sense. The very project of fashioning distinct objects, each of which occupies its own place in space, betrays the intention of competing with nature where space is filled with such objects. Moreover, as far as conjecture is possible, all the most ancient modelled or sculptured objects known to us represent animal or human forms. In any case, it would be arbitrary to claim that the mimicry natural to man has not played a decisive role in the origins of statuary. Without wishing to make a bald assertion on the basis of what after all is an unverifiable supposition, it seems at least reasonable to glimpse a degree of kinship between the first modellings and the almost instinctual movements with which listless fingers model the bread crumbs lying on the table into tiny animals. Primitive sculptors perhaps simply yielded to the same tactile and muscular urge. Anyhow, mimicry seems essential to statuary in the sense that the sculptor or modeller, himself surrounded by things, yields to the desire to add to the objects surrounding him other objects of which he is the maker and, specifically, the cause. Even today when sculpture has freed itself from the urge to imitate to the point where it flees from it rather than goes in search of it, the artists representative of this tendency publicly declare that their intention is to make sculptures which are actually "things" among things and which can be left on the ground of a garden like a stone or a rock. But making a "thing" is still an imitation of reality.

This basis of statuary in imitation is a salutary warning against overdoing the systematization of philosophical reflections on the fine arts. It is possible that all the arts tend to liberate themselves progressively from imitation,

but some of them cannot achieve this goal completely because their origins lie in imitation itself. We can even
ask ourselves whether, in the case of some arts, the concept
of matter should not be divided in two, so that it can include the imitated form itself. As we can imagine it in its
beginnings and as, in any case, we see it reproduced in all
sculpture workshops, the sculptor's operation consists in imparting a form to a matter sculptured or modelled by analogy with the form of a given natural being. It is a commonplace that the artist never plans to copy the model exactly.
Even if he is working from a live model, as the phrase
goes, his purpose is not slavishly to reproduce a human
body, since all he would need for that would be a cast. It
has been shown on occasion that some sculptors have done
just this (like Clésinger for *The Woman Bitten by a Ser-
pent*), but it is never meant as praise. One point on which
everybody is agreed is that the art of imitation aims to go
beyond the level of imitation and that the inventiveness
of the artist is to be measured by the transformation he
imparts to the model in order to guide its natural form
to the plastic perfection of the work of art. As was suggested at first, if we consider all its determinable elements,
including its natural form, as the matter of the work, it
seems reasonable to include in the same notion the very
model from which the artist works, in addition to the material which he models or sculpts. The sculptor who sculpts
a man or a horse submits the form of his models to the
determinations which his mind imparts to them as author-
itatively as his hands mould or sculpt the matter of the
statue. Assuredly, to sculpt a man is tantamount to giving
the stone the form of man, but it is also tantamount to
giving the form of the real man the form of the statue of
man which is fitting only to the work of art. The very
possibility of statuary as an art requires this. In this sense

it becomes conceivable that an art as intimately related to imitation as is statuary is, nevertheless, a genuine art. The fact is that what it includes of imitation in itself is only matter, even if it is a form which is to be imitated.

This sort of primal destination of statuary to the imitation of living beings, from which it disengages itself with great difficulty and at the cost of efforts not at all natural to it, exercises a deep influence on the plastic quality of its works. Let us repeat once more that the artist is free, that we can scarcely talk of rules in these matters, even barely to the extent where the question of exceptions could arise. What is at stake here, as is always the case with the philosophy of art, is to extract by reflection some ideal essences in relation to which the works will find their place. Each one of them is beautiful if it achieves the perfection of what it wills to be; those which find their beauty in a proper conformity with the essence of their own art are not necessarily more beautiful than others, but their beauty is of a specifically different kind. Any sculptor knows what it is for a statue to be pure sculpture; any musician immediately recognizes the tone of pure music; any real poet infallibly perceives the tone of pure poesy, in Racine, La Fontaine or Mallarmé. Art is pitiless toward its practitioners; good intentions are worthless, final success alone counts, and all that can be said is that fidelity to the essence of its art always confers upon some work a particular dignity which, if the work is beautiful, can only ennoble its beauty.

Thus there is a pre-established harmony, one that is easily discovered by man, between the distinct unities, or living beings, situated in space and the existence of blocks of solid matter also situated in space by means of which such beings can be represented. In conformity with this prime purpose, statuary in principle prefers to produce unique beings, that is to say solitary or isolated beings. The great majority of statues that fill the museums depict only a single personage. Some depict groups of two or more personages, but besides the fact that the proportion of the latter is not very high with respect to full-round sculptures, the impression they produce on the beholder is accompanied by a specific feeling of disquiet. Two, three or four personages grouped in a single work must either be arranged so that they are perceived as one, as is the case with all beautiful statues depicting Mary mourning the crucified Jesus, like Michelangelo's *Pietà* in St. Peter's,[5] or the work breaks up into juxtaposed figures each of which is set apart from the others and demands to be seen as such. Despite the consummate harmony of the arrangement of the figures in Rodin's *The Burghers of Calais,* they are not wholly unified to the point where this obstacle is overcome. This is due to the fact that when statuary represents, or creates, discrete objects in space, it cannot avoid juxtaposing them in the void. This is not the case with real objects given together as a group; in reality, which painters luckily can follow more closely in this respect, individuals are linked to each other by the forms and lines of objects against which they are profiled as against a stage backdrop. Statuary does not have this resource at its disposal; its personages must by themselves compose a definite space in which they take their place but which itself is suspended in the void, or they must be set side by side like full solids, juxtaposed in the void with no formal intermediary relationship, no bond uniting the whole.

The situation changes when we go from full-round to low-relief in which sculpture juts out against a background.

5. Let us mention further the genre "The Entombment," so popular toward the end of the Gothic Age. Some criticize the particularly dead aspect that "tableaux vivants" often present.

The artists of the great Greek epoch knew how to utilize the background to good advantage, arranging friezes in which the personages, though distinct in space, nevertheless form a whole within it and are endowed with a certain unity. But the problem subsists even here, for the undifferentiated background of the stone or marble does not allow a link between them through intermediate forms. We often delight in the ingenious devices to which the artist at that time had recourse in order to avoid this difficulty as much as possible. Here personages form a group while another who precedes them turns to face them, as if leading them; here all one of them has to do is to look backward to unite himself with those whom his movement designates. In another case, through a new slackening of the very idea of statuary, the artist sketches on the low-relief a kind of background composed of trees or buildings which brings the personages together in the unity of décor and consequently of form. This genre reached its peak of perfection in the famous doors of the baptistry at Florence in which each panel constitutes a sculptured painting, or a picture in relief. Ghiberti's dazzling art abundantly shows that the less pure modes of art do not necessarily produce the less beautiful works, but there is a hierarchy of purity between these modes and the eye is not deceived. Going from Ghiberti's doors to the *Throne of Aphrodite* at the Termi museum in Rome, we experience the sensation of entering a sphere in which beauty wills to strip herself of all incidental ornamentation; when the statue stands apart and alone finally in the sufficiency of its perfection, its beauty is that of sculpture grasped in conformity to its proper idea. It is in this sense that we can place such works in the first rank of their art.

Another observation on sculpture draws its inspiration from the same principle. We have already noted that

this art is alien to movement. Not all sculptors gave up the
idea of expressing movement, of course, and here again we
cannot censure them in the name of any principle. The
artist has the right to attempt everything for the simple
reason that if he fails he will be the only one to suffer from
his failure. It is therefore conceivable that an artist can be
tempted, in default of being able to do more, to grasp and
to reproduce some special moment of a movement in the
process of being accomplished. It is a known fact that he
can even invent the figuration of one of these movements
and substitute for the real position of the legs and arms of
a man in motion an imaginary but synthetic position whose
effect on the beholder is to suggest a man walking, as in
Rodin's statue, *L'Homme qui marche*. Actually, the man
is not walking at all, and no effort of the imagination
enables us even to imagine it, beginning with the actual
position of his limbs, that is to say what this position would
be in the following instant: if he were walking. The beauty
of a statue of this kind depends on the spectator's aptitude
to perceive it as a real immobility, and as enduring as that
of stone or bronze. The best that the sculptor can hope for
is to represent the motionless instant of an uninterrupted
movement. For the success of such an enterprise it is important that the spectator, instead of imagining that he
sees a movement—which he cannot really believe—must
content himself with thinking that he is grasping one of
its successive moments on the wing. Thus it can be maintained without paradox that far from wanting to compel
what is motionless to represent movement, statuary tries
to impart to movement the appearances of immobility.

It is not always easy to convince the spectator of this.
The very nature of the statue militates against this. Too
many props remind him that the arm of the *Discus
Thrower* threatens to break under its own weight and that

the two forward legs of the prancing horse threaten to fall back on the ground, in which case the statue will be no more. But the problem is posed earlier and on a less material plane. By its very form, the solid is an enemy of dispersion, of fragmentation and of the appearance of movement. It "hates" movement which displaces lines. This is why the statue, alone, one, immovable, which desires to cling as closely as possible to its essence avoids even the appearance of gesticulations. It concentrates itself, so to speak, in space, like the charioteer who, standing on his chariot without stirring, his hands closed in front of his body, to this day drives invisible horses. If it is necessary to have an appearance of movement, the sculptor most often will try to include an infinity of successive positions in the unity of a circular form. India knows the secret of endowing some of her deities with motion in this way. Here there are neither laws nor rules. Generations of art critics and estheticians have halted before the famous *Laocoön Group* in the Vatican Museum as before the loftiest achievement of statuary. Indeed, it is a beautiful work in its fashion. It materializes the idea of what sculpture can offer when it handles subjects which are as incompatible with its essence as can be imagined. The *Laocoön Group* is an anecdote told in stone, in which two monstrous pythons, while strangling Priam's son and his children, hold them together in the unity of a single group. It is a well-wrought work and admirable in its order for those who find this kind of problem-complex of interest.[6]

6. The name of the Laocoön group sculpture evokes the title of Lessing's book, but it did not treat of statuary. The complete title exactly describes the subject: *Laocoön, or the limits of painting and poetry* (1766). Lessing was very concerned to know whether the author or the authors of Laocoön were directly inspired by Homer or rather by Virgil. A good question for archeologists and philolo-

It is not of the order of pure sculpture which is less
rhetorical. Michelangelo's *David* does not hurl his stone;
he is content to hold his sling, a motionless and concen-
trated threat within the unity of a simple form against a
Goliath who is not even there. This is great sculptural art.

With statuary, our analysis of works whose substance
is an inorganic, solid volume and whose form totally
occupies a definite space, comes to an end. The primary
competence of the sculptor, as of the architect, is the
imaginative conception of volumes. Both must "see in
space" and, if it can be said, "think in space." It is no
disadvantage that the one uses plans and the other drawings or sketches, provided that these auxiliaries of the
imagination come after the fundamental act of directly imagining the future solids which will project and
balance their masses in the air in the play of the ceaselessly changing light and shadows, so geometrical by
nature that they will enliven their surfaces. The preview
of the volume sculptured in the stone must precede and
determine the sketches in which the future status strives
for self-realization. From the moment in which the fac-

---

gists but one of no interest to statuary itself. Lessing moved in the
wake of Winckelmann and of the painter Mengs, who contributed
to the taking over of the plastic arts by the university by taking them
back to everything that one can say about them when one does not
practice them oneself. For example, Winckelmann thinks that the
object of art is to express corporeal beauty; in consequence, to reproduce the supreme beauty of the body is the supreme object of
art; now this supreme beauty of the body is found in the human
body and, for man, it exists only in the form of the envisaged idea;
therefore the proper object of art is the representation of the ideal
form of the human body. This conception of art is altogether reasonable and it responds to a certain moment of Greek statuary, but
we can clearly see what it neglects, even in statuary, and for greater
reason in art in general.

torial order tends to reverse itself, the two arts stray from their essence. They can still produce beautiful works which are not only charming but powerful. We have said that in art success alone counts. Therefore it suffices to justify everything, but it remains for philosophical reflection to seek the particular relation of the works to the art which they belong to and which they illustrate, each in its own manner. The time of judging them comes inevitably later, but then judgment judges itself. And once this judgment becomes aware of its principle, it also, at the same time, recognizes its justification and its limitation, as is shown in the unwavering tolerance of those who, knowing why they like what pleases them, also know why others like what they themselves do not like. Even the intolerance that some exhibit in matters of esthetics is easily intelligible to them, which makes them particularly insufferable to impassioned absolutists. But this is not proper either to architecture or to sculpture. Painting and music offer a preferred battleground to these personal certitudes.

It is only in very recent times, indeed in our day, that statuary has produced works wholly in keeping with its proper essence, by setting itself the aim of obtaining a purely formal beauty free of any imitation of natural objects of any kind, save that of the ineluctable necessity of being an object. This observation does not imply any esthetic judgment whatsoever on the works of non-representational sculpture. Their greatest merit in the view of some persons of taste is precisely that which disconcerts the taste of many others for whom formal beauty ceases to be perceptible when it presents itself alone, without the support of some natural form of which it is an interpretation. What we are here discussing is simply a fact, but one that is extremely important. After having worked for centuries in so many schools and trying so many different styles in order to extract a formal beauty in its pure state from the matrix-ore of natural forms which contain its principal elements, the Western world in the twentieth century has tried to bring the experiment to a close by inaugurating a sculpture free of any representation.

It is not certain that this phase is destined to last, because we cannot know whether a large enough public will be formed to encourage the production of works of this kind. No art is more costly than statuary. Many more statues would be made if there were more art-lovers willing to defray the costs. The existence or the absence of a public directly conditions the possibility of the practice of an art, and this fact is all the more brutal the more expensive the art in question. If it should pass never to return, the present phase would remain crucial for the philosophical interpretation of statuary. The fact that a non-representational sculpture was possible at once discloses the unity of this art and the principle of this unity. Let us recall that sculpture has existed, in an infinite diversity of styles, in all times and in all countries, to the measure in which men strove to create in space solid objects whose forms would be beautiful to behold, that is to say, the sight of which would be desirable for its own sake. Herein lies the essential element, the presence of which in any work makes sculpture of it. A Zeus, a Christ, a Buddha, an African fetish, all belong to the art of statuary if the beholder desires to prolong his view of them and to renew it when the object is no longer before him, independently of what they represent, provided only that the artists subjected the material on which they worked to the requirements of formal beauty.

All these statues, however, represent living bodies, particularly human bodies. There must be some reason for this rooted in the very nature of statuary, for even if, as we see it today, it is possible to make a statue which represents nothing, the fact remains that for centuries, or rather for millennia, statuary has represented living beings, preferably man. By defining it as the "chosen imitation of living forms," the classics of the philosophy of art assert an indisputable fact.

A prime reason for this fact is that living beings have their natural beauty, hence it is inevitable that sculptors draw inspiration from them to create objects endowed with a beauty proper to them. An animal is the preeminent type of a distinct being, situated in space and whose being is defined, inasmuch as it is the object of a possible perception as a plurality of parts arranged in the unity of a form. Pigeon, bull, or man—the living being is an organic unity given all at once. Thus we can imagine that an artist should conceive the project of creating forms, solids like those of living beings, and like them endowed with a distinct unity with proportions that are pleasing to the eye.

It is more difficult to say why man, among all living beings, should have enjoyed a marked preference. It is tempting to assert, for example, that "free through its movement, superior through its beauty, the human form, of all the living forms, is the only one capable of fully manifesting the idea." Above all, if we admit that statuary is an art of expression and of signification, it is natural to think that man by preference imitates the human body "to arrive at expressing his own thoughts." Indeed, to represent a man who experiences or personifies human thoughts or human feelings is the natural way of expressing them. But the problem assumes a different character if the object of statuary is the creation of beautiful forms. We can easily find in nature living beings whose plastic unity is at least as manifest as that of the human body. But it is not so easy to let forms such as the trunk, the members and the head of a human body really "hold together." The head and the neck, Ingres would say peevishly, "never mesh."

Sculptors therefore have not found the ready-made model of artistic beauty in the human body. To explain the preference which sculptors have shown in this regard, it must be recalled that man above all is an intelligent and talking animal. Now man tries to talk in all possible ways, in words, gestures, attitudes, actions and operations whose products speak for him. Speaking is not the function of an art of the beautiful, but man naturally avails himself of it for this end, and sculpture can be of service here. Since man is that which most interests man, sculptors have represented him, in one or the other sex, in all attitudes, performing all the acts, fulfilling all the functions of public or private life. The artist found therein the double pleasure of imitation itself and of the imitation of human life, to which he is attached by his deepest instinct. All this was only indirectly related to the production of the beautiful, but it has been within this frame that the arts of the beautiful have progressively recognized their proper object. It took a very long time and seemingly it is only in our day that this search has finally identified its object.

By placing man at the center of its interests, the art of statuary found itself led to interpretations of the human body such as would satisfy its taste for plastic beauty. It was not enough to search in nature in order to discover corporeal beauty that would also be a thing of beauty for art, for beauty was abundantly found in nature and in all varieties. Human bodies are principally made for life and health, not for beauty. Nature has produced different human types according to the different great races of man, and even a great number of varieties within each race; every human family secretes its own beauty. Statuary has done the same. A history of the nude [7] in art clearly shows the variations undergone by the canon of typical beauty in Greece, in Rome, in the western Middle Ages, in the Renaissance and in our day. Scholars and academies have vainly tried to fix an artistic canon of the human body, of the face and of the members, that would have a universal validity. Experience has shown that the genius could violate every canon of this kind with impunity. Statuary created the beauty presumed natural which it needed for the ends of art.

Whatever the reason for this choice, once it is made there remains nothing else for the sculptor to do but to draw out from the human body the form of art which it has the vocation to assume. The permanent danger presented by the nude is the error to which the statue-maker is exposed as much as the spectator, which turns the interest of art toward sexuality. The esthetic-sexual ambiguity of the nude is coessential to art. Some think that under the circumstances the average taste has hardly any chance to be mistaken; on the other hand, we can ask whether in reality it is not mistaken rather easily on this score since one of the difficulties which the artist has to overcome is that of inducing the average spectator to view the nude as a work of art. And much could even be said on the value of natural taste itself. Many consider as artistically beautiful the sculptured body whose living model they would consider captivating and desirable if it existed as such, but natural beauty has its order as it has its ends, which are not those of esthetic beauty. All Venuses are not desirable, all those who trade on their beauty are

7. Herbert Read, *The Art of Sculpture,* vol. 3 (New York: Bollingen Series, 1954).

not Venuses. Even the kinds of beauty found in the *gabinetto oscenico* are at times artistic, but only by accident.

By using natural beauty as material for a possible artistic beauty, statuary remains in the line of beauty. The same is not true of the various utilizations of this art having ends in view specifically different from its own.

The art of the sculptured portrait, or the bust whose proper end is to represent a personage as he was, is the most difficult to distinguish from pure statuary. The art of making medallions, including that of striking coins, which is allied to sculpture, is naturally connected with that of the statue-portrait. We immediately see that it is a very great art, but it once again confirms the assertion that the purest forms of art are not always those which give the spectator the most intense or the most complete esthetic pleasure. We cannot look upon a bust without asking ourselves what kind of a man the model was. The classic Greek statue, pure sculpture, seems cold to many moderns; it is "expressionless." The representation of individuals such as they are or were, or would like people to believe they are, necessarily includes elements of imitation. This approach does not exclude pure plastic invention; we know of busts or of medallions of living personages, genuine works of art, which nevertheless are "bursting with truth" as the saying goes. It is no less true that the concern to achieve a likeness limits the plastic freedom of the sculptor by forcing him to seek the beauty of form within an ensemble of given volumes whose curves and proportions are to be respected, at least to a degree below which there is no longer a likeness nor a portrait. This other end, which is added to that of the plastic art as such, and which threatens to replace it, is the representation of a human face or body as expressive of an individual

personality. It could be that the model may no longer be
living at the time the artist sculpts the bust or the statue;
in that case he strives in the beginning to create an image
resembling a type fixed by tradition and expressing the
characteristic commonly attributed to the person being
represented.[8] The same applies to statues designed to
represent a type rather than an individual: Man, Woman,
The Boxer, The Thinker and others of the same kind.
In a sense such "subjects" leave a greater freedom to the
artist by virtue of their very generality, but he is still
caught between two dangers, one of which is to lose
himself in the vagueness of some symbol whose banality
leaves a feeling of unreality, and the other—which aims
to avoid precisely this danger—is to make the portrait
more or less a faithful likeness of some individual gratuitously raised to a type or class of the species. The greatness characteristic of Greek and Renaissance statuary is
attributable to its discovery of a middle way between
these extreme dangers. Its exponents knew how to create

8. Sculpture sometimes creates artistic types which serve as
historical types about whom we know nothing: Jesus Christ, Saint
Peter, Saint Paul and others. While writing these lines I am thinking
above all of the extraordinary ancient busts of illustrious personages
whose photographs are reproduced in Jérome Carcopino's *Profils de
Conquérants* (Paris: Flammarion, 1961). Compare Caesar and Pom-
pey on page 143; without knowing whether they are historically
faithful, we could no longer picture the models to ourselves otherwise. The most curious thing is that the remark would be true even
if the modern attribution of busts to this or that model was not
made by the artist but by some modern museum curator. The
Brutus and above all the Cato on page 302 suggest similar remarks.
This reminds me of the remark of my distinguished teacher Lucien
Lévy-Bruhl who one day, while showing me some photographs of
statues on one of the portals of Chartres, exclaimed: "What psy-
chologists these sculptors!" In fact, one does not exclude the other;
many essences can be united in a single concrete entity.

human types of an unsurpassable plastic perfection while giving the impression that they were working from nature, as though in reality Apollo and Venus had been their models. Greek statuary has been much imitated; to this very day it still represents to the great majority classic art *par excellence,* and rightly so, for it found the secret of producing statues in which likeness, reduced to the role of being the simple material of the work despite its extreme perfection, is completely dominated by plastic form. The spectator, blind to art, enjoys the pleasure of believing that he responds to it because he takes the beauty of statuary for that of nature, which the statue imitates by leading it to its perfection. The triumph of Greek art rests, to a certain degree, upon the most felicitous of misunderstandings.

Starting from the pinnacle, only a decline was possible, but when a decline begins from so great a height it can go on for a long time without sinking into mediocrity. Innumerable statues are dedicated to propaganda of all sorts. That they often pursue ends that are not specifically artistic does not prevent them from being works of art, at times even of the highest quality. Let us discard the mass of *kitsch* that encumbers the churches or claims to adorn public places. Taking into consideration only statues in which artistry is dominant, we will have to recognize that art is not the only element involved. The statue of a god, a saint, or hero belongs to statuary proper in the degree to which the creation of a plastic form has known how to utilize as material, in addition to the natural forms imitated by the artist, the religious or patriotic emotion associated with the memory of the personage whom the work intends to represent. In such cases (the *Pietà* in St. Peter's, the *Moses* in the church of St. Peter-in-Chains, the Colleoni equestrian statue in Venice) the formative power of the art so visibly dominates the material (marble or bronze in the body imitated, the scene depicted, the emotions evoked) that no doubt is possible; art is so manifestly the dominant factor here that we ask ourselves whether religion and patriotism are still involved. It is very difficult to be stirred by the image of Jesus Christ when we stand before Michelangelo's *Pietà*. The esthetic emotion occupies too much place to leave much more for the religious feeling, unless the very opposite occurs and a Christian heart is so moved at the very remembrance of the Passion of Christ that it no longer is concerned with the masterpiece.

The religious feeling in that case plays a role similar to that of natural beauty in other works; the emotion which it engenders is taken for esthetic enjoyment of the beauty of art. And this is all to the good, for while the art-lover enjoys the work of art in his own way, the faithful enjoys it in his, and no doubt most people find in it this mixed, but often intense, gratification of a sensibility divided between its religious faith and admiration for the sculptured masterpiece which places the object before him. There is no measuring instrument to determine the proportions of such mixtures. A phenomenology of esthetic experience would perhaps find in it material for many interesting observations, for it would seem that statuary, having little confidence in its power to hold the attention of men by itself, sought in subjects of all kinds something with which to ensure itself an emotional involvement on the part of the spectator which plastic beauty hardly has the right to hope for. Here again misunderstanding reigns, but it is the soil from which the art of the beautiful bursts forth now and then in its pure or nearly pure form.

The artist comes up against this problem only from the point of view of his poietic activity; he alone knows

what he would like to do, what he is permitted to do in the
concrete conditions in which his art is brought to bear—
in short, what he can in fact realize of that which he
desires to accomplish. This explains why some masterpieces are still but compromises between the demands of
art and those of the causes that an artist must serve in
order to ensure his livelihood. The artist cannot live on
commissions rejected by those who assign them to him
and who pay for them. But here the poietics of sculpture
is without resources; being philosophy, it has no direct
bearing on any particular case.

FOUR

Painting

UPON APPROACHING the subject of painting the reflective mind immediately senses the haunting presence of the notion of another art, poetry. *Ut pictura poesis:* poetry is like painting and, inversely, painting is a kind of poetry. It would be easy to compile a book of writings devoted to this subject; indeed a whole series of books would be necessary were we to add to such a compilation writings whose authors labored hard to compare the dignity of these two arts.

To the degree in which considerations of this kind cite Horace as an authority, which they do all too frequently, they are just so many commentaries on a misinterpretation. Let us say, rather, that they comment on three words whose meaning it is impossible to misunderstand when read in their context. In this passage of the *Epistle to the Pisos,* Horace perceptively remarks that poetry is akin to painting. As is the case with some paintings, some poems should be read from close up, whereas others are best appreciated from afar; some court the shade, others endure scrutiny in full light unfearful of the demands of the most penetrating criticism. Setting aside Horace's personal preference for this second kind of poetry (and of painting) the

106

fact remains that his verses do not authorize any assimila-
tion between the ends of painting and those of poetry, nor
vice versa:

Ut pictura poesis. Erit quae, si propius stes,
Te capiat magis, et quaedam, si longius abstes;
Haec amat obscuram, volet haec sub luce videri,
Judici argutum quae nom formidat acumen;
Haec placuit semel, haec deciens repetita placebit.

Therefore this precedent can be ignored; it is wholly
imaginary, but it is impossible not to take into account
what these three words by Horace have suggested to the
imagination of critics and philosophers. We come upon
the doctrine in its perfect form in the *Réflexions critiques*
sur la poésie et sur la peinture by Abbé du Bos, one of the
forty "Immortals" and permanent secretary of the French
Academy. The seventh edition is dated Paris, 1770. The
success of this work clearly shows that, in matters of taste,
it was in keeping with the aspirations of the age. In any
case, the Abbé's doctrine is exemplary in that it compiles
and arranges ideas which in fact conjure up each other
and which a logical mind refuses to disassociate.

Let us first of all note that painting and poetry are
here treated jointly as two arts which, though using different means of expression, have the same end in view.

The stand taken by du Bos can be traced back to the
following principles: poetry and painting aim at stirring
the emotions of the spectator and pleasing him; the principal means of being pleasing which they have in common
is the imitation of objects naturally capable of stirring
human emotions and of being pleasing. Above all it is important never to represent objects and events in a poem or
in a picture that are not by nature interesting. "The imitation would not be able to move us if the object itself is

incapable of doing so." Hence the conclusion common to the two arts: "Poetry is akin to painting and the imitations that poetry makes of nature stir us only in proportion to the impression that the object imitated itself would make on us."

The consequences of this perfect poietic art of painting as a pure intellectual pictures it to himself becomes apparent in the judgments on taste which it inspires, or better put, which are deduced from it. First of all, art is declared incapable of matching nature in the power to please the human eye and to stir human emotions. Quintillian gives the reason for this in his famous treatise on the training of an orator. *Quidquid alteri simile est, necesse est minus sit, eo quod imitatur* (X, 2). Indeed, if works of art are homogeneous to those of nature, being of the same order but consecutive to the former, they are necessarily inferior to them. Secondly, since their efficacy depends upon the interest inspired by their models, it is the personal interest that we entertain for their models that becomes the rule of our judgments. Thus, in agreement with Louis XIV and almost all his contemporaries, Abbé du Bos set a very low value on the art of the minor Dutch masters, such as Teniers and Wouvermans, whose work could not affect us very much because "there is nothing in the celebration of a village feast or in the coarse pastimes of a group of foot guards that could stir our emotions." Communist criticism in our day would condemn a favorable portrayal of bourgeois manners exactly for the same reason. In both cases the judge would say with Abbé du Bos: "We praise the art of the painter for his excellent imitation, but we must reproach him for having chosen as the object of his work subjects which have such little interest for us."

A final consequence of this primacy of the imitation

of natural beauty is the essential superiority of so-called history painting in which the human figure always occupies an important place and often the first, over landscape painting. Indeed, we do not speak with trees; they say nothing, nor do they express any feelings, emotions or thoughts. "The most beautiful landscape, even if painted by Titian or Carracci, would not interest us any more than the sight of a dreadful or delightful country district: there is nothing in such a picture that talks to us, so to speak, and since it scarcely affects us, it does not hold our attention very much." Abbé du Bos must be given credit for his consistency and logic. He does not deny that the artist's achievement can interest us, but he contends that "imitation never makes an impression on us greater than the imitated object would be able to make." Moreover, he has a criterion for the appreciation of a beautiful painting: the time spent by the spectator in looking at it; and since this time is proportional to the reflections which the subject suggests, assuming an equality of artistry, we would tarry less before the landscape of a picture by Poussin than before the personages whom he has placed in it, and less before a representation of a basket of flowers than before one of the Seven Sacraments.

This view of art prevailed in the history of French painting, as well as in that of some other countries, practically up to the beginning of the nineteenth century. In the name of these principles a painter as accomplished as Chardin was for a long time considered to be a second-rate artist. There is no assurance that this philosophy of art is dead in all minds, but few understand the error upon which it rests. Starting out from the primacy of natural beauty which dominates it, it necessarily follows that the painted image imitating it cannot have a greater value than the model from which is draws its substance. Hence the fidelity of painting in its imitation of natural beauty is the measure of its beauty.

It is impossible to introduce more coherence in this confusion, for everything here is bound up with the initial error which by substituting natural beauty for artistic beauty fatally condemns the artist to the role of being the more or less faithful imitator of a ready-made model which nature suggests to him. This initial error involves him in numberless complications which are all the more super-fluous because they are without object. It is this notion that makes him despair of ever being able to match nature and gives him the impression of a failure which he really has not undergone. In fact, it is quite natural that he should not succeed in this enterprise because art's essen-tial purpose is not the imitation of nature. The matter of ascertaining whether or not natural beauty surpasses artistic beauty is not in question here, for they cannot be compared; what is important is that the beauty which the artist pursues, such as he can produce with the means avail-able to his art, is something specifically different from that which nature produces with her own.

The nature of this difference is made very clear by an experience familiar to all of us. After walking through end-lessly long galleries and enormous rooms filled with mas-terpieces of the art of painting, our gaze suddenly falls upon a young couple making a tour of the same museum. Our hearts are stirred by a very strange emotion: a feeling that our musings have been disturbed mingles with a feel-ing of relief as when we arrive unexpectedly at the end of a search unaware of its real aim. Living creatures, at last! In this instant of clairvoyance granted by chance, who would not give all the painted beauties in the museum's collection for the beauty of these two real faces where nature seems effortlessly to have found what so many artists

have vainly pursued? But this is an illusion, for nature is
as incapable of producing a painting by herself as the
painter is of creating a living being with colors and brushes.
If the work of the painter should come to life like Pygmalion's, it would constitute a total defeat of his art, for it was
hardly necessary for him to bring into the world the living
beings surrounding him. To console himself for a non-
existent failure, the artist thereupon embarks on the pursuit
of an "ideal beauty" destined to remain inaccessible to him,
since in order to bring it into being he would have to effect
the contradictory synthesis of natural and artistic beauty. It
can be called contradictory not because the one is opposed
to the other or because the beauty of art cannot fruitfully
be inspired by that of nature, but for a much deeper reason:
in the last analysis it is a question of two orders which can
only subsist if each respects the specificity of the other.
Among the proliferating bastard arts the art of make-up
makes it quite clear that by dint of painting a face we
cannot make a natural beauty of it, but neither can we
create a masterpiece of the art of painting unless, of course,
we confuse painting and daubing.[1]

1. As far as I know only Baudelaire has treated the subject
seriously, "In praise of make-up," in *Curiosités esthétiques*, XVI, 11
(Paris: Pléiade), pp. 911–914. Note, by the way, the poet's remarks on
fashion (pp. 912–913); on the specificity of the end of make-up, p. 913
(woman fulfills a kind of duty "in applying herself to appearing
magical and supernatural . . . an idol, she must adorn herself in
order to be adored"); and above all the remark following (p. 913):
"Thus, if I have well understood, the painting of the face must
not be employed for the vulgar, unconfessable purpose of imitating
beautiful nature and of competing with youth." "Who would dare
to assign to art the sterile function of imitating nature?" (p. 914).
Baudelaire is very right to disdain those who would judge him to
be unduly grave on such a subject. Truth with respect to art depends entirely on each of the particular truths that refer to it.
Paul Vuillard, in his decors for the *Théâtre des Champs-Elysées*

The irrepressible vitality of the doctrine of art as imitation is attributable precisely to the fact that it occupies two terrains at once and, by seeking refuge according to the situation in one or the other, it seems to justify the espousal of an order of factivity which could compete with it for the reason that it would also be the order of natural fecundity. The awareness that there is something incongruous about this position becomes apparent in the attempt, the reverse of the previous one, to exploit art's presumed self-styled power "to embellish nature." This is the same illusion but in an opposite sense, for the painter can neither embellish nor disfigure nature for the simple reason that he does not produce nature but paintings. The most beautiful of painted nudes will always arouse misgivings in the mind of an anatomist.[2] The possibility of cooperation between the two orders presupposes the respect for their specific distinction. If we were to proceed here from the philosophy of art to esthetics the same remark would apply to the respect that must be accorded

---

(*Le maquillage*), has well illustrated the magic feeling of the operation.

2. We know what liberties Ingres took with anatomy: added vertebrae, disproportion of members, etc. No one, however, has preached more convincingly on the duty of following the model, and along with it, nature. But he was more subtle than that: "The ancients never corrected their models," he said; but he added, "by that I mean that they did not denaturalize them." That's a difficult margin to measure. "The principle and the most important part of painting is to know what nature has produced that is most beautiful and most fitting to this art, in order to make a choice following the taste and the manner of feeling of the ancients." And further: "One is always beautiful when one is true." But true in relation to what? To given reality, or to the choice exercised according to "the manner of feeling of the ancients"? And which ancients? And, if the manner of feeling of the Greeks, of which Greeks?

to the necessary distinction between the two orders in the principles that should preside when pronouncing judgments upon a painter's work. What mishaps occur in both directions! All the cosmetics of the world will never do more than postpone the moment in which the most beautiful of real faces will have to fall back on its natural beauty exclusively, in regard to which the beauty of art is an illusion, though real in its own order.

The only honorable way out of this confusion is to return to the true principle, that is to say to the very essence of the art of painting such as it is in itself. By this we understand that essential element without which painting as one of the fine arts is not possible, neither more nor less. If other determinations can be added to it they will not be excluded if they qualify this art as one of the possible modes of painting, and do not constitute it as such.

Reduced to this essential, a picture is a solid surface which the artist covers with colored forms whose arrangement is pleasing to the eye through the unity of the form, the harmony of the parts and the perfection of the execution.

The art of painting therefore produces material objects located in space like the creations of statuary; but even though the painted wall, the painted wooden panel and even, in a sense, the painted canvas are solids, painting is concerned only with their surface. Painting does not even capture the surface save to the extent that it is visible, so that pictures, precisely as works of art, offer themselves to view in space as objects endowed only with the dimensions of length and breadth, but without depth. Pictures, being inorganic bodies, are immovable like statues. Practically speaking, they are two-dimensional solids. The achievements of modern technology have made this truth clearly evident. The currently practiced technique of recanvasing a picture shows to what extent the substance of a painting can be reduced to a thin film of pigments. When a painter represents tri-dimensional solids on a two-dimensional space, he embarks on a path wholly different from that of the sculptor. Convention plays an initial role in it as a foregone conclusion. As in the theatre where it is understood in advance that nothing that transpires on the stage is real, any normal viewer of a painting will unquestionably grant that the artist has no intention of letting him take the image of a man for a man. In this sense the *trompe l'oeil* represents an exception, but it rarely aims at producing a complete illusion which, even if it is successful, hardly lasts.

Painting is abstract by nature, for it abstracts from one of the dimensions of our space; and in another aspect it is inevitably conventional in the sense that, if its aim is imitation, only lines, curves and colors are at its disposal for the representation of solids. Either it must apply itself to illusionism to create the impression of depth—necessarily absent—through relief and perspective, or deliberately practice a painting that is indifferent to the third dimension and freely reduces volumes to surfaces. It is only very recently, that is to say with the advent of so-called abstract (non-representational) art, that we have seen the appearance of pictures which, by going beyond mere decoration, claimed to be what any painting essentially is. Maurice Denis, who never practiced abstract art and who did not even know of its existence at that time, correctly defined it when he came up with his now famous definition of a picture: a plane surface covered with colors arranged in a certain order. A picture exists from the moment these simple conditions are fulfilled. If Maurice Denis was right, painting by definition is abtract and not representational.

What is even more remarkable about painting is that

like sculpture it has almost always been representational.
The origins of this art are lost in the mists of time. Its
date is of little importance; when we speak of fifteen thousand years before our era, a few millennia more or less do
not make much difference. On the other hand, one fact
should hold our attention: whatever the date may be when
painting was first produced, those who have left us the
most ancient attestations of the art confront us with an art
that is already fully established. Its representational character is already evident. Painting, like sculpture, was born of
imitation, perhaps even more obviously. Moreover, these
painters or other artists were also sculptors. The admirable bisons of Altamira, and of the grotto of Font de Gaume,
and those of the Lascaux caverns in particular confirm the
existence in these remote times of painters who could draw
stylized animal forms, compose groups and paint them
with the aid of simple but lasting colors, and arrange them
on broad surfaces whose irregularities, curves and planes
they knew how to put to good advantage by making them
serve the ends of their art. A frieze of deer, with antlers
erect, who seem to be emerging from a stream or a lake,
one behind the other; a horse depicted falling into a hole
because a real hole is there and suggests the image of a fall.
After them, it is hard to see what there remained to invent
in the art of representing solid forms on a plane surface by
means of lines and colors arranged in a certain order.

As far as is known, given the present state of our
knowledge of prehistory, no art of painting has ever existed without imitation. Indeed, it would appear that man
imitated before writing, for writing does not figure in
these grottoes except in the form of elementary symbolic
signs of whose meaning we are not certain, and the immense variety of painted forms at that time by far exceeds
the number of signs known to us. But this is not the most

surprising feature. What is particularly striking is the fact
that by inventing an immovable art, exactly in the same
sense as sculpture, these first artists were already obsessed
with a desire to represent the appearances of movement.
The deer of the Lascaux caverns gallop; the horses walk,
trot or jump; the cows and bulls assume varied poses and
move in many ways. To suggest solids in motion by means
of immovable spots was a doubly paradoxical enterprise.
We cannot go into finer detail here on these facts which
are outside a philosopher's sphere of competence but we
must add this supplementary question: why did these men,
already masters of the art of stylizing animal forms, who
drew bisons worthy of the greatest Chinese painting, seem
to be indifferent to the human form, or unable to draw it?
The human beings in these paintings resemble the crudely
drawn figures produced by children: a tube surmounted by
a ball and flanked by two lines at the end of which shorter
ones protrude. We cannot help but wonder about the plastic poverty of this human form, the exploitation of whose
formal possibilities required the advent of Greek genius.
Reflection upon these facts can lead only to the conclusion
that, from the beginning, man the artist proceeded as
though he had read Ingres. He chanced upon art in imitation itself: in the construction of a figure, he did not "proceed piecemeal" but "drew the whole." Finally, in the
same spirit with which he first grasped the whole, he already dealt with the "breadth of form and breadth of form
again," for in Ingres' own words form "is the foundation
and the condition of all things." The painter of the black
bull in the Lascaux caverns already presented it in a full
run; indeed Ingres himself who was so primitive in his
own fashion might have painted it. On one occasion he
voiced the deep meaning of this wholly spontaneous decision on the part of the artist: "When sketching a figure,

apply yourself above all to determining and fully characterizing its movement. I can't stress too much to you that movement is life."

Indeed nothing interests man as much as life and the movement which is a sign of it, or resembles it. Let our gaze roam over a vast plain and the least thing that stirs in the landscape makes us fix our eyes upon it. Animals perceive the surrounding world in the same way. Here again we are face to face with a prime fact, beyond which we cannot go. From it we must deduce that painting, like sculpture, works on a two-fold material substance constituted by the canvas with pigments of which pictures consist, and on the ensemble of natural forms which it submits to the artistic form born of imagination. Whether directly or indirectly borrowed, whether from the organic or inorganic world, all the lines and forms employed by the painter derive from natural objects and beings. Among the latter, living beings hold his attention first and foremost. At least it would seem that such was the case with the artists who decorated the grottoes of Vézère and elsewhere. Their paintings are the creations of hunters, like all the paintings since then which have been inspired by that pre-eminent hunter, Eros, the god of desire and of love.

Of this two-fold material substance, that from which the artist extracts the very substance of his art is inseparable from the technique of art about which the philosopher has no experience and consequently knows nothing. Like everybody else he knows that this matter, through its natural forms, exercises a determining influence on what the finished work will be. A drawing will have a beauty all its own, which is not that of an engraving or of an oil; a painting will also have its own beauty, though the beauty of an oil painting will not be that of a fresco.

Thus each work will find itself classified in a genre, in a family or in a definite species among which all possible varieties are to be found, including highly individual creations, depending upon whether the draughtsman uses this or that charcoal or pencil, and treats his pastel in this or that manner which can be personal to him. For in the last analysis every artist is a distinct person and his means of expression belongs to the world of nature in which everything that exists is particularized.

The material of the painted work differs from that of the statue by virtue of a remarkable characteristic. In painting, the material of the work of art is itself a human creation.[3] The sculptor must choose the piece of wood or the block of marble upon which he intends to work; certainly in making this choice he thinks of the form that he plans to impart to it but he does not produce the

3. In consideration of the "formal vocation of material substances," demonstrated by Henri Focillon, the invention of new pictorial material, like that of oil color by the same token, opens a new era in the order of formal invention. This platitude in the history of art is recalled here only for its principle. If styles are closely related to techniques, the history of techniques presides over that of styles. At a certain level, these notions are confused with each other. The philosopher, however, cannot fail to observe that the painted work has progressively escaped from the initial plenary authority of the painter in the measure that the fabrication of color escaped him. In the beginning it was almost the whole of art. We owe to the enigmatic monk Théophile (eleventh century A.D.) a *Diversarum artium schedula* in which the manner of mixing and applying colors according to the subject to be represented occupies the foreground. See the *Traité des divers arts* (Paris: Emile-Paul, 1924), particularly Book 1. Let us note in passing that this very rare bird, a theoretician of the arts of the beautiful in the Middle Ages, gave himself the pleasure in his Prologue to the First Book (the beginning) of outlining a theology of art. A Greek source seems to have been at the origin of the work.

material of the future statue, contenting himself with taking it just as nature offers it to him. Even terra-cotta and bronze, which are artificially fabricated materials, were not first made with artistic ends in view. The artist may use the techniques of iron and copper but he utilizes them pretty much as though they were materials that would be offered to him by nature whose ingenuity in this respect he does not find essentially distinguishable. Artistic creation begins earlier in painting, for although the colors used by paleolithic painters seem to have been simple natural oxides or charcoals, those used by their successors had first of all to be deliberately produced with future coloring and painting operations in view. At the beginning of modern painting, the substitution of the fresco by the oil, and that of mineral colors by vegetable colors, placed at the artist's disposal a whole range of new materials expressly conceived and produced with an eye to his specific purposes. At the present time the oils, gouaches, and pigments of all kinds, not to mention the glosses, lacquers and other products equally necessary to the painter, as well as those required by the art of engraving and of drawing, are furnished by specialized industries at the service of these different arts. This is even true of colors, for the separate preparation of the three fundamental colors, red, blue and yellow, such as the painter needs to find in their pure state so that he can proceed, if he so desires, to the preparation of fragmentized tones, is itself the object of an industry expressly created to service the art of painting. In painting, even the material of the work of art is an effect of art.

The notion of form [4] common to all the arts assumes

4. The excesses to which the notion of "form" lent itself formerly in the interpretation of nature has afforded much amusement; it is just as comical to see fine minds, who intend no malice, riddle

its prime and proper meaning, which is that of visible form, when it is applied to painting. There it belongs to drawing which many consider as a distinct, self-sufficient and definable art in itself. This is a legitimate approach which it would not be difficult to justify, or at least uphold with sound arguments, for the domain of drawing goes beyond that of painting in all respects. There is line drawing, architectural drawing, sculptural drawing; in short, there is drawing whenever the representation of some object is involved through the imitation of its visible appearance by means of lines. But the role of drawing in what are called "the arts of design," namely architecture, sculpture, painting and their derivates, is merely that of a means which is not always indispensable and which can even be harmful in these arts. At times we deceive ourselves about the role drawing plays in them because we fail to examine it in itself. In philosophical terminology "in itself," of course, will be understood to mean in its essence and in its concept.

---

it with their sarcasms, as though they were Descartes or one of his contemporaries. "Doubtlessly Claudel has become a prisoner of of the scholastic notion of *form* as many passages of his works will show," recently wrote an excellent literary critic. The notion of form, which goes back to Plato and Aristotle, is a common patrimony of Western thought. It was wrong to take the word for an explanation, but what it signifies is a reality to be explained, and in this sense it has become evident to all minds still in our day. André Saint-Lague writes *Le monde des formes;* Henri Focillon writes *La vie des formes,* not without correctly specifying that those about which he speaks are not those of scholasticism (and he believes it); modern psychology becomes *Gestaltpsychologie;* in short, no one dreams of avoiding an inevitable notion closely related to the notion of being and of thing of which it defines the constitutive law. In any case, if he was ever a prisoner of the notion of form, the author of *L'oeil écoute* is rather comfortably ensconced in his prison, so that we may have no fear of being imprisoned there along with him.

When concepts are in question we must always take recourse to Socrates' method which on the whole was taken over by Aristotle. What do we mean here when we say *drawing?* Chateaubriand, whom nothing daunted, gives a fairly good idea of it in that passage of the *Génie du Christianisme* where he describes both its nature and its invention (III, 1, 3). "A young girl, perceiving the shadow of her lover on the wall, drew the contours of this shadow." Happy lover, happy young girl, happy Chateaubriand who seemingly did not himself try this operation which is not as simple as he thought! All we should retain of this fantasy is the seemingly natural bond which associates in the mind the notion of drawing with that of contour. Drawing is the delineation of figures, of contours, and the "contour" itself is "that which marks the circumference of something." Now the circumference of any object, even in connection with the contour of a solid, say a column or an edifice, can be marked only if we trace it by means of a line. The latter does not exist in the solid of which it is the delineation, but rather it results from the act of the mind abstracting from the material mass one of the ideal limits which, by determining its form, defines it. This is why drawing is rightly described as the act of tracing the contours of a figure. Where this act is sufficient unto itself it constitutes a distinct art, drawing.

Thus viewed, drawing, taken in itself, is necessarily imitation, for tracing the contour of an object is tantamount to imitating the appearance of this object. At the same time, it is creation because the contour of the object to which the draughtsman limits himself is not a datum of reality. There are no drawings in nature and this is why every time some are discovered after millennia on the walls of an unexplored grotto, the inference is immediately drawn that men once lived there in the dim past. Like any art drawing is not a natural but a human fact. It must be added that the act of creating an outline by drawing it is not limited to the faithful reproduction of the outer limit of a natural form. The mind intervenes directly in the operation so that the outline can be made in such a way as will be pleasing to the eye. At least this is what happens when the hand spontaneously defers to the mind's suggestions. Ingres, whose memory hovers like a ghost over every discussion of drawing, constantly counselled the imitation of nature: "One is always beautiful when one is true," he said. But he was not aiming so much at literal truth as at that of the perfect form of which the live model is like a sketch. Every real form attests to an ideal form which it more or less resembles, the idea of which, however, it never perfectly actualizes. "Health must be imparted to form," Ingres said further. Drawing in this case becomes the medium of a plastic creation and one of the arts of the beautiful.

We must pause a moment here for this seemingly simple determination in reality assumes that we have just made a crucial choice. Drawing may belong to the fine arts, but not necessarily so. For there is another manner of drawing which consists of observing the object in order to reproduce it exactly as it is, that is to say as it naturally offers itself to the eye. Thus conceived, drawing is the expression of a cognition: therefore it belongs to the order of language and no doubt constitutes the most direct manner of signifying reality since it depicts it just as it appears. Thus we enter into the order of the true, which is a distinct order of that of the beautiful and where fidelity to the object becomes the rule of the act whose end is likeness. A moment's reflection suffices to see that the most exact drawing is not necessarily the most beautiful, but it is assuredly the most true because it is the most faithful reproduction of the object that it portrays. In such a case the eye must limit itself strictly to observation, and the hand must retrace exactly what the eye sees. Here the danger to be avoided and overcome if it arises is the inevitable temptation to neglect some aspects of the object and to modify others in order to "impart health to form," which is the beginning of art. We are in the realm of observation and of the mind's effort to describe it. In short, we are in the order of signification in which drawing is irreplacable, for all the descriptive talent of a Buffon would not suffice to give us the precise idea of "the most noble conquest of man," whereas prehistoric drawings suffice to put troops of horses under our eyes.

In practice it is impossible to avoid mixing the uses that are made of a same technique having distinct ends in view. Audubon's animals (when their models existed) [5] were portraits as much as documents, and when Ingres asserts that he scrupulously observes the human body, he is telling the truth, but this does not prevent him from giving a member the length, and a body the number of vertebrae that either must have so that the drawing may be beautiful. Thus cognition will often be blended with art, but the artist will always make artistic use of it, and it is precisely this that earns him the censure of the spectator who is more oriented toward truth than toward beauty. Once again, by reflecting upon the essence of these two acts, we can conclude that the opposition between the ends pursued discloses the presence of two specifically different activities. It may be useful to stress this distinction of

5. Audubon, an excellent observer and meticulous draughts-man (he was a pupil of David), at least once amused himself by describing and drawing a North American quadruped which every-body generally agrees existed only in his own imagination: the re-venge that invention takes on the discipline of observation and that art takes on knowledge.

essences through that of names, reserving that of *imagery* for the technique of drawing whose principle object is to reproduce as faithfully as possible the outer appearance of a form exactly observed. As a technique integrated with the fine arts, drawing has no other destination save beauty. To the extent that its object is to produce an image, drawing can certainly achieve the perfection proper to imagery, but plastic beauty is not necessary to the perfection of this order. Without being at all paradoxical, we could say that it is always indifferent to it and in some cases actually excludes it.

The specific distinction between artistic drawing and imagery can easily be discerned if we take the latter as a term of comparison. Photographs are perfect images by definition. Provided that the negative and the proof are good, the object that a photograph represents is represented as well as is possible. This is why good photographs are the most satisfying documents in all spheres, whether in the sciences, history or the fine arts. No other kind of image is more informative, no verbal description, no artistic reconstitution of the event or of the object which they represent can match them as regards objective information. But precisely such images belong in the category of information, which is the transmission of knowledge. Thus there can be imagery without the art of drawing or of painting. Now it remains to be seen whether the art of drawing or of painting can exist without imagery.

It can be said that today the question has been decided by facts. The advent of non-figurative painting, still of recent date, no longer permits doubt regarding the possibility of imageless drawing and painting. The existence of both should be enough to put an end to the debate. But it continues no less because many confuse the question of determining whether an art of drawing without imagery is possible with the wholly different question of determining whether it pleases them. It is legitimate to think all the bad things one wants to about abstract art, and to say so, but after all is said and done the fact remains that this art has been conceived, realized, savored and preferred to that which is called "museum art" by a considerable public which at times goes so far as to refuse to recognize any art other than abstract art as worthy of being called painting. All the pejorative explanations of this phenomenon, such as the decadence of art and taste, snobism, the mercantilism of some intermediaries between the artist and the public, are tenable and in part justified, but causative factors of this kind are found at the birth of all artistic modes, good or bad. None of them suffices to explain why in the case in question these influences favored precisely a form of art which, paradoxically, was far removed from the public taste, especially in its beginnings.

Upon closer examination we see that the crisis was latent at least since the sixteenth and seventeenth centuries in the form of a basic conflict between drawing and color painting. In the eighteenth century, Abbé du Bos, whose perspicacity often went far beyond the prejudices of his time, was already of the opinion that the debate could not lead to any conclusive decision. Some people, he observed, favored drawing, others preferred color, and no reasoning could prove that one group or the other was right. Should Titian be preferred to Poussin? Each one is free to make his choice, but the choice itself is inevitable. At the time he wrote these words, du Bos could not foresee to what point the future quarrel between Ingres and Delacroix would one day prove him right.

Let us try to see why this choice is ineluctable. Those who discuss drawing and painting as dialecticians sometimes raise the objection that there is a simple answer to the problem: all the artist has to do is to balance the two tendencies, thereby sacrificing neither color nor drawing. But this is merely verbiage. Actually, all the arts are based on the aptitude of certain classes of sensible qualities to move our sensibility or, if preferred, on that of our sensibility to be touched by them. Those whom sounds leave indifferent never show an interest in music, and the same remark applies to colors: those who are not affected by the simple perception of a pure color will never take pleasure in any combination of colors. Now individual sensibilities to color vary.[6] A person whose mind is primarily speculative cannot live in the company of painters, or even read the writings produced by some of them, without confirming how his own sensibility to chromatic sensations and shading is inferior to theirs. Whoever has a "painter's eye," especially if he is a colorist, constantly experiences pleasure and pain—sometimes to an intense degree—at the mere sight of the colored objects around him, whereas the ordinary mortal watches this spectacle without really noting it. Thus it is easily understandable that some experience a keen pleasure at the sight of pictures deliber-

6. By way of example, Baudelaire's predilection for violet. In it he saw (as we see in it in fact) its two component colors, red and blue fused as a qualitative unity of a new color. By itself, violet evoked in his imagination many moving ideas: "Of violet color (contained, mysterious, veiled love, color of a canoness)." A canoness whose blue still affords the glimpse of glowing embers. The mere perception of this color kindled a very general notion in him: "I have found the definition of the Beautiful—of my beautiful. It is something fiery and sad, something somewhat vague, leaving scope to conjecture." One could show how this elementary reaction to a color is related in him to his ideal of feminine beauty, to his predilection for the art of Delacroix, etc. But the origin of all is the spontaneous harmony between a definite sensibility and a sensible quality. For many, violet, as some dictionaries say, is the color of the violet.

ately calculated to give the eye the kind of pleasures it
prefers. We cannot blame those who do not experience this
for expressing their disapproval of a painting of this
kind. In order to give them a reasoned doubt, the most we
can ask them is whether they do not judge these combinations of color arranged in a certain order on a plane surface somewhat like a deaf person would judge a musical
work whose effects he can neither perceive nor imagine.
There is in fact a blindness to the nuances of color just as
there is a deafness to the nuances of sound. This kind of
blindness, like the other, is in no way shameful. But those
who are afflicted with it ought to be aware of it and not
base the validation of their judgments upon it.

Here we come to the crucial point: why does it seem
as though a perfect balance between drawing and color
would be, if not impossible, at least always precarious and
tending to disruption? The answer involves the very object
of the art of painting, for it is very far from requiring that
all painters conceive the object in the same way, or that
all agree that this object is painting. For the great majority
of those engaged in painting, or those who view it, the
important thing is not to arrange colors on a canvas in a
certain order but to arrange these colors by surrounding
them with lines in such a way so that they represent an
historical scene, a familiar event, a known person, or
merely a recognizable object. Color in that case serves to
perfect the resemblance already assured by the drawing
which represents the object. Very few people are endowed
with a sensibility so refined that the mere sight of a simple
harmony of tones is a source of pleasure to them. Hence
they and the painters who appeal to their taste seek support
in the wholly different pleasure of recognizing represented
objects and of deciphering the meaning of the pictorial
scene. We pass then from the order of pure painting to

that of imitation, representation and signification. In this order the artist uses his technique as a language with which he speaks to the spectator. This wholly special language is not composed of arbitrary and abstract signs, and bears no necessary relation to the objects which they signify; on the contrary it is this which confers a superiority upon it which painters frequently have claimed for their art over that of the poet, because painting puts the spectator directly in front of an object as real in itself as objects of nature. When the poet says "bird," those who do not know the language in which he writes will not know what he is talking about. But the painter simply paints a bird of any kind on the wall and everybody understands. By directly representing the appearance of visible reality, the painter uses a language composed of natural signs intelligible to all.

The sole condition required for effecting this kind of communication is that the spectator must already know the meaning of the signs that are being used, that is to say, he must already know what the painter is representing. This is why so many painters choose their subjects from historical events that are known to a broad public, such as those taken from religious or natural history. As the memory of these events fades, the images representing the chosen episodes lose their meaning, which it then behooves scholarship and iconography to restore to them. When painters worked for a learned élite steeped in the classics, the mythology and the history of ancient peoples were the inexhaustible reservoirs of the "subjects" of paintings; nowadays most of the subjects of this kind have no meaning for the great majority of spectators unless they are explained. But why go so far back? Who among us, without being informed beforehand, would understand that one of the first canvases painted by Degas depicts the

queen Sémiramis supervising the construction of the ramparts of Nineveh? Having never seen Sémiramis or the
ramparts of Nineveh, we would be unable to surmise this.
But neither had Degas seen them.

On the other hand, once we are alerted the nature of
the problem undergoes a change. The painter in that case
communicates to us information concerning a possible
scene, representing an event that is at least believable, and
the "meaning" of his picture consists in furnishing us with
the necessary elements so that we may be able to picture it
to ourselves. From this moment, the spectator's role is to
"understand" the picture, that is to say, to interpret the
whole and relate the details to the subject which the work
represents. The principal accomplishment of the painter
in that case becomes what formerly was called "poetic
composition," understanding by that the choice and the
arrangement of personages and objects to the extent that
they contribute to the good representation of the subject
chosen. Everything counts for those who espouse this conception of painting: the choice of figures, their attitudes,
their facial expressions—differing in accordance with the
nature of the emotions or feelings which they are supposed
to be experiencing—as well as the characteristic costumes
of their time, and of their people. In short it involves both
expression and local color. It is no longer enough to be
able to identify Jesus, St. John and Judas, in the representation of the Last Supper; far too many conventional signs
easily permit us to guess; we must still be able to explain
why each personage expresses the particular emotion depicted on his face, why such an object is painted in a certain style. The critics in such cases never fail to do for the
painter what they have done a thousand times for Corneille and for Racine: namely to object that their personages did not live at the time in which the author situ-

ates them, that he endows them with a language they did not speak or with customs that could not have been theirs. When a picture cannot represent, it changes into a rebus, marking the triumph of allegory which prevails in all the arts of drawing. By signifying the Nile through a statue whose head is enshrouded by a veil, says the good Abbé du Bos, Bernini "nobly designated that the Nile wished to conceal its source." So be it! But today when the sources of the Nile are known, this veil would lead the spectator into error, were he to ask the question.

The most striking feature of the comments made on pictures by those who judge them from the viewpoint of poetic imagery is that, valid or not, they bear no necessary relation to the art of painting and would apply just as well, or better, to an historical essay on the events depicted. This is a sure sign that the artist and the critic have surreptitiously shifted the problem and substituted knowledge for art.

It is from this starting point that the celebrated conflict between color and drawing finds an intelligible meaning. All that is required to discover it is to listen to the painters who have given thought to their art. The more the painter inclines toward historical painting, the greater importance drawing has in his works. This is a self-evident proposition for the reason that so-called history painting (religious, national, ancient or mythological) is necessarily representational and nothing can be represented without drawing it. Why does this necessity force color into second place? Naturally, it is not a question of abolishing color, since color perfects imitation and resemblance, but in a genre as essentially representational as history, whether it be anecdotal or merely topical, credibility imposes itself with such absolute necessity that the painter must stay approximately within the limits of the natural colors that to the eye are characteristic of objects. To follow the play of color for pure optical pleasure is to make use of it against likeness where color, on the contrary, ought to lead to its perfection. In this case, color, like drawing and form, is compelled to imitate nature; it cannot be an end in itself, and there is no reason to invent one.

Both painters and drawers of historical subjects have clearly understood this fundamental aspect of the problem.

"Avoid too ardent color," said Ingres, "it's anti-historical. Fall into grey rather than into ardent tones if you can't make it just right, if you can't find an absolutely true tone." Such words are revealing if interpreted in the light of this spirit of submission to the real and the credible which characterizes this genre of painting. Again Ingres: "The historical tone leaves the mind tranquil; have no more ambition on that score than on any other." Should we underline this marvelous phrase, *historical tone?* A kind of color that knows how to be inobtrusive because it is the color of things themselves! "According to many persons," wrote Ingre, "Raphael was not a colorist. He did not use color as did Rubens or Van Dyck. I certainly agree, indeed he guarded himself against it very well!"

Here then it is not the reflection of a philosopher but that of a painter upon his art which sets two principles of painting against each other, each one of which tends to dominate the other and finally to exclude it. As often happens, the most beautiful accomplishments, or at least the ones we savor most, have always been compromises. In Ingres we desire no color but his, and in Delacroix no other drawing but his; the latter, through his painter's drawing responds to the former's draughtsman's coloring. We would betray a poor understanding of the astonishing evolution of modern painting if we did not see in it an almost necessary sequel to the duality of tendencies inherent in the traditional notion of painting. Ever wavering between two possible arts, imagery and painting, which for a long time he was content to combine into different proportions, we have seen the modern painter engage himself in compromises that he himself did not have the patience to endure. The beginnings of "Fauvism" are instructive in this respect. The sight of the first trunks of trees painted blood red or raw green provoked hilarity among some and indignation among others. These painters protested against this reaction, but neither reason nor art were entirely on their side. They had the right to represent trees, but if this was their intention why did they retain the form of this representation without the color? They likewise had the right to place red or green streaks on their canvases, but if color alone interested them why give it the form of trees? They or their immediate successors sided with one of the solutions to the problem: Vlaminck returned to landscape painting and to its naturally grey-green tones while Derain went back to classicism with an obstinacy which his first admirers have often regretted. The partisans of color liberated it no less from form but also from the imitation of natural forms to which painting had always more or less strictly compelled it. Whence stems the non-figurative art of today, whose mere existence constitutes a convincing answer to the second question that we posed: if imagery is possible without painting can we say that painting without imagery may be equally possible? The answer is yes and the objections that have been raised to this answer up to now are rooted more in emotionalism than solid fact.

The common fault of these objections is that they discuss art from a viewpoint other than that of its essence. For example, personal taste has no role in the discussion of this problem. Those who tolerate only non-representational

painting pontificate as arbitrarily as those who refuse to
consider it painting at all. Tastes are free, painters are free.
Colors arranged in a certain order on a plane surface always
constitute a painting, whatever the colors and this order
may be. Whether or not the result is pleasing depends not
only upon the artist but upon the spectator as well—and if
there are many people who cannot endure the sight of
abstract canvases, there is no lack of those who shrink at
the mere thought of seeing some of Horace Vernet's compositions again. To argue about such matters is a complete
waste of time.

The objection drawn from the very nature of art in
general is more subtle and takes its point of departure at
a much higher level. Art is declared to be all the more
lofty the more its operations fully utilize the ensemble of
the resources at the disposal of the human mind. Indeed
it cannot be denied that painting, by achieving an increasing awareness of its proper essence, has considerably
lowered its former requirement. By recognizing the essential nature of its proper good with an ever greater clarity
it has progressively lost the remembrance of the techniques
formerly practiced in the ateliers and allowed to perish its
manual skills and the perfections of method to which we
owe the greatly admired beauty in the art of the old masters. It has been said that an exceptional general culture
of the gifts of mind and hand was necessary to conceive
work such as those executed by Veronese, Tintoretto or
Tiepolo, in which the artist proved his ability to create a
world of human beings, of gods and of goddesses, not to
speak of the palaces they inhabited, of the objects with
which these palaces were furnished, and of the animals
who graced them. This is incontestable, and the virtuosity
of the technicians who knew how to execute these works

with almost infallible mastery attests to the perfection achieved at that time by an art that perhaps will never find it again.[7]

If, however, we persist in conceiving of the art of painting in terms of its proper essence and idea we may doubt whether all the perfections of these pictures were the perfections of painting. By judging it as a harmony of forms and colors arranged on a plane surface, this or that predella by Sarsetta or this or that tiny interior by Bonnard or by Vuillard holds no less perfect joys in store for the spectator than the contemplation of so many enormous compositions ideally suited to feed the descriptions of them purveyed by writers and the commentaries of historians or of guides. Historical knowledge, psychological penetration, ingenuity in the conception and arrangement of the parts are so many precious perfections in themselves: their importance grew to the degree that painting further assumed the functions proper to imagery and poetry and undertook to represent or tell a story. It was then that this creator of immovable visual appearances willed to give the illusion of movement and that this great silent art aspired

7. A position defended several times by Paul Valéry and which is certainly justified in its order and on its plane. But the art of this or that artist includes a great number of elements that merge with the fundamental art from which his work derives. To paint like Veronese, Tintoretto or even like Tiepolo at Stra, is manifestly to testify to an ensemble of cognitions and to the mastery of necessary techniques which imply a human perfection which is difficult to attain and which will probably never again be equalled. In the past there was one country, Italy, where geniuses of this kind found all the artistic and social complicities favorable to their flowering. Such an art in effect is difficult and very lofty. But in another sense, an art so simple in appearance which has bequeathed us Vermeer's *The Lacemaker* or Watteau's *The Indifferent One* is at least as close as *The Wedding at Cana* to the essence of pure painting.

to speak. In order to compete with history it had to compose "scenes" conceived as so many talking images which as a result have become numerous subjects for explanatory texts and lessons. Is it really so surprising that this admirable figurative technique, priceless in its order and worthy of the sincerest admiration, has in fact been neglected and lost in a time like ours when the least interesting thing about a picture is the subject matter? We can therefore ask ourselves whether this decadence of technique is also a decadence of painting. This does not require us to draw a conclusion, but to effect a disassociation of ideas.[8] Neither does it require us to pronounce judgment, inviting us rather to reflection.

The evolution of modern painting forcibly poses a final question. To speak of non-representational, non-imitative or abstract painting is not to speak of an amorphous painting. No painting is more abstract than Mondrian's, but this geometric painting is also the most formal of all. Like formal logic itself, it is form without content.

8. Writers have a weakness for this part of the art of painting because on this particular subject they are as or more competent than the painter himself. Nobody reads Diderot's "Salons" today. He was strong on the description of the subject of pictures. But we can still see him, in the anthologies of his writings, giving Pigalle a lesson on the manner in which the sculptor should conceive and compose the *Monument de Reims.* The passage is grandiose in its unconscious presumption: "Pigalle, my friend, take your hammer and break this group of bizarre beings into pieces for me" (Diderot, *Essai sur la peinture,* in *Oeuvres* (Paris: La Pléiade), p. 1181. The preface to the first edition (1798) entirely shared this feeling. In this essay, according to the preface, it will be seen "what help the arts can draw from this perspicacity of the true man of letters and the reflections of the philosopher." This incredible pretention has not ceased to show itself in some men of letters, but we can hope that philosophers will be more and more inclined to obtain instruction from artists and less and less inclined to lord it over them.

Everything which preceded effortlessly accommodates itself to a painting of this kind, but a later development has led our contemporaries to eliminate even form from painting. We hesitate to describe works of this kind, which seem to be reduced to colors arranged without apparent order on a plane surface. Some of these paintings look like wall panels covered with a layer of almost uniform paint, without any diversity save that of the brush strokes. It could be that this is still painting, but we can no longer be certain that it is art. The objection is not that the sight of these panels arouses no feeling of pleasure, for they must give some pleasure to their authors and no doubt also to those who buy them.[9] The question, rather, is to determine whether this pleasure is that of a pure apprehension of color, hence natural, or of the apprehension of a work of art proper in which pleasure is born of the intelligibility of a form made perceptible to the senses through its material. There is no work of art without matter, and the cognition of artistic beauty is always essentially a perception, but in order to be an apprehension of the beautiful, this perception must necessarily be that of a matter intentionally impregnated with intelligibility. Art and the

9. As determined as I am not to attribute any privileged value to my personal esthetic experiences, which for that matter are in detail so unstable, I must, however, recognize that these recent developments have somewhat disconcerted me. In 1963, in Washington, a very enlightened lady art-lover placed me before some canvasses where I saw only a form similar to that deposit of dust that spontaneously settles on the top of some radiators. In the face of my all too obvious dismay, she charitably left me as a hopeless case. In the same city, an admirable private collection placed me in the presence of large colored panels which bore not the slightest trace of a line or spot. Why judge? Would Baudelaire perhaps have been happy before a beautiful violet panel? True enough, the canonesses in that case provided him with some distractions.

beauty proper to it disappear along with form and order.
The pleasures of matter are all that remain, stirring to be
sure and rather too much than not enough, but they
scarcely lead beyond the level of animality. An ethics of
art, perhaps, would seek purification of the ever confused
emotivity of our sensibility passively subjected to material
stimuli of all kinds. Art in that case would have the function of furnishing the sensibility with objects worthy of it,
that is to say the sensibility of an intelligent being.

Painting is found only rarely in a pure state, but what
an artist introduces into the conception and execution of
a painting is what authorizes the work to lay claim to the
art of painting. For a great number of spectators, probably
the great majority, painting can only be taken in small
doses, and they prefer the elements of imagery, sentimen-
tality, romanticism or anecdotes found in it. The remarks
which were made on statuary in this connection are
scarcely less true with respect to painting.[10] This kind of

10. In Baudelaire's *Salon de 1846* we come across a chapter
title which promises much: "Why sculpture is boring." The prom-
ise, however, is imperfectly kept. The fact itself is hardly con-
testable; in a museum or at an art exhibition when we want to
breathe better than we do in the picture galleries, all we have to
do is to go see the sculpture. The first reason that Baudelaire gives
for this is rather disconcerting. Sculpture, he says, "is an art of
Caribbeans." All peoples knew how to sculpt long before they could
paint (he did not know Altamira); sculpture is closer to nature
than painting, and this is why "our peasants who rejoice at the
sight of a sculptured piece of wood or stone remain in a state
of stupor in the presence of the most beautiful painting. Therein
lies a singular mystery which we cannot put our fingers on" (*Oeuvres
complètes,* Pléiade), p. 671. Let us admit that we see nothing here
which can make sculpture boring to the public. A more serious
attempt at explanation states that sculpture "brutal and positive
as nature, is at the same time vague and ungraspable because it
shows too many faces at once." We can read other reasons in this

art triumphs principally in the form of mixed modes which achieved their peak of perfection among the masters of the Italian Renaissance, among the first Flemish masters and those who perpetuated their tradition in different countries. It would be all the more bad grace to criticize them because it was probably by offering us doses tolerable to our weakness that these admirable painters progressively led modern man to the discovery of a pure form of their art. In admiring their works the important thing is not to let the admiration lose itself on the ore, but to concentrate on the gold.

The discernment of works of art is the province of art criticism; the philosophy of art has but one general rule to set forth in these matters: everything which enters into the composition of a picture, not only the materials, the tools and the traditional techniques of execution used, but further the model, the subject, the obvious meaning or the symbolic signification, in short everything therein, forms part of the material of the work, except for the plastic form which the painter has conceived and progressively imparted to these different elements in order to integrate them into the unity of an object the sight of which would be desirable for its own sake. What is involved in

---

particular chapter, in which the conclusion is drawn that "it is as difficult to be knowledgeable in sculpture as it is to make bad sculpture" (p. 672). But this assertion also would lead us to expect that we take pleasure in looking at it. The real question, perhaps, is that the incontestable fact, which is the point of departure, is itself ambiguous. The multitudes perhaps go to see pictures for the sake of the imagery rather than for the sake of painting; without the charm of color, deprived of anecdotal interest which for many spectators constitutes the principal charm of the picture, sculpture proper is perhaps no more or no less faithful than pure painting. Baudelaire, obviously, does not seem to be of their number: *non omnia possumus omnes.*

this case is an object which is called beautiful, that is to say a sensible object whose intelligibility is in some way visible, as something wholly impregnating a material for the exclusive purpose of embodying it.

Hence it is always to be feared that the material may seduce the spectator away from the form, all the more so because the plurality of forms seems to be the rule in the order of art in contrast to what occurs in the order of nature. In art the higher form does not replace the lower forms which it takes possession of; all it can do in its supreme determination is to unify them without suppressing them. Therefore each form remains present, animated by a natural tendency to self-assertion, not without some danger to the unity of the whole.

Virtuosity in the technique of execution can tend to affirm itself for its own sake; indeed it is natural for it to do so because it is a good thing, constitutes an art in itself and can legitimately pursue its own beauty. Skill in imitation, which is also an art, can tend to seek its own satisfaction in an increasingly perfect imagery, up to the perfection of a reproduction or even of *trompe l'oeil;* this too is an art capable of achieving beauty of its own, and we see no reason why we should deprive ourselves of it, or even simply limit its rights. Above all, natural beauty is permanently present as an irresistible invitation to the artist to carry it over just as it is into his work, which will thereby turn out fully wrought. He can certainly consent but on the condition that he does not believe that the copying of a beautiful landscape is the same as making a beautiful painting, nor that painting a beautiful live model is by the same token the painting of a beautiful nude. The artist is less exposed to this danger than the spectator, for one of the surest means of purifying the sight of a living beautiful body is the effort that must be exerted to make of it a picture whose beauty will be that of art, its very own, and not that of nature which is that of the model. The spectator most often judges only the result: an artistic beauty, obliging complicities, which lets itself be admired as a natural beauty. It is in the nude that the art of painting achieves the most complete triumph of form over pictorial matter by proceeding to a kind of purgation of the passions; but it is also the terrain of its most frequent defeat, for it is scarcely possible to fashion an art free of all sexual complicity with an object so closely bound up with sexuality. Eroticism is the shoal on which painting, which deliberately makes the natural beauty of the human body its subject, runs the risk of foundering.[11]

All the other "subjects," depicting emotions, passions, history, patriotism or religion, are of another nature, but their effect is similar. Each time the artist stirs the spectator's emotion through the subject matter, it is not art which moves him but the subject. Each time that he proceeds this way the artist cheats, but since it is the spectator who often demands to be tricked and becomes

11. The history of modern painting since Cézanne offers a very important subject of reflection to the philosopher. It is the artists, not the philosophers, who by their investigations have demonstrated the non-imitative character of plastic art. The painter Ozenfant's book, *Art* (Paris: Jean Budry, 1928), is rich in philosophical reflections on this point. This book, which has been out of print in France since 1930, unfortunately has never been republished. I first learned about this book through its American edition: Amédée Ozenfant, *Foundations of Modern Art*, tr. by John Rodker, new edition (New York: Dover publications, 1952). I quote, nearly at random: "The Cubist attitude; the effort to evoke emotions without resort to representational form" (p. 51). "One definition would be: Cubism in painting conceived as related forms which are not determined by any reality external to these related forms" (p. 76). "Cézanne gave us pears and apples that owed nothing to Eve; it was a brutal interruption to a flesh diet" (p. 82).

indignant if painting is offered to him instead of the pictorial, sentimental or anecdotal imagery that he expects,
it would be bad grace to blame the artist who seeks a compromise, inasmuch as the artist himself often desires it. It
can be truly said of the art of painting above all that it is
useless to try to prod nature out of sight, for she makes a
quick comeback. This is the bastard condition in which
the art of painting has lived and endured for centuries. It
seems doubtful that it could ever live differently, save for
the brief periods during which it wages a heroic struggle
to realize itself in the purity of its essence. The example
of our time abundantly shows how little recognition painting attracts to itself by an effort of this kind, but since
universal art must nourish itself on its lessons later, it is a
good thing, indeed it is necessary that, from time to time,
some artists have the courage to repeat it.

FIVE

Music

SOUND IS THE MATERIAL of musical art. Since noises are also sounds, the term "musical sound" is used at times for greater precision to mean the sensible quality or impression produced on the nerves and auditory centers by the vibrations set up in the atmosphere, whose frequency ranges between sixteen and sixteen thousand double vibrations per second. The numbers of these vibrations can vary slightly according to individuals. Acoustics is the science of sounds as optics is that of colors; in both cases art has preceded science and, with even greater reason, philosophy. The latter takes the properties of musical sound into consideration only insofar as they directly affect the essence of music.

The three principal qualities of musical sound are pitch, timbre and intensity. Their importance is attributable to the fact that these qualities, taken together, make it possible to identify a given musical sound. The existence of distinct sounds identifiable by their pitch, timbre and intensity ensures the material possibility of the very existence of music because it enables us to distinguish sounds and to combine them without the possibility of confusion.

In this respect musicians are more fortunate than painters, for if the distinction between lines is clear that between forms and colors is much less so. Delacroix deplored that the average spectator was not as capable of perceiving tonal harmony or discordancy in painting as he was aware of those qualities in music. Indeed, sounds seem to be the most distinctly differentiable of sensible qualities; whence derives the possibility of the unconscious calculus to which the ear spontaneously surrenders upon perceiving them and which is the basis of the pleasure we take in music.

Although no sustained experiments have been made to prove it, it would appear that on the whole sensitiveness to the emotions aroused by the perception of sounds is more widespread and keener than sensitiveness to forms, lines and colors. This is not to say that a monument, a statue, or a picture cannot intensely and deeply move some spectators endowed with a special sensitiveness to visual images. If painting were not so commonly confused with imagery it would be easily seen that the number of those who love painting for itself is relatively small; thousands of visitors spend pleasurable or painful hours in a museum and leave it without suspecting that they know nothing about the real nature of painting. On the other hand, nobody is ever mistaken about the nature of music, for it cannot be confused with any imagery. As to its effects, all we have to do is compare the crushed air of patrons leaving a museum with the shouts, even the howling, that greets the end of many concerts to convince ourselves that music can unleash violent reactions of an emotion of the most obvious visceral character. Those who are visibly annoyed by this wild disorder and who do not give vent to their feelings are exceptions and are exposed to the hostile glares of the other concert-goers. Perhaps this is the secret revenge that noise takes against sound! In any case, the sudden release of an excess of emotion repressed during a musical performance sufficiently confirms the intensity of the emotional states normally associated with sounds. Painting unleashes no such uproar. If we look daggers at someone in a museum, our disapproving glance is much more likely directed against the visitor who has given vent to a soft cry of delight upon a sudden encounter with beauty.

Just as painting at the start requires a void of visual forms, music likewise can be created only in a void of sonorous forms. Imperfect as the traditional formula *esse post non esse* is when applied to the creative act, it is justified here. First there is silence, then the song which the lonely man invents to fill his solitude, or the music suddenly released by the conductor of the orchestra after he has obtained almost total silence from the audience.[1]

The analogy ends here. The forms which the architect, sculptor or painter create in space are forms proper, visible and endowed by their creators with a total and simultaneous existence which is also definitive for as long as the material out of which these forms have been fashioned lasts. In fact, the mode of being and of duration of a work of art are those of its material. Sound is not a solid; it is caused by a sonorous vibration, hence by a movement in the atmosphere, and its duration is that of the movement causing it. Actually, this is not altogether correct for a sonorous sensation in its unity already combines a multiplicity of elementary physical movements that have been set off in the atmosphere out of which they make a single sound. Below sixteen double vibrations, the ear perceives only discontinuous pulsations, the elements of a potential sensation which our ear does not perceive, being unable to

1. The minute of silence in the darkness demanded by Wagner before the beginning of every musical drama at Bayreuth, can serve as a symbol here.

bind its elements together into the continuity of a definite single sound. We sense we are on the threshold of this transition, on the very border between sound and noise, when listening to an organ pipe 32 feet in length.

This is why music is called an art of time in contrast to the plastic arts whose works subsist in space. The distinction between the arts of time and the arts of space is certainly a meaningful one, even though all the arts by virtue of their materials are dependent simultaneously upon time and space, as has already been noted, for where are sonorous vibrations produced if not in space? And where do the temples of Egypt endure if not in time? But the true meaning of the distinction lies elsewhere. Sound has no physical substance of its own, it does not continue to subsist by itself after being produced, rather it ceases and is heard no more.

The consequences ensuing from this fact deeply affect the structure of musical compositions, for they would vanish into discontinuity like the physical elements of vibration if sensation did not grasp them in the unity of sound. Sounds likewise would be lost in the void of discontinuity, as Saint Augustine pointed out fifteen centuries ago,[2] if memory did not harbor and measure them so that the mind, aided by the imagination, can arrange them into distinct groups each one of which constitutes a sonorous form. This form passes away in turn and dissolves, when upon reaching its limit the sonorous images of which it is composed fade away and their order escapes the memory. The fluid and successive being of musical substance entails its intellectuality since the work, inasmuch as it forms a whole, requires that it be structured in the memory by the mind. Thus, the mind affects the totality of this art in all its aspects and its minutest details.

2. Augustine, *Confessions,* Book XI, Chapters 27–28.

Music is essentially an art of time in the specific sense that it has no actual physical existence save during the time of its actual execution. The sculptor sculpts, the painter paints, the architect builds in time; they leave behind a work which lasts and subsists without them, sometimes for millennia. The singer sings and each note dies as it leaves his lips. Not only is it an art of time, but an art of the moment, whose existence as art is of the same nature as that of the dance, poetry, the theatre. The unity of these actions is but that of a duration whose elements would fall back into the void of silence as they fade if memory did not forget this unity by endowing these elements with at least a temporary subsistence and a mode of intellectuality.

Music, being essentially ephemeral, is the art of that which is to die, but it is also the art of that which wills to be born and its victorious ability to affirm the being that it creates is inseparable from its essential resignation to its own demise. Music not only accepts passing away, it aspires thereto; its parts must fall back into nothingness one by one so that the whole, of which they are the elements, can come into being. There is no point in stressing the intimate relationship with the human condition whose unceasing changes, as Saint Augustine frequently noted, are so many successive deaths. Nobody knows this better than the musician. He never ceases to annul the sound which he has just produced by producing another which cancels its predecessor. He simply cannot fix musical sound in an immobility of any duration. There are sustained notes, of course, and chords whose prolongation seems to want to impart a feeling of stability, but they announce a change unless they serve him only like the pedal notes as a support for their very immobility. Absolutely motionless music would be like the music of the celestial spheres, the ear

would cease to perceive it. Therefore, from the beginning
of our reflection upon this art we must accustom ourselves
to the fundamental notion of musical occurrence. Music
is essentially a sequence of sonorous occurrences which the
artist perforce creates without let-up so that the substance
of his art may exist. He knows well that his listener will
live in the expectation of the unexpected, in default of
which even the return to the expected would not be possible. Music therefore is an art of time to the same degree
that it is an art of change and of becoming.

Its material is sound, as we have already said. By
virtue of this it is the creator of its own material, for
strictly speaking there are no musical sounds in nature.
All we hear in nature are noises, that is to say sounds generally produced by irregular vibrations without a definite
timbre and without a pitch that is exactly locatable on any
recognized scale. In this sense everything is created in
music, even its material, for noise is merely the material
of the sound which itself is the material of music. But now
for the first time since the beginning of these reflections
we must confirm the existence of a human artistic material
all the elements of which are furnished by the human body
in its natural condition and functioning without the help
of any artificial means. In this sense, music introduces us
to a new order which we can call that of the arts of man.
The human voice is the first of all musical instruments;
most musicians are also agreed that it is the most beautiful
of all of them. This is understandable in view of the
sounds that it is capable of producing, its flexibility and
the perfection of the most varied sonorous forms that it
can be made to execute at the price, naturally, of considerable effort and well-directed training.

The body is the singer's instrument. We can very
rightly say this of the body, for even the parts that do not

directly contribute to forming the voice play a role, even if only as a sounding board. Vocal music because of its material is the most moving of all forms of musical expression. The listener to whom a human body addresses itself responds to this call through his own body. Nothing which makes of him an animal body remains indifferent to this experience. If we restrict ourselves to voices taken at the peak of their development, at their optimum age (there are young voices and old voices, like the bodies they inhabit), and disregard the numberless individual or racial variations distinguishing them, human voices are divided first of all into the voices of men, women and children of both sexes. Voices have a sex, indeed to such a degree that the removal of the sex of some adults resulted in the creation of a special type of voice, that of the *castrati,* some of whom had brilliant musical careers. The disappearance of this type of voice brought the end to a definite type of musical beauty. The part of Orpheus in Gluck's opera is most often played by excellent artists, expert in the art of of *bel canto.* Whether they are contraltos or counter-tenors these remarkable singers leave many listeners dissatisfied, although they are in no way to blame. What is missing is the vanished "treble-singer," a representative of the breed of Guadagni for whom Gluck had written the part and whom he himself could not listen to without weeping. These asexual voices, first subjected to twelve or fifteen years of study, no longer exist. In contrast to musical instruments, every human voice has a sex and it is probably useless to maintain that the physiological relation between singer and listener in no way affects a musical performance.

The case of singing offers an exceptionally favorable occasion to pose some problems and to understand the answers to them.

First of all it helps us to give its true meaning to Keat's poetic utterance "a thing of beauty is a joy forever"—itself so beautiful. Indeed it is this for as long as it lasts and we last to behold it; but we pass on, works of art fall into ruin and their very ruins perish. Innumerable beautiful creations no longer exist for us save as names of musical compositions. They are no longer performed because there are no longer any artists such as the ones for whom they were written nor, of course, a knowledgeable and appreciative public to listen to them.

From this follows a second observation. Singing assumes a singer and this becomes the source of problems in the musical art that do not arise in painting. The painter is his own executant, he is his own virtuoso and his work is uniquely his own in a sense in which that of the musician's is only rarely—perhaps even never. In music, the actual existence of the work depends most often on some person other than its creator; now the art of execution is distinct from that of composition, it is learned, acquired and displayed separately. A contemporary reproached Liszt for "playing the piano" and recommended Chopin to those who wanted to "hear music played." In part he was right, yet it must be admitted that the two arts are closely related, whence the source of the problem of the virtuoso that inevitably rises in all orders of the musical art, for the executant must acquire the virtuoso's skill to be able to play the musical works that are entrusted to him. It is not necessarily the problems of a difficult execution that are in question. The way one strikes a keyboard or a violin by itself permits an almost infallible forecast. One must be the master of an instrument in order to be truly able to play music. Listeners do not always know where to direct their attention, nor to what to address their admiration or criticism. Most of the time they

focus their attention on both at once, that is to say on the
execution in the music, or inversely since the execution is
the actualization of a potential music which would not
exist without it. A great number of esthetic judgments are
misdirected because the actual addressee is not clearly
identified.

This initial imprecision affects a vast sector of music
in the case of singing. By its very tradition, opera is inseparable from the art of singing. Italian opera of the
eighteenth and nineteenth centuries, up to Rossini and
perhaps Verdi (minus *Falstaff*), can be more or less accurately described as an art of *bel canto* as much as an art
of music. We cannot read a history of this opera without
constantly coming upon the names of some male or female
singers for whom some operas were written to measure,
that is to say by taking into account the individual particularities of their voices. For even in the class proper to
them the voices of men, women and children are distinguished by their texture, ranging from the absolute so-
prano to the contralto for women, and from the absolute
tenor to the deep bass voice for men. Given the same texture, furthermore, the voice of each individual is distinguished from others by characteristic qualities such as
power, richness of timbre, the brilliance or volume of the
sound. Vocal instruction, the study of which is a world in
itself because of the great variety in methods and aims,
results in the production of voices whose instrinsic perfection constitutes the material of a distinct art. We speak
of singers such as Elisabeth Gafforini, Adelaide Melanotte, Marietta Mariolini (for whom Rossini composed
l'Italiana in Algieri), and further of Pisaroni, Judith
Negri (Madame Pasta), Alboni, Malabran and so many
others as artists "placed at the service of music by the art
of singing." The very opposite is true. These are the names

of artists for whom music was placed in the service of the art of singing.[3] The score was written for the singers and the singing itself took into the greatest consideration the quality of each voice, even the quality of the chest or head notes of this or that female or male singer, as well as the transitional notes, so important for ensuring the consistent quality of voices. It is merely an expression of taste to say that the opera at that time was a false genre and that the scores of Jonelli, Piccini, Sacchini, Trajella or Hasse betray a distressing musical poverty. This judgment may be correct in itself, but it neglects the fact that works of this kind were written with the art of singing as such in view, and for a breed of singers now extinct whose names no longer mean anything today. Who remembers the eunuch Farinelli, the tenors Babbini and Babbi? Yet it was their art of singing which in their time served so many operas nowadays wholly out of fashion. Their art died with them. What is particularly striking is that it was killed by composers, first because of their persistent demand that the singers sing the music exactly as they had written it and then because they wrote music conceived with its own beauty in view rather than with that of its execution. Mozart, perhaps, began to open up this path, not without

3. The fact strikes the reader of old theatrical criticism in France, for example, written in the second half of the nineteenth century. See the criticism in the *Revue des Deux-Mondes;* Paul Scudo, *Critique et littératures musicales* (Paris: 1852, 2nd ed.), in which chapters are dedicated to the "art of singing in Italy," "Angelica Catalani," "Henriette Sontag," "Story of an opera-singer" (Rose Niva). The same author's *L'art ancien et l'art moderne* (Paris: Garnier, 1854) comments on Grassini, Céleste Coltellini, Faustina, Caroline Duprez, etc. In *Les écrits de Paul Dukas sur la musique* (Paris: *Musique et Musiciens,* 1948), the selection of criticism stretches over the period from 1892 to 1932; I noted that there was not a single article dedicated to a singer, male or female.

running into a resistance from singers which continues to this day; Wagner led the trend to its limit by personally teaching his own singers how his music was to be sung. This endemic conflict between the art of music and the art of singing merely illustrates the specificity of the creative arts and of the performing arts, which in themselves entail a degree of creativity in their own sphere. When we say that a work was "created at La Monnaie" in Brussels, we thereby mean to fix the place of its first performance. A certain kind of art of singing had to die in order that a certain kind of music could come into being. Nothing else distinguishes the difference between them more clearly.

The same observation could be made in connection with any performing musical art. The case of vocal art is simply the first one that offers itself to scrutiny, but the eternal quarrel between composer and virtuoso has no other meaning. It is, perhaps, no mere accident that the age of Italian virtuosi singers was also that of the virtuosi of the violin: the singing instrument. Yet in this golden age, and perhaps because of the possibilities inherent in the instrument itself, the virtuosi were often composers: Corelli, Tartini, Pugnani are names still laden with musical associations for us. In the field of instrumental music, Paganini would be the counterpart of the singer whose artistry is virtuosity itself. Ingres was already wary about this, and today when a young violinist announces that he will play a concerto by Paganini, whose artistry formerly was enough to overwhelm audiences, we understand that his intention is to prove to us that he too is capable of executing it.

The voice and its music constitute a class apart, specifically distinct from the ensemble of sounds produced by the instruments that were invented, perfected and

constantly multiplied precisely for the purpose of producing such sounds. Singing is the living music of the
human body; like the body it is animated by an intellect
which commands the emissions, the inflections, the variations of intensity and, as is said, the slightest "expressive"
nuances. Whatever its nature and range, which can be
extremely broad or almost nil, the instrument introduces an
inorganic intermediary between the musician and his music.
Therefore he does not command the sound like a singer,
who as the master of his voice animates its inflections
from within. This duality of nature between vocal and
instrumental music is reflected in the musical works themselves. Broadly speaking, it can be said that some composers write for instruments, others for voices. More
exactly, some of them treat voices as instruments, as
Johann Sebastian Bach did so often, whereas others do
the opposite, as did Mozart, many of whose orchestral
themes ask only to be sung. This is indeed why Bach's
music, as beautiful as we know it can be, is always
inhuman (non-human) whereas Mozart's is essentially
human.[4] Mozartean music is always human because it
always sings, it is impossible for the musician to play
it without singing it.

Any material that can set off regular vibrations
in the atmosphere perceptible to the ear is a musical
instrument, or can become one. The classification into
three main families is well known: wind instruments,
string instruments and percussion instruments in which per-

4. Mozart can give proof of cruelty toward his singers, and
perhaps even more towards those of the female sex. At times we
sense in him an intention to do so, but more accurately it is a
cruelty which brings itself to bear on singing as an emission of the
human voice, not as a substitute for an instrument.

haps we can separately classify some instruments whose
strings are struck into action, such as the piano.[5] The
history of instruments is part of musicology; psycho-
physiology studies the different ways in which each kind
of instrument affects the listener's sensibility; the knowledge of their characteristic textures and timbres is answerable to the science of orchestration which presupposes such
knowledge although it is not reducible to or deducible
from it. The philosopher is most interested in the fact
that, regardless of the instrument, the sound produced is
already a musical creation. The painter's colors are also
human products, but they have their models in nature
where we find reds, blues, and very bold yellows as well as
the broad spectrum of their possible combinations. It is
much more rare to find ready-made musical sounds in
nature; sometimes the songs of birds contain them,
especially to the ear of a musician. The sound of drops of
water falling one by one in the silence of the night is not
organized into a melody except by those who are already
knowledgeable about music: [6] it would require remote

5. Electric music, improperly called "electronic," enables us
to assist at the birth of a new musical building material. Here what
is at stake is the creation of new instruments, in which sound is
produced by oscillators, by photo-electric cells, etc. Electronic organs, the "Martenot waves," have taken their place in the curric-
ula of the conservatories. A considerable musical literature has
already been written especially for electric waves. This is a particular case of the problem, general in the fine arts, which consists
in determining whether a new technique involves new forms.
Architect Lloyd Wright's remark: we have building materials for
which we do not yet have forms, is valid in all the arts.

6. Experiments are actually in progress to introduce noise into
music, or even to compose music with noises (typewriters, explo-
sions in motors, or noises artificially produced *ad hoc*). Any experiment is legitimate in art; its success or its failure with the public
alone will decide the fate of "concrete music." We will at least

analogies to find in natural noises anything resembling the sounds of a violin. Men have invented musical instruments of all kinds for the purpose of producing sounds that are the very material of music.

This inventiveness continues. There is no end to imagining new ways of producing musical sounds of a new type which themselves suggest the invention of new musical forms. The history of music confirms this. Bach is inconceivable without the organ, Chopin without the piano, Mozart without the violin, and the ensemble of modern symphonic music without the string, wind and percussion instruments that make up a large orchestra. If its details were known, the history of the invention of musical instruments would perhaps make us see more clearly that there has been a frequent exchange between the imagination of composers in search of new sounds with which to structure new musical forms and that of instrument makers who by creating new sonorities opened and revealed unsuspected formal possibilities to composers.[7] Who can say what modern music owes to Adolph

---

point out that the case is not the same as that of so-called abstract painting because the concrete element of which the building material of abstract painting is composed is still the line and the color which imitative painting makes use of. Noise, on the contrary, is not a sound. The tom-tom produces sounds, not noises, hence it is put into music; a percussion orchestra is a genuine orchestra, it plays music. Not only does noise not lend itself to the construction of musical form, but it prevents it from being born or destroys it. Noise is the enemy of sound. But artistic invention consists precisely in drawing the possible from the impossible. The philosophy of art does not enable us to predict its future.

7. The remark that without the bass clarinet one of the preludes of his opera *Fervaal* would not exist, has been attributed to Vincent d'Indy. If this remark is correct, it well illustrates the fruitfulness of the creation of instruments, since it invites composers to create new sonorous forms. Let us note in this connection that

Sax who, in the period between 1840 and 1845, invented the family of seven instruments which quite rightly have been called "saxophones." Conversely, the way in which certain composers employed new instruments in their works made them so particularly their own that it is practically impossible for anyone else to use them later without appearing to imitate them. It is difficult to assign a bare theme to tubas without seeming to plagiarize a passage from the Wagnerian tetralogy; no sooner do we hear tubas by themselves, some Valhalla seems to be crashing into fiery ruin. In short, the very possibility of musical forms is closely related to the existence of sounds created by man with these forms in view. There are no conceivable limits to the possibility of new musical sounds, but there are to the constant training of new artists to produce them since performing artists do not like "their fingering to be changed."

The details of the problems connected with musical forms are of a more complex character, but the only one that the philosopher can pose in regard to them concerns the meaning of the very notion of sonorous form. We can talk about it only by way of analogy with visual forms. Whereas it is easy to conceive a principle of unification arranging a plurality of simultaneously given points in space, it is more difficult to imagine how we can unify and arrange a plurality of elements whose characteristic

---

the formal vocation of a particular instrumental sonority is indestructible. Eliminated for a time by the piano, the harpsichord tends to resume its place; not only is it being manufactured again, but music is composed for it (M. de Falla, *Concerto for harpsichord and five instruments;* Francis Poulenc, *Rustic concerto for harpsichord and orchestra*). A more modest example is the flageolet which, considered to have been definitively eliminated by the German flute, begins to be played again in many countries (recorder in English). The fact is that its timbre has never been replaced.

feature is precisely the fact that they are not given all at once since they follow each other in a temporal sequence. Yet the simplest of songs, followed by its refrain, unquestionably solves this problem. All we have to do is reflect upon the theoretical conditions that ensure the possibility of this solution.

If musical sounds fade into the nothingness of oblivion at the moment of being heard, no relation between them would be possible. Saint Augustine long ago observed that the perception of a single sound requires the intervention of memory: how could we perceive that it lasts, that it is the same if we do not already remember it at the moment the ear perceives it? Like the relation of a sound to itself, the interval between this sound and another assumes that, in some way or other, the two successive sounds are simultaneously present in the hearing. In the case of a simple melody, the perception of the interval between two successive sounds therefore implies the persistence in the memory of the previous sound when the subsequent one supervenes. Thus the possibility exists of a kind of sonorous space, in which successive sounds coexist in a certain way thanks to the imagination which is itself the most immediate form of the memory of sounds.

The confused awareness of this truth explains why music is so often described as a purely intellectual and immaterial art despite the fact that its instrumental body can achieve a considerable mass—what are the dimensions of the organist compared to those of the organ? Like all the arts, music consists of sensations which are produced only in the mind. The very setting in which sonorous sensations are produced has neither substantiality nor extension. Sounds, like thoughts, succeed one another in the mind where they determine their relations, arrange themselves without letup, and finally set up orders in the process of breaking up and reforming. In this respect music, like poetry, is truly an art that is intellectualized even in its material. In a sense this most stirring of all the arts is also the most intellectual of all. For as soon as we proceed a bit further with the analysis of its material we find a structure composed of mathematical relationships whose intelligibility had been perceived by the sensibility long before the reasoning of the ancient Pythagorians had discovered it. The birth of musical form requires matter which, in this case, exists only in memory; hence it requires a mind.

Space permits the orderly arrangement of distinct elements by fixing them in an orderly relation to each other or, more simply, in relation to the same center of reference. Music is also not possible unless there are sonorous elements that are audible and arrangeable by virtue of some law. The principle of the discernment of sounds is what is called pitch. From the cradle, the infant shows a capacity to produce a multitude of sounds of different pitch, even more than he will be able to produce later. The infant's "warbling," like that of a bird, is characterized by the fact that it does not contain fixed intervals, and we would be quite surprised to hear a regularly structured melody come out of a cradle. Thus for singing to be possible it was first necessary to create musical sounds distinguished by intervals separating them, by way of simple definition. What we know today about the musical systems prevailing among different peoples suffices to make it clear that the imagination has enjoyed free reign in this domain. The distinctions approved in our musical system between whole notes, half notes and quarter notes are the product of a collective education. This education has led to a variety of listening habits, capable of perceiving *the same* sounds. This first formal inven-

tion was of considerable importance, since we owe to it the
possibility of a common musical language whose terms are
identifiable and linked to each other through identical
relationships by all those who listen to them. The possibility for each one of us to produce definite sounds, main-
taining determined relations among them which are the
same for those who produce them as for those who hear
them, is due to this condition. The frequency of a sound
wave determines the pitch of the sound that it produces;
hence any variation in the frequency of vibrations causes
a difference in the pitch of the sound, and is called an
"interval." A sound remains the same as long as it is not
distinguishable from itself; the perception of an interval,
no matter how short, produces *another* sound. Therefore
the elements joined together by sonorous forms are these
units which, above all, are distinguished by their different
pitches.

How are these elements to be arranged? A major
fact to consider if we want to understand the problems
posed by the music of our own time is that there exists
no absolute necessity for constituting groups of musical
sounds arranged according to this or that order of definite
intervals rather than any other. This indetermination,
which modern music considers as its most valuable discovery, seeing in it the foundation of its freedom, was not
favorably viewed at first, but rather it was seen as a serious
difficulty from which it had to extricate itself. The very
possibility of a music art was at stake. Any sonorous
order presupposes that a choice has been made among a
certain number of distinctly identifiable sounds, and that
the sounds thus chosen can be situated in an orderly
relation to each other on a common scale, constituted by
the ensemble of these sounds on which they can then be
assigned a definite range or, as is said, a "place." A "tone

scale" is necessary. The extreme limits of this scale are
the octave intervals which nature herself imposes, but the
intervals can be freely chosen within the octave. Moreover,
the intervals chosen can be arranged differently, starting
from any determined sound or note. Since antiquity, the
different groupings of regularly constituted intervals permitted the arrangements of musical sounds by situating
them in a place determined by their pitch within the
group. These were the different Greek "modes," whose
study is the concern of the history of ancient music. After
being later replaced by the actual tone system established
on a diatonic scale, they are progressively resuming their
place in musical creation, thereby giving modern music a
freedom of language of which the tyranny of tonal music
threatened to deprive it. Today all the known modes,
practiced by all peoples and in all times, have regained
their right to be heard, even though all may not enjoy
the same success with an audience. The reason for this
is simple. A habit must be created before a sonorous
order perceptible to the ear and recognizable by the mind
can be instituted; it is possible for several different habits
to coexist, but beyond a certain limit the multiplicity of
orders gives the impression of disorder. Different sonorous
systems get into each other's way once they are no longer
simple modifications of the others. Hence the feeling of
strangeness we get upon hearing systems fundamentally
alien to our own systems of scales, tones and modes. But
they are no less viable since they exist, and legitimate as
such since there are auditors who find their sounds
pleasing. The only problem they pose is that of the
possibility of coexistence with respect to the same musical
sensibility. It is hard to imagine that any answers other
than particular ones can be found to this problem which is
a personal one by definition. We all know what music we

like, but none of us knows what music we could develop a
liking for.

The question is posed in an acute form in our day.
Ever since Claude Debussy demonstrated to the Western
world that any musician who is master of his art can use all
possible modes, an inexorable logic has led musicians to
ask whether it is necessary to be restricted to any order
arbitrarily chosen in order to structure a musical composition. Music thus arrived at the concrete formulation of
a question of the highest philosophical interest. Just as
painting that is wholly formless and reduced to a mere
juxtaposition of colors, hues and shadings, makes us
wonder whether painting may not have ceased to be an art
by renouncing not only imitation but any form at all, so
does the "atonal" music of our day which contents itself
with juxtaposing the intervals of the diatonic scale, pose
the question as to whether a musical art is still possible
in the absence of all objectively necessary formal elements.
The philosophical import of the problem is considerable
for it comes back to the question: is the form of the
sensible quality necessarily required for art to be possible?
Now the determination of form is ultimately intelligible.
Therefore we raise the final question: is art possible
without intelligibility?

In keeping with what we have said about art in
general, our answer to this question can only be in the
negative. If artistic beauty is an intelligible entity posited
in sensible apprehension, the beautiful would disappear
with the intelligible, and since intelligibility offers itself
to the sensibility only as form, without it artistic beauty
would disappear. Yet we would not dare to resolve a
question of fact with purely *a priori* arguments. There are
many more real things in the world of art than are
dreamed of in our philosophy. The recent history of

musical art fortunately provides us on this point with an almost experimental confirmation of the impossibility of art without intelligibility. A completely atonal music has been conceptualized and tried. Tonality has been abolished, that is to say the choice of a note whose absolute pitch determined the relative pitch of the other notes. Since all the diatonic or chromatic intervals could be equally utilized as the musician pleased, the result was complete sonoric freedom.[8] The formal frames of musical thought ceased to exist at the very same time that these restraints were lifted. By losing the laws which it had imposed upon itself, precisely so that it could exist as form, music seems to have experienced great difficulty in being. Therefore it has restored frames. "Serial music" has decided to choose freely each time a series of notes previously deduced from the diatonic and chromatic scale without any other obligation—but a strict one—than that of employing them always in the same order.[9] The phil-

8. Whence the name of "dodecaphonic" music given to this kind of music which is based on the systematic and deliberate use of twelve half-tones.

9. Dodecaphonic music can also be called "serial" music, but for a particular reason that is of the greatest philosophical interest because composers had to look for a formal principle of order other than the tonality which had been rejected, so that a sonorous structure perceptible to the senses could again become possible. In other words, it was necessary to emerge from pure atonality and re-invent a new system to replace it. This is the series. This is the name given to the sequence of the twelve successive sounds on the chromatic scale; the order of the retained sounds is chosen by the composer; once chosen, the order remains the same from the beginning to the end of the composition; however, a note can always be replaced by its octave (since it is the same); in addition, the classic procedure of variation (multiplicity in the unity of the form) remains applicable to the series, but in a discipline that is much more strict because the musician cannot go back to the first

osopher as such has no opinion on the experiment's chances
of success, but to him it is the visible sign that music
cannot exist without some formal structure perceptible to
the ear. Only the future can tell how far this freedom can
be pursued without leading music back to the void of
forms from which it emerged thanks to the musician's
art. While waiting, it appears that the rejection of a
certain number of conventions has at least had the effect
of destroying the common musical language which all
Europe heard and understood since the sixteenth century
and which, beyond Europe, has been heard in all civilized
countries. Finally, we can ask ourselves whether music that
is good only for the person who has composed it may not
be as legitimate as that whose language is known by
millions of listeners? But this question brings us from
poietics to esthetics and although there is a close kinship
between the two orders, they are different.

Assuming a sound scale whose intervals are definite,
included within a gamut of some kind and arranged
according to a tone, mode or series, the succession of
sounds must still form discernible unities composed of

---

note without first having let all the others be heard. Hence they
are not variations except in the mode of presentation of the series.
The latter can be presented in a direct form, in an inverted form,
in retrograde form, in an inverted retrograde form. Inasmuch as the
series of twelve sounds can be treated in four different forms, it
is conceivable to obtain forty-eight possible forms from it (R. de
Candé, *Dictionnaire de la musique*, art. "*Dodecaphonisme*"). These
elementary notions suffice to illustrate the important philosophical
fact that the pure negativity of atonality taken by itself has made
it necessary to invent new laws of composition. The name given
to the series by the musician Hauer, *Grundgestalt,* admirably illustrates the necessity of a new formal element in the art of sound. The
transition from atonality to dodecaphonic series that has occurred
in Schoenberg's work is an event of primary importance for the
philosophy of art.

intervals of which the ear approves and even desires to hear again. Such a sequence of different sounds, perceptible as an apprehended sonorous whole, is a "melody." No music is possible without melody, except pure rhythm which irresistibly calls for melody, and which we shall discuss later. Any melody whose notes are retained in the memory can be heard as a harmony since the ear has a spontaneous loathing for sounds in close succession which it would not like to listen to simultaneously. Melody and harmony are creations of the mind inventing rules which are in keeping with the physical nature of sounds and the structure of the human ear which perceives them. Modern Western music, established as an art since the sixteenth century and as a science since Rameau's *Treatise on Harmony* (1722), is based on a melodic and harmonic language whose fruitfulness confounds the imagination and which is by no means exhausted. The effect of the rules of this language is to impart a formal consistency to musical sounds enabling them to be joined in sonorous structures endowed with a distinct unity and which start out from a life all their own.

But this is not all. Inasmuch as sounds succeed each other in time, they share in the properties of motion, notably velocity, measure and rhythm. All three properties contribute to the formal determination of the musical sound. The fundamental distinction of velocities are designated by the vague but expressive words which Western music borrowed from the Italian to signify them: *lento, adagio, andante, allegro,* and *presto.* The imagination not only retains the memory of the pitch of sounds but of their duration as well. This makes it possible to form groups of sounds of an equal duration. Hence in music there is a "measure" of time as there is one of space in geometry. Moreover, the time measure can be symbolized by agreed upon divisions of space: each group of notes forming a unity of duration is called a "measure," distinguished from the preceding and following one by drawing a vertical line called a bar. Finally, each note within the measure or series of measures is distinguished from others by its characteristic duration and forms, with some of them particular groups or musical phrases proper which are the very stuff of which music is made. A musical phrase is a form, a compound of sounds which succeed each other at a determined velocity (tempo), according to a definite measure (quarter time, triple time, etc.) and whose characteristic rhythm is attributable to the succession of long or short durations as well as to their variable stress in strong or weak beats.

The musical phrase is the pre-eminent sonorous form, complete and perfectly defined. The plurality of its constitutive elements, the ever open possibility of imparting individual variations to them which, beyond the notation, even modify the execution, ensure this seemingly strict system of formal determinations with a flexibility that confounds the imagination, and at times the ear. To symbolize the complexity of this problem, it is useful to picture to ourselves the reader of a musical phrase, complete in itself and furnished with all the required indications—notes, key, bar lines, general indication of the tempo—being reduced to guessing at the form of this phrase because he has not also been furnished with true indication of the manner in which the sounds are to be grouped. The first phrase of Beethoven's Sixth Symphony ("The Pastoral"), in itself so simple, changes character depending upon whether we read it in an edition in which all its notes are *legato,* emerging smoothly as though out of the same mould in the tradition of Kalkbrenner, or in an edition that makes a staccato note of the "C" of the second measure and which, by detaching it in some way, imparts a different articulation and sonorous form to the phrase. Any consonance can be altered and re-established, any movement can be accelerated or retarded, any measure can be slowed down gradually (but at the same time stressed) through syncopations and breaks of all kinds, any musical phrase can be transformed through a simple variation of its rhythm and through the shifting of one of the accents around which the other sounds group themselves and receive their total unity and intelligibility as a musical phrase. The amazing complexity of these formal structures is seen in the simple inspection of a score, in which the sonorous order is expressed in the form of a visible spatial order. It has been rightly said that music must even be beautiful to look at.

The essential fluidity of musical substance explains the continuous invention of procedures of all kinds accumulated by musicians in order to endow music at least with a relative consistence, solidity and stability without which it could not have form but which its nature, however, seems to refuse. The whole history of music can be summoned to testify on this point: the repetition of the motive, of the passage (*da capo*), imitation, the canon, the major and minor variation, the use of the musical theme up to the invention of the cyclic form as well as the creation of the major genres of musical composition. All these, as Schumann rightly observed, have a virtue of their own. In fact, for the composer they define forms ready to receive his ideas, and often they are even invitations to think musically so that these forms may be given the content they are waiting for: the suite, with its international dance styles, the prelude, the fugue, the sonata and its three movements, and the symphony which is merely a sonata for orchestra. Within each of these forms, the

artist's inventiveness is ceaselessly working to press into
service the play of tones, the modulations and infinite
resources of orchestration. This attempt to impart the
maximum formal coherence compatible with the maximum variety and freedom is truly the musical art itself,
taken in the totality of its history, which is here in question.
Even the art of improvisation has its forms and rules; its
apparent license is made up of formulas and tricks of which
the musician's inventiveness makes skillful use. The very
possibility of creating music is at stake here. Hence there
is no reason for taking a tragic view of the revolt of each
generation of composers against forms bequeathed to it
by the previous generation and against the restraints that
such forms imposed. Forms are vexing only to those who
lack the genius to fill them or to subject them and bend
them to their personal requirements. If Bach were still
living, he would continue to invent fugues, Haydn and
Mozart would still find unprecedented themes in the hackneyed intervals of the scale, and even more probably they
would invent new forms. This is the whole problem. The
musician is free to reject forms bequeathed by the past,
provided only that he create others in their place. What is
inconceivable is a music without form, because this would
be a music without being, and one which has reverted to
the status of noise. Noise can also have its charm for a
while and by chance, but noise is of the order of nature,
and music is an art.

This analysis seems to neglect all too much music's
power to stir the emotions and to signify. It is a problem
that must be dealt with inevitably, for music by its very
nature is at the very center of the controversy on the role
of imitation in the fine arts. Those who believe that imitation is not essential to art gladly invoke the example of
music to buttress their thesis; on the other hand, those

who contend that there is no art without a certain measure of imitation labor hard to prove that imitation exists even in music, for if it can be found there it will certainly be found everywhere else.

The problem partially bears on questions of language, which is a matter of convention, and anyway does not confine itself to strictness in the use of terms. In contrast the philosopher must be demanding toward his use of them. Therefore if musical sound does not exist in nature as we have said but is a creation of art, neither could a natural musical beauty exist. The beauty of a bird's song belongs to the order of natural beauty, not to that of art. The ear hears it. Attempts have been made to pitch the song of a nightingale to orchestral music but the two registers remain alien to each other: the orchestra furnishes only a kind of sonorous background which is not even an accompaniment. This is why the attempts of musicians to insert natural noises, or their imitation, in the web of a musical discourse merely end up as anecdotal and picturesque curiosities. The genius of the artist is not here in question; all that is at stake is to determine whether noise and sound can be mixed without creating incongruities. The distinction between the two orders is so obvious that in our day there have been increased attempts to compose music out of sound effects, which would replace music itself. However the ear may react to this music, which would be a problem of esthetics, the mind could not disapprove of a separation in keeping with the distinction of essences. Imitation will be better served by noise than by music because there are noises in nature, whereas even if music likes to make use of them it can only do so after it has first fashioned them into sounds.

The case of so-called "imitative" music is a corollary

of the previous one. The reproduction of natural noises rarely goes further than the imitation of a rhythm, such as that of the gallop of a horse, or the thunderbolt of lightning suggested by the violins. Immediately we see that no real formal imitation is involved, but only a more or less remote analogy of which the listener would not even be aware if the composer and the program did not tell him by a literary title or an explanatory note what he was being invited to imagine. Actually, music succeeds only in imitating itself: it imitates a hunt by sounding French horns, the fanfare in Siegfried is a fanfare, a peasant dance is a dance piece, etc. The rest is a matter of convention and complicity acquiesced to by the listener. The storm being the domain of noise, composers have often written "storm" music, but it requires a great deal of goodwill to take even the storm in the Pastoral Symphony seriously at the level of simple imitation. As for the Royal Hunt and Storm staged by Berlioz in "The Trojans," the composer was manifestly hoping to kill two birds with one stone, and even his orchestral imagination could only suggest to him remote analogies of rhythm and noise in regard to the imitation of nature. On the other hand, the fanfares of hunting horns with the help of French horns are a real imitation of musical themes which real hunting horns would have found very difficult to execute.

It is much more difficult to realize that music's function is not to signify or express anything any more than its function is to imitate something in nature. The difficulty derives from the fact that visual imagination and intelligence never stand still; it is practically impossible to hear any kind of music without it making us "think of something," from which we conclude that since it makes us think of this something, it therefore is an expression of it.

Implicitly we concede that this is what the music "wants to say," but the fact is that music "says" nothing because it does not speak and it is not a language.

It is not a language of ideas. Language indeed expresses ideas inasmuch as it is made up of words or of conventional gestures attributed to the expression of certain concepts. Moreover these words are grouped among themselves according to rules fixed by usage, which permit the signification of the relations established by the mind between the objects or actions which the words signify. Each "part of speech" fulfills a precise function which contributes to the definition of the meaning of words and of the sentences that make up language. Nothing of this sort exists in music. There is no "musical language" proper. First of all, there is no system of musical sounds whose function is to signify definite concepts or feelings. We cannot say *father, mother,* nor *filial love* in music. Consequently, even if such a dictionary of sounds existed, the relation of the signs between them would be so different in music from what it is in language that we would have no trouble in seeing that musical sounds do not have a signifying function. The notion of "sentence," a musical period formed by two phrases, is equivocal in language and in music. Molière unwittingly gave a decisive proof of this. No matter how we may recast and rephrase M. Jourdain's sentence "Beautiful marquise, your lovely eyes make me die of love," it will always be the same sentence. The meaning is the same. On the other hand, we cannot change the order of sounds in a musical motif without making it into a different motif. If it was originally the theme of a fugue, it will be a different theme and you will have a different fugue. In fact the musical motif consists of its form and this form consists of the order and of the very relationships of the sounds by which it is structured.[10]

These observations are confirmed by experience. The hearing of a symphonic work presented as pure sound does not offer an intelligible meaning to the mind. If the composer is thinking about something while writing his music, he is as incapable of expressing it as the listener is of understanding it. This is why music, when it undertakes to address itself to the intelligence, enters into a partnership with written, spoken or sung language, and from the moment words are involved there is intelligible language and signification. In this case there is no question of exceptions. Just as painting cannot expect to find a great number of spectators sensitive to the pure plastic quality of forms and colors but must seek the vehicle of the characteristic beauty that it wills to create in the imitation of nature, likewise music, though perhaps with less inevitableness, does not always dare to present itself alone with the hope of being loved for itself. Hence it looks for the complicity of the word, to which it commits itself ever more deeply by proceeding from the song and the ballad to the *Lied;* [11] or to that of the song wed to spectacle in which

10. On this question see Susanne K. Langer, "On Significance in Music," *Philosophy in a New Key, A Study in the Symbolism of Reason, Rite and Art* (New York: New American Library, 1948), ch. VIII, pp. 174–208. The problem is viewed here in all its aspects. The book is rich in insights and moves with a remarkable ease through the vast literature on the subject. See in particular p. 178: "Music, on the other hand, is preeminently non-representational." Let us note from this moment that insofar as poetry is music, hence a formal art, it does not tolerate any change in the order of the sounds of which it is composed. In that case one would be treating it like prose, and it would cease to exist.

11. Everything that has been written about music belongs to the history of music, and rightly so, because history perforce must

case it becomes theatre, free to organize itself according to the system of leitmotif. In this way it becomes a kind of language and makes possible a musical lexicon in which sonorous forms signify personages, situations, objects and even intelligible notions such as "the curse of gold." Music often joins with the dance even though in this case it is the dance rather which needs music for reasons which shall be pointed out later in their proper place. Whatever the particular form of association to which it consents, or which it desires to produce, music never enters into it on the strength of being a language which by itself is capable of signifying any intelligible notion. This is what is meant when it is said that music does not *speak,* or that, by itself, it *says* nothing.[12]

---

seek music where it is; now music has gone to take up its abode everywhere, but evidently it is in its pure form that it reveals its essence. From the moment the word is mixed with it, or the program, or any sensible emotion linked to what is something else than musical form alone, the object of the esthetic experience is, if we can say so, music +x. The study of these hybrid forms constitutes nearly the whole history of music, and how many the masterpieces that we owe to them! We can see how captivating the history of these mixed genres is by reading one of the most modest treatments of this subject: "Esquisse d'une histoire de la romance, depuis son origine jusqu'à nos jours," in P. Scudo, *Critique et littératures musicales,* pp. 282–312.

12. The classic exponent of this truth is the former celebrated professor at the University of Vienna, Edouard Hanslick, *Du beau dans la musique: Essai de réforme de l'esthétique musicale,* tr. by Charles Bannelier, 2nd ed., revised and modified according to the 8th German edition (Paris: Ph. Maquet, 1893); later sold by Fischbacker, the work is out of print in French and in German. Paul Hindemith has assured me that at present (1961) the work is simply not to be found. Hanslick wrote against the one generally accepted opinion that "music should express feelings" (p. 9). "I don't have to trouble myself moreover about the fact that one may see (in this essay) the doctrine of an absolute negation of feeling in music.

The rose emits a fragrance, but the *expression* of the idea of fragrance is not inherent in it; the forest spreads a shady freshness, but it does not *express* the feeling of shade and of freshness" (Ibid.). "A positive proposition corresponds to the negative one which I formulate thus: *the beauty of a musical work is specific to the music,* that is to say it resides in the relationships of the sounds, without any connection with a sphere of alien, extra-musical ideas" (p. 10). Hanslick has made the most felicitous usage of the decisive yet only slightly effective argument that is drawn from the indifference that music demonstrates it has toward those feelings that it is supposed to express. Boyé, a contemporary of Gluck, "presumed to point out that the melody could be equally fitting, and even more so, to the following utterances which say the very opposite, 'I have found my Eurydice!' 'Nothing equals my happiness!'" (p. 36). Naturally, the mimicry of the singer can change all that, but it is not music. Another example: Winterfeld has observed that several very religious portions of Handel's *Messiah* are taken from a collection of "very secular, indeed erotic" duets composed by Handel in 1711 and 1712 for the Princess-Electress Caroline of Hanover based on madrigals by Mauro Ortensio. The music of the second duet: *No, di voi non vo' fidarmi,/ Cieco amor, crudel Beltà;/ Troppo siete menzognera,/ Lusinghiera Deità!* passed without the slightest modification into the chorus of the first part of the *Messiah,* which is especially popular: *For unto us a child is born"* (pp. 38–39). "And did not Sebastian Bach put into his *Christmas Oratorio* madrigal-like snatches borrowed from his secular cantatas?" (p. 39). In fact, André Pirro informs us, for example, that in the *Christmas Oratorio,* the alto's aria of the second part "comes from *The Choice of Hercules.* It was already a lullaby in this work; here the mother of the child sings it near the crib. It has been pointed out that Bach transposed this melody through which Pleasure sought to seduce the young Hercules into a more solemn tonality. In addition he added the oboes and a flute which plays one octave above the voice. The coloration of the accompaniment thus becomes more sombre, and the voice wed to the flute assumes an almost supernatural character" (*J. S. Bach,* Paris: F. Alcan, 1910), p. 191. Thus Pleasure is metamorphosed into the Virgin Mary thanks to a flute and two oboes. Let's change the subject, but I must confess that the example of Handel affects me personally. I heard *The Messiah* for the first time in my life in Toronto, many,

As inevitable as it may be, this proposition naturally leaves the mind in a state of disbelief; consequently it is joined with a corrective asserting that music is not the language of ideas but that of feeling. Nothing would seem to be more obvious at first sight, for is not music according to the circumstance gay or sad, passionate or stirring? In short is it not made to express the affective states by which man is ordinarily moved? Indeed some theorists go even further and point out that music has the gift of expressing a thousand nuances of feeling which language, and the words of which it is composed, cannot. As proof of this they point up the fact that nobody has ever been able to describe exactly in words the gentle or violent emotions, in any case ceaselessly changing and infinitely nuanced, with which music affects the listener's sensibility.

This is correct, but while music may not express these feelings, it causes them. The storm, the sea, the mountain do not express the emotions engendered in us when we behold them. These natural phenomena affect us with multiple, fleeting or durable impressions, endowed with characteristic affective tonality which the word is power-

---

many years ago. The annual performance of the work there is a rite. I distinctly remember that this chorus was an enchantment from the very first note; what especially struck me was the *child-like* happiness which this exquisite page breathed. But this is not all, each time that I hear it again, I succumb to the music. "Blind love, cruel Beauty," the child Jesus each time receives the homages first destined for the Princess-Electress of Hanover. Only the words have changed. Hanslick is correct, but even those who approve do not believe what he says. A different thesis, expounded with as much ingenuity and penetration, will be found in the writings of Susanne K. Langer; for example, in her *Problems of Art* (New York: Charles Scribner's Sons, 1957), pp. 80–81; notably this definition of art which the author suggests: "All art is the creation of perceptible forms expressive of human feeling" (p. 80).

less to express. This is why so many writers begin their
descriptions of these "spectacles of nature" by frankly declaring their inability to depict in words the emotions they
experienced. Yet, if expression is at stake, this noble role
falls to them because they, at least, say something about
what they see, whereas nature allows herself only to be
seen: she herself says nothing. The same holds true for
music. Besides its formal plasticity it has naturally the
power to stir the emotions of most people; indeed with
some of them it wields an almost unendurable power over
their affective states. A composer, if he so desires, has the
right to use the power over the emotions of his listeners
that sound gives him. Richard Wagner, who handled this
affective power of sounds with sovereign ease, knew how to
retain much pure music in the most impure of musical
genres. Each time music addresses itself principally to the
emotions, whether by itself or in connection with other
arts, its own contribution is not of the order of signification
but of that of efficient causality. The composer in that case
draws on the reserve of tones, modes, musical instruments
and rhythms at his disposal,[13] in short on all that which can

13. Everything essential on this point has been said, and better
than I would be able to do, by a musician who has deeply reflected
upon his art: Roland-Manuel, *Sonate que me veux-tu? Réflexions
sur les fins et les moyens de l'art musical* (Lausanne: Mermod, 1957),
particularly ch. II: "The Fourteenth Fauteuil." In it I found what
for me was a discovery, penetrating and sprightly observations on
the ideas of Guy de Chabanon, *Observations sur la musique et
principalement sur la métaphysique de l'art*, Paris, 1779 (no author's
name is given). *De la musique considerée en elle-même et dans ses
rapports avec la parole, les langues, la poésie et le théâtre*, quoted by
Roland-Manuel, op. cit., p. 50. I have not had this latter work in my
hands, but I was able to find in addition to his *Observations*, the
Mémoires sur les problèmes d'Aristote concernant la musique . . .
in *Histoire de l'Académie des Inscriptions et Belles-Lettres* . . .
tome 46 (Paris: *Imprimerie Nationale*, 1793), years 1779, pp. 285–

engender in the listener's sensibility an emotional state
attuned to those in keeping with the words or situations on
which his music comments. The language of such works

303; 1780, pp. 304–325; 1780, pp. 326–335. Autobiography: *Tableau
de quelques circonstances de ma vie. Précis de ma liaison avec mon
frère Maugris* . . . Paris, 1795 (posthumous, published by Saint-
Ange). Roland-Manuel elsewhere cites an article by Mathis Lussy,
"Chabanon précurseur de Hanslick" in *Gazette musicale de la Suisse
Romande,* May 7, 1896. I do not know this work. Let us note Roland-Manuel's observation (p. 50): "Chabanon is apparently the
only practitioner of the musical art who has ever succeeded in
piercing the defenses of the French Academy." This is true. The
French Academy to this day remains a group of men of letters and
personalities who feel no sympathy at all for artists. His election
to the Academy in 1780 was greeted by a chorus of witticisms. No
other musician, as far as I can see, replaced him: Berlioz, Saint-
Saëns, Debussy, Dukas, d'Indy, and still others, have at one and
the same time honored their art and the French language; it seems
that the Academy has never given them a thought. Without asserting it, I must say that I see only one painter accepted among its
members, Albert Besnard. Neither Poussin, nor Ingres, nor Delacroix were members. Delacroix had enough difficulty in piercing
the defenses of the Académie des Beaux-Arts. Many personal
attempts to interest some colleagues in the possible candidacy of
some artists met only with indifference marked by a touch of
astonishment. Since he is no longer with us, and moreover never
knew it, I can now say that I tried to arouse some sympathy for
André Lhote as a likely candidate. The author of several works
such as *La peinture, le coeur et l'esprit* (Paris: Denoel et Steele,
1933), or *De la palette à l'écritoire* (Paris: Correa, 1946), would not
have disfigured a society of servants of the French language; the
last person to whom I spoke replied drily, "He's a pretty bad
painter!" The question was settled then and there. To know how
to talk is to know. The traditional recruitment for the French
Academy is a concrete experiment in favor of the real distinction
between the fine arts and the arts of language. Among the latter,
the modest place assigned to poetry attests to the same direction.
Mallarmé entered the Academy through the efforts of the charming
person of Henri Mondor.

furnishes the meaning, whereas the music furnishes or reinforces the appropriate emotion. Moreover, the music can remain clear by itself, even when we do not hear or understand the words. It is clear each time, while acting fully on its own, that it imposes its authority upon the sensibility of the conquered listener. Whatever his emotional state may have been during the musical composition, the artist does not try to make us privy to it, but rather to engender in us the feelings that he wants us to experience.

Where, then, must we look for pure music? Wherever it presents itself, whether by itself and for the sake of the beauty of the constitutive sonorous forms, whether in association with other arts but in a way that preserves its full autonomy therein and where while playing its role it nevertheless pursues its proper end. Less abstractly, let us say that we can witness the unfolding of the purest musical beauty when for the first time we look at the libretto of the *Marriage of Figaro* without hearing its music. Never has so much tonal inventiveness, winged grace, or aural seductions ever gushed forth so abundantly from such an unpromising beginning in terms of potential musical material. To achieve a proper awareness we must try to place ourselves in this musical comedy libretto just before the moment when Mozart's genius, "music itself," fused this dust of insignificant words into the unity of sonorous form with which they have become inseparable for us. This necessity, created by the artist, masks for us the total contingency to which it succeeded at that time and which it will eternally preserve as long as there are musicians to play this music and listeners to hear it. Music is pure to the degree in which, existing only for its own sake, it is at one and the same time its own cause and its own end.

This truth is equally valid in cases where music presents itself alone. It is easier to discern this clearly despite the fact that music of this kind is not the most popular. For this very reason all we have to do is turn our thoughts to the superiority of the string quartet in the order of symphonic music. The composer has at his disposal for the creation of beauty only four homogeneous instruments, covering the entire scale of sounds from which he must write his music without recourse to the charm of the diversity of timbres, the resources of orchestration, or the suggestions of the voice. String quartets are grey, dismal, in a word boring, to those who do not find sufficient satisfaction in the pleasure of listening to musical forms emerging into chiselled fullness, breaking up and ceaselessly being born again under the fingers of the artists, or rather of the artist in four persons, who brings the sonorous structure conceived by the composer into temporary being. But for the listener whose intelligent attention in some way keeps ahead of the composer's intentions, the string quartet clings as much as possible to the very essence of music. Art gives to each only that measure of it which he can receive. Moreover music contents itself with a single listener, who can be the executant himself; it is in that case entirely present, provided that it is accepted as it is. The *Well-Tempered Clavier* is an outpouring of sonorous intentions, rhythms and melodies of which a knowledgeable ear never wearies. Yet these preludes and fugues do not aim at pathos and, when this effect is obtained, it is that of pure formal beauty whose presence ends up by stirring the heart. Hence the emotion is born of the mere presence of an object which transcends the order of simple nature and of a material made exclusively for the purpose of satisfying the demands of the mind of whose expectations it is the climax. Yet these forms express nothing, and say nothing else but what they are; indeed, they never give as much pleasure as when they are listened to for their own sakes more than

for the joy we expect them to give us. Everything transpires there in the order of pure spiritual gratuitousness.
To the question "What after all does music contain?"
Edouard Hanslick answered simply, "Nothing else but
sonorous forms in motion—*tönend bewegte Formen.*" [14] It
would be a waste of time to attack the opposite opinion.
Even for the creative genius, music is never anything else
except what he can do; all the more reason then for the
modest listener to content himself with receiving it in the
form that is accessible to him. There are many kinds of
music. No doubt it is even a good thing that there is a
kind for all tastes, for the changing moods of each taste
and for all of life's circumstances. No kind of music ought
to be excluded, for in the measure that they exist all are

14. E. Hanslick, op. cit., p. 49. The notion of form being derived from visual sensations, it is not applied to sonorous sensations except as pure metaphor. Since they contain no meaning,
they resemble "words denuded of meaning." At times, therefore,
we say that sonorous forms are "empty forms." Hanslick seems to
have foreseen the criticism: "The idea of form is realized in music
in a wholly special way. Sonorous forms are not empty, but perfectly filled; they cannot be likened to simple lines limiting a space;
they are mind which is embodied and draws its embodiment from
itself" (op. cit., p. 51). A musical "thought," a musical "phrase" is
a musical form, that is to say an ensemble of sounds whose relationships are such that the ear and the mind perceive them as a unity.
In this sense, "music, among all the arts, is the greatest user and
destroyer of forms, and in the least space of time. Modulations,
cadences, melodic and harmonic successions are so used up in a
period of fifty or even thirty years that the composer who is anxious
to avoid platitudes ends up by not being able to make use of them
and all his efforts tend toward the discovery, element by element,
of a new musical phraseology. Without being unjust to a mass of
compositions placed well above the average of their time, it is permissible to say that they *were* beautiful" (Op. cit., pp. 58–59). Hanslick speaks of "the plastic quality of the relations of sounds" (p.
72).

legitimate.[15] The philosopher does not judge the composer's art; he tries only to arrive at its essence for the purpose of knowing it in itself, such as it is.

No other art has a richer phenomenology. In truth, it is inexhaustible and its detail goes to infinity. The reason for this lies in the ambiguity that surrounds the ontological status of the musical work. Its sole stability comes to it from the system of written signs which sym-

15. Hanslick, beyond reproach in his notion of pure music, made the mistake of wanting musicians to write no other. He blamed Liszt's program symphonies: "since then, we have also had *Tristan and Isolde, The Ring of the Nibelung* and the Wagnerian doctrine of *infinite melody,* that is to say the absence of form erected into a principle, the intoxication of opium in the singing and in the orchestra, for the worship of which a temple has been especially erected at Bayreuth" (Op. cit., p. 10). It would serve no point to discuss it. Wagner revenged himself by representing Hanslick, it is said, in the features of the pedant Beckmesser in the *Meistersinger.* He was also mistaken and in the same way, because both confused music and musical drama. Musical drama includes its music, but it is there as an integrating part of the drama, and in view of its proper end. *The Ring* is certainly not an opera, but it is a *Buhnenfestspiel,* and where there is a stage, there is theatre, actors, décors, represented action. Wagner was extremely aware of it; the musician in him is inseparable from the man of the theatre, and to wish that theatre music be pure music is a contradiction in terms. Hanslick rightly states: "It is in pure contemplation (*Anschauung*) that a listener enjoys a musical work" (p. 18), and to define the latter as "the act of attentive audition, which is nothing else but an attentive consideration of musical colors"; but Wagner above all desires to interest the spectator in the whole drama ("Lettre sur la musique," in *Oeuvres en prose de Richard Wagner,* tr. by J. F. Prud'homme and F. Caillé (Paris: Delagrave, s.d. t. VI, pp. 177–250). The fascination exerted on him by Weber, whom he saw conduct his works at Dresden, when he had not yet heard *any-thing* of Beethoven (op. cit., p. 189), is at the cradle of his art. Hanslick's criticism was mis-addressed, but he was right on the essence of music.

bolize it. By writing in an agreed upon language the artist
indicates the sounds that must be produced so that his art
may exist as a tonal fact.[16] Incapable of executing it by
himself since it often requires more than one executant,
he would even be incapable of doing so with the desired
perfection even when one executant suffices. Musical
thought must therefore be embodied in human voices,
each one of which reflects a certain personality and marks
the work so deeply with its imprint that we never again
find it as it was at first, when the "creator" of the role
revealed its beauty for the first time. Often, this will require instruments which are different even within their
species. Even more, differences will exist to such a degree
among the performers who play them that the great executant leaves a unique mark on the work which he inter-
prets, sometimes even on the instrument. I think of the
special quality of "Louis Diener's piano." If it involves
an orchestra, there must be a conductor, without whom the
orchestra hardly exists, but who in turn does not exist at
all without his orchestra. We do not dare to dwell with
our imagination on the fragility of these ensembles endowed with an intermittent existence, each member of
which is a human being dedicated to the practice of a certain musical instrument. Such ensembles are formed or
dissolved through many economic and social contingen-
cies in response to the decision, itself born of the desire that
certain virtual kinds of musical beauties accede to the actuality of being. A concert or an opera requires listeners who,
motivated by a similar love, set out at the prescribed hour,

16. Just as literary art, in its fully developed form, presupposes
the invention of writing, musical art calls into being a musical
notation in order to fix forms and to transmit them. For the medi-
eval origins of modern musical notation see *Histoire de la musique*
(*Encyclopédie de la Pléiade*, I, pp. 689–716); bibliography, p. 716.

interrupting their professional activities and suspending their family life for a few hours to go to the place where the music they love to hear will come into being, thanks in part to the modest financial contribution which they will make on their own volition. At the moment the performance is scheduled to begin, we observe the extraordinary spectacle presented by a concert hall or an opera house peopled with men and women who have left everything to take part in a wholly useless work. "Peopled" is indeed the right word, for they do constitute a people, temporarily but intimately joined together by their common love for beauty and united in the disinterested homage they render to it. This social grouping, fortuitously brought into being, lasts for two or three hours, it lives a communal life and expresses its emotions and passions, after which it breaks up and disperses in a kind of devout silence, still full of the music which has just died away and with the hope that it might be reborn again some day. Music is social by essence, vocation and destination.[17]

17. Such was not Kant's feeling. Music makes noise; in making music for oneself, one obliges others to listen to it just as the person who takes a scented handkerchief from his pocket obliges others to smell it. In 53 of the *Critique of Judgment* there is a priceless observation on the impertinence of those who sing spiritual hymns in their homes, during their family devotions, without considering the noise they inflict on their neighbors. Here we would be entering the domain of esthetics. Let us merely note the necessary consequence entailed in the traditional conception of art as expression when its champions come to judge musical art. Kant recognized that music is the most agreeable of the arts, but it is enjoyment rather than culture ("mehr Genuss als Kultur"); judged from the point of view of reason, its value is less than that of any other art of the beautiful (53). In that case we enter the domain of esthetics: "Like every pleasure it demands frequent changes and does not endure being repeated many times, under pain of leading to satiety." The art of sound is "the language of affective states." Hence

That music which is bought on records, and which is reproduced mechanically without even leaving it a chance
to make a possible mistake—which is the mark of life—
or worse still, that which is purveyed at home to idle and
distracted listeners, none of whom would make the least
personal effort to participate in the solemnity which is
a public musical performance, is only a shadow of music.
Here poietics must halt at the threshold of esthetics and
even of the phenomenology of musical life. Let us bear in
mind, however, that the vast mobilization of human lives,
of persons, of talents, of material resources answerable to
the most diverse orders of the economy, industry and
finance, is the concrete result of sonorous images invented
in an earlier time by a Bach, a Mozart, a Beethoven or a
Wagner, and which are still being created today by those
through whom the tradition of the masters is perpetuated.
The fact of Bayreuth is unimaginable, but it is incontest-
ably real. It would be difficult to find in nature a more
striking image of this creative impulse whose matter, Bergson said, lies in its wake like a fallout of the mind.

Kant has the great merit of seeing that since music involves neither
concepts nor definite ideas, its form is that of combined sonorous
sensations, which is the pure truth, but precisely for this reason: "if
we measure the value of the fine arts against the culture which
they impart to sentiment, and against the enlargement of the facul-
ties which must be combined in judgment for cognition, then music
immediately passes into the lowest place among the fine arts . . .
because it brings only sensations to bear" (Ibid.). In addition to
the lack of urbanity which we have just talked about, and which
is attributable to the noisy nature of the instruments it uses, music
therefore is sure to see itself despised by those who judge art by
knowledge. As Voltaire said: "One sings what is too silly to be
said."

SIX

The Dance

MAN'S OWN BODY is one of the materials that he can press
into the service of art, and it was one of his first discoveries.
The dance brings us to a wholly special order of the arts
whose aim is to impart a formal beauty to the human being
himself: to his body, his soul, or to both taken together.
Arts of this sort raise special problems for those who practice them as well as for those who merely enjoy their creations. Man is universally viewed as something more than
the other creatures in the world, and somehow he is, because he is an object of respect or ought to be. Man cannot be played like a piano, nor can he be turned against
a wall like an unfinished canvas, and if what was hoped
for is not obtained from him he is not a rough cast to be
smashed into pieces with a hammer, as Michelangelo used
to do at times. The matter of all the arts of man, as defined
in the last chapter, is a living being which alone would
suffice to distinguish them from the other arts, but it
shares the special dignity that is bound up with the nature
of a being endowed with intelligence and a consciousness
whose destiny, according to philosophers, is in a sense

unique, and who has the right, as Kant asserted, to be treated always as an end and never as a means. These considerations need not necessarily be explicitly present in the mind of the practitioners of the arts of this kind; an arcane instinct unfailingly apprizes them of it.

The infant begins to move around in space as soon as he is able to do so; it walks, and the grown man continues to move around in a like manner in order to go from one place to another. If he is in a hurry, he runs, if the object to be taken is out of reach, he leaps towards it from where he stands; he jumps forward to clear an obstacle, or turns around and goes back to his point of departure. All these are natural movements and they can be improved in terms of speed and precision by practicing sports, but they are alien to art and to the dance because their end is utility, not beauty.

The same movements can be made for the simple pleasure of doing them, as can be seen among young animals, and often among children, not to speak of adults whose only interest in sports consists in reading the sport pages. Nothing is more pleasurable for a youthful or still agile body than to bring all its latent possibilities to bear. Even the spectator enjoys the sight of a sudden leap which clears the hurdle. But all this still belongs to the natural pleasure that follows upon exercise and the easy performance of a natural function. It is not yet art.

We are much nearer to art, and perhaps have already come upon it, when we see a child play at moving itself in a certain manner and instinctively calculate the movements it plans to make in such a way as to take pleasure in them. The streets of Paris abound with tiny ballerinas who, while their mothers are chattering away, sketch the *pas de fuite*, with a *battement* on the right, a *battement* on the left, and a yanking of the held hand after which the choreography starts all over again.[1] Rarely do children run without embellishing their course with fanciful steps invented at pleasure and for pleasure's sake. All the games related to hopscotch, and they are legion, are as many miniature ballets involving their effective entries, exits and sequences of movement regulated by a law. At times we even wonder whether some children, seemingly absorbed in themselves, attain altogether by chance this immobility and this perfect carriage of the head where, their faces bent forward and lit up with an almost imperceptible smile, the eyelids seem to fall like veils over some secret. Nothing is lacking to make of it a dance except that all these patterned movements must be willed, sought for and found, having in view the beauty proper to them.

The dance is the art which orders the natural bodily movements by imparting to them a form which is pleasing in itself, independently of any other end. There are religious dances, war dances, erotic dances, but it is not in terms of their ends that they can be art; when they are it is only as dances. Even those dances that are performed almost everywhere as artful accomplishments for social or worldly ends remain alien to the order of the fine arts regardless of how perfectly they may be executed or the pleasure they may give, for there is no art without pleasure,

1. I recently watched a girl, about five years old, invent a dance step while her mother was engaged in a conversation in front of the steps to a large post office. She placed herself in position on the bottom of the first step, then she stood on the toes of her right foot; at the very moment that her foot resumed its normal position, up came her left foot which she placed flatly on the step; once more she stood on the toes of her right foot, as her left foot again hit the ground. Then she stood on the toes of her left foot, with her right foot on the first step, etc. Only a film could show the successive attempts which the little girl made "to perfect" this step which she had invented. A simple game, to be sure, but it contained the material of a possible dance.

or without pain, for that matter, but the only pleasure of art as such is the pleasure of the beautiful.[2]

    2. Here I should like to express my appreciation for the chapters in *Système des beaux-arts* in which Alain reviews "the dance and all its varieties: namely *politesse,* acrobatism, fencing, horsemanship, and in general all the arts that rid us of timidity, fear, vertigo and of bashfulness." These "arts of motion" are those which "regulate the human body according to ease and strength, first of all for its own sake." They are "arts of mimicry," thus called "because imitation is the principal means. (*Les arts et les dieux,* Paris: Pléiade), p. 245. Alain is obviously following a wholly personal path here which it would be useless, and slightly ridiculous, to discuss. But what does he mean to say? That imitation is the principal means of learning these arts? Indeed, but this is true of any act of learning. To learn is first of all to imitate. Or does he mean that the very substance of these arts (we mean, what they are) is imitation? But horsemanship doesn't imitate anything, one simply rides a horse. Politeness doesn't imitate anything, it merely manifests respect for others through agreed upon acts and attitudes. We teach a child to remove his hat, but once the habit is instilled, he is no longer imitating anyone, he bares his head, etc. This does not prevent chapters such as II, ch. 2, "On equestrian art and others," to formulate remarks that are correct, penetrating and worthy of reflection. There is an art of horsemanship, and even several. Elements of the useful and of the beautiful are found in it (as in fencing); these arts therefore belong to esthetics (to which all the beautiful is answerable; but the beauty of the riding-master is that of horsemanship in its most perfect form; it is this perfection which is desired for its own sake, beauty being given only into the bargain. Alain takes no account whatsoever of this fact, but he perceived it, and this is why any discussion would be futile. Alain even observed with perfect accuracy that in horsemanship the spectator must often make something of an effort to discern the hidden elegance "which at first sight often seems awkward and ugly" (p. 250). To which, by digging deeper into truth, he adds these profound observations: "The same difficulty will be found in mime and in studied dances, where it happens that one first gets a painful impression. And that is proper to this kind of art which is a spectacle only by accident, and in which the man who dances or acts is the best judge; therefore we should never judge a dance

It is easy but futile to speculate about the origins of the art of dancing. As with the other arts, all we know about the dance is what it has become, particularly in the West where its technique has been enriched with all the perfection that the creative genius of generations of dancers and dancing masters have bequeathed to it. The latter deserve special mention, for teaching and the schools play a decisive role in the creation and the preservation of the art of the dance. This teaching also explains the local, national or continental character of the forms of this art. Western dance is a natural subject for the considerations of a philosopher living in the West, but in no way does it exhaust the possibilities of the dance. The European dancer, or the dancer of European tradition, dances mainly with his legs; the dancers of Asia instead dance primarily with their arms, hands and fingers, but everywhere dancers tend toward a complete art which would be a dance involving the whole body.

Since the body is the dancer's instrument, the choice of a body with an aptitude for dancing plays the same role and has the same importance as that of any material in any art. The sculptor carefully chooses his stone, his marble, his wood with the work to be wrought in view; so a dance is not executed with a body chosen at random, and dances that are different in style will be obtained from different bodies. Here, as elsewhere, the material of art

---

unless we dance ourselves. This genre of art has for its object the human body, and as a spectator the very person who dances or practices" (Ibid.). Alain seems to be thinking of the *Bal de l'Ecole normale,* but the dance as an art of the beautiful is "a spectacle only by accident," and its spectator, in the strict sense, is not the dancer himself. We understand Alain's conclusion at the end of Ch. V: "There is nothing more silly, anyway one looks at it, than the person who watches dancing." From this correct observation it follows that the dance which Alain has in mind is not one of the fine arts.

exists with the form in view and in turn determines the latter.

It is useful to recall that the art of the dance requires an ensemble of exceptional physical qualities: strength, speed, suppleness and endurance which will enable the dancer to exert the efforts demanded by this art in which the spectator sees only facility, grace, ease of movements, and absolute mastery over a body free to move at its pleasure. The Radio City Music Hall Rockettes, famous for their perfect precision, are never on stage more than twenty minutes which in effect represents a considerable physical strain, especially on the part of a group in which no individual failing is permitted. A doctor's advice is required in connection with the choice of a future dancer, male or female, and his advice and at times his intercessions will all too often be necessary in the course of a career in which accidents are to be expected. It is not enough to want to be a dancer in order to be able to become one. Here the body has the first and final word.

Different bodies make possible different dances. To avoid going into detail, which would be interminable since it involves individual differences, we shall at least note the primary difference which sex introduces between the art of the male dancer and that of his female counterpart. Some men have an almost feminine suppleness and grace and some women, especially by dint of hard work and training, can equal or surpass some men in strength, but the general rule is that the male dancer excels in efforts that require power, vigor and solidity in terms of balance. If he moves, he will excel in the leap, or *ballon,* and most often will be what is called an "elevation" dancer. All this can be briefly described by noting that the role of "porteur," so frequently assigned to the male dancer, has no equivalent among female dancers. As a general rule there is no "porteuse," and manly strength is always used to show womanly grace, not inversely. Despite all the reservations that we may make, it must be recognized in the end that the physical differentiation of bodies entails a corresponding differentiation in dances.

The same observation applies to individuals. Although natural beauty is a useful asset to the dancer,[3] it is not indispensable; certain defects can even be advantageous provided they facilitate the effort and movement proper to the dance. A feminine dancer with a fairly small head on a fairly long neck, with legs and arms that are longer than the average can achieve effects that would be otherwise impossible. But we also see male and female dancers with small builds who turn the particularities of their physique to good account. We should especially bear in mind that here bodily movement outweighs bodily structure. The most beautiful Apollo must also be beautiful in motion if he wants to be a dancer. The history of

3. On the contrary, natural beauty doesn't harm; but it is neither enough nor necessary. The "danseuses" Degas so cruelly but so perceptively reproduced give rise to the notion that a woman is not a "danseuse" except when she is dancing. Marcelle Bourgat, herself a dancer, has stated that while examining those who are gifted for the dance "one observes that they do not always have a well-proportioned figure, but that they are endowed with special qualities" *Technique de la danse* (Paris: Presses Universitaires de France, 1946), p. 13. The following remarks, however, leave nothing more to say: "Njinsky had a below average build. In soul and body he was professionally deformed. His Mongol-type face was tied to his body by a very high and large neck. The muscles of his legs and those of his calves stretched the material of his trousers and gave him the appearance of having legs arched backward. His fingers were short and as though cut at the phalanges. In short, one would have found it hard to believe that this little monkey with sparse hair . . . was the idol of the public . . ." etc. Jean Cocteau, *La difficulté d'être* (Monaco: Editions du Rocher, 1957), pp. 73–74.

the great artists of the dance could provide us with numberless examples of a fact which everybody has been able to observe, no matter how slight his interest in this art may be.

When we say that the body in motion is the material of the dance, we must not forget that a human body is in question. Intelligence therefore is another requisite of the would-be dancer, and the gifts of the body must be complemented by the gifts of the mind. In the first rank of these gifts must be placed a particular kind of plastic imagination which enables the individual to see in his mind the exterior aspect of his body in each of its movements and each of its possible attitudes. This gift must be common to the body as well as the mind in order to ensure its effectiveness, the body being capable of patterning itself according to the wishes of the mind, as the latter is of picturing to itself the attitudes and movements that it wills to obtain from the body. But language is too analytical to make a faithful translation of reality. The dance is pre-eminently the domain of the union of body and mind, or as traditional philosophy—ever so close to reality —expressed it: their "substantial union." The born dancer thinks with his body the way he dances with his mind. No other art is so completely and integrally an art of man, understanding thereby the human being in the organic unity of all his constitutive material and spiritual elements. This is the reason indeed why there is no human activity which the dance cannot honor with its contribution. David dancing before the ark is man offering himself in homage to God. To any degree that he possesses this gift of imagining his body in space, and even that of inventing in his mind new plastic forms and new movements possible from it, the born dancer, *homo saltator,* is in the highest degree that soul which "makes use of a body" mentioned by

Plato, or that body which moves like a soul thinks, as Aristotle put it, because all is mind in an intelligent being. Like any other art, the dance can be prostituted, but in the eyes of the philosopher nothing can strip it of what its essential nobility confers upon it. It is pre-eminently the art of the human structure as such, or to express it more simply, the art of the whole man.

Every dancer is a distinct human being and his art will necessarily bear the imprint of his personality, his body as well as his soul or his mind. By electing to dedicate himself to the art of the dance, and in consequence to a life of arduous training and increasing effort—not without its rewards, to be sure—the artist nevertheless cannot even imagine to himself that he will ever dance as he would like to, but only as he will be able to. His physical and intellectual predetermination can go just so far, and he is wise to see it beforehand as a genuine fate. The traditional classifications of dancers into "noble," "character," "semi-character," "burlesques" and other distinctions of the same kind are reminders that, at least to a certain degree, the dancer's physique will inevitably control the development of his career. Among dancers endowed with eminently superior gifts, the imprint of personality affects the art of the dancer so deeply that it becomes well-nigh impossible to bring two topflight artists together in the same recital. Neither the artist nor a public could endure the absolute dance executed simultaneously in two different manners, in which both styles bring each other into question through their very perfection. The history of the dance provides frequent examples of one of these brilliant dancers driving out the other by his mere presence with the help, if necessary, of a generally keen tactical sense.

Assuming all these gifts are combined in one person,

which in fact can never be known beforehand, the would-be dancer must still learn how to make good use of them.[4] The desire to be a dancer does not excuse one from learning to dance any more than the desire to paint, to sculpt or to write excuses one from learning the techniques of these arts. This is the moment when the phenomenon, well-known in the apprenticeship of all the arts, occurs: the apparent loss of the natural gifts upon which the hope of a vocation is based. Nothing can be done without these gifts, but they will bear no fruit if they are left to themselves. In order to obtain art from them a passage must be opened to a genre of beauty different from that of nature and which cannot be achieved without effort and sacrifice. The person who runs, spins around or jumps for his own pleasure does not perform movements that enable him to obtain from his body those positions, attitudes, and movements necessary to the ends of the dance. The passage from nature to art requires a technique transmitted through teaching. It was therefore necessary to create the elements of an art of human movement which would enable the prospective dancer to obtain from his body the desired attitudes, positions and actions with the minimum of

4. Here we are considering only the dance of the professional artist, because his life is consecrated to the dance and because beauty is the end which he pursues. But we do not at all deny that social dancing has a beauty of its own. This was even more true when dances called "low," or at times "noble," were performed, which were only studied manners of walking or bearing oneself. Going back only to the Middle Ages, such were the gavotte, the minuet, etc. Even today, danced by professionals, they have a great charm but their ends are more directly social than artistic; they are not arts of the beautiful. It is here that Alain's observations on the dance as a "purification of passions" is applicable, *Vingt leçons sur les beaux-arts*, "Deuxième leçon" (*Les arts et les dieux*: Pléiade), pp. 484–485. In order that no truth deprive other truths of their salience, it suffices that each one be in its place.

fatigue and the maximum of precision. Hence this sort of grammar of motion, progressively invented and codified by artists and teachers, which the would-be dancer must learn because it contains the constitutive elements of the dance. These movements themselves vary according to different national schools and traditions (Balinese, Hindu, Spanish, Russian dances, etc.) and the grammars of motion which teach its elements vary within them. Borrowing between schools and traditions occurs but less frequently than we might imagine. Each part of the speech in motion, which is what a dance is, bears the mark of a definite style which is that of this speech itself; introduced into a different speech, it tends to break its style and substitute that of the school of dance from which it derives. The constitutive motor elements of a style of any dance share in the formal unity of the style and do not easily lend themselves to disassociation.

The example closest to us is the style of dance common today to the countries of Western Europe. It can be said that it is the joint creation of Italy, France, Spain,[5] European Russia and that, more or less, all the peoples of European civilization have contributed to it. The grammar of this speech is represented by five elementary positions of the feet to which as many elementary positions of the hands were later added. They are far from being the positions easiest and most natural to man, but experience and study have shown that those positions, now become tradi-

5. If one were to object that the Spanish dance represents a style all its own, I would not contest this; but in its essence, perhaps, it has remained a popular dance and in some way natural rather than artistic. Neither would I object if one were to add that in this respect it is often more beautiful than the art dances. Natural beauty often surpasses artistic beauty, but it is not of the same kind. The "European" style of which I speak includes the Spanish dance only to the extent that it is not a national dance.

tional, are the most favorable starting points for the execution of movements whose sequence, combination and concatenation constitute the very substance of the dance. A description of them can be found in the treatises dealing with the techniques of the dance as it is practiced in the West.[6] Some examples are the *battu,* the *jeté,* the *jeté battu,* the *entrechat,* the *pirouette,* without forgetting the *pointes,* i.e. supporting the foot on the toes, this least natural of all ways to carry oneself or to walk, and which partly for this very reason is most manifestly dedicated to art. These willed restraints are to the dance what the rules of versification are to poetry. Whatever the school in which the would-be dancer may be trained, a private course, a troupe which adopts him or the quasi-official school of a great opera house, he will progressively have to master this gymnastic training and learn this syntax of motion. This will require years of effort, beginning sometimes in early childhood and extending from the age of five or six to twenty and beyond. As with all the arts worthy of this name, the apprenticeship of the dance never in fact ends except at that age when the strength of his body fails the dancer. This time comes tragically all too soon. The violinist's instrument improves as it ages, whereas the dancer's tends to grow heavy and stiffen after a period of perfection which is coeval with its successes. Every art of which man himself is the instrument is born, grows, ages and dies with him.

Whoever says art means technique, and since the means necessary to create beauty must be first acquired as though they themselves were the end of art, they tend to replace it everywhere. It is then that the virtuoso appears, excellent in himself and necessary because virtuosity is the freedom

6. Marcelle Bourgat, *Technique de la danse,* ch. IV, "Vocabulaire traditionelle de la danse classique," pp. 44–84.

to create beauty. Left to itself it ends up by substituting the perfection of the means of execution to that of the work. In this case the virtuoso puts the resources of a technique, rightly qualified as "transcendent," at the service of futility because it enables him to cope with any difficulty of execution, however general it may be. The artist proper does not delude himself on this score. Scudo counselled his contemporaries to go listen to Chopin rather than Liszt if they wanted to hear real music being played; although they differed in matters of painting, Ingres and Delacroix were both ill at ease when listening to Paganini; on the other hand, those who knew César Franck assure us that he was not a particularly brilliant organist, and today we are amused by certain extraordinary fingerings which he used in order to get by. But he was a musician.

The dance also has its virtuosi and the dancer is naturally tempted to show off what he can do. Therefore he does so not because the arabesque designed by his body will be beautiful to behold but because the effort necessary to achieve it will be crowned with success. Hence the highest possible leaps, the interminably repeated pirouettes and other exploits of the same kind. They remind us of the unpleasant impression singers produce when they manage to hold on to a high note at the highest range of their voice or hold it for as long as they can hold their breath. What a relief when the former become silent and the latter breathe again! The male dancer is more exposed to this kind of danger than the female dancer. His normally greater strength tends to bring itself to bear by itself. In that case his virtuosity takes the particular form of acrobatics. The latter is also an art of the body in motion which has a beauty of its own, but it is not one of the fine arts because its principal end is not to create beauty but to give proof of skill, strength, suppleness and courage pushed, if necessary, to the point of rashness.[7] The beauty of acrobatics, like that which accompanies the exercise of gymnastics and sports, belongs to the order of natural beauty. The acrobatic dance, in which powerfully muscled men of Herculean strength throw female dancers of average weight back and forth between them like a ball, has no relation at all with the art of the *porteur* whose object is not to display his personal strength but rather to show, if only through a simple effect of contrast, the grace of a female dancer whom he can set into motion merely by lending her the support of a finger. Acrobatics has its place in the music hall or the circus—only fools would disdain its merits; but it is one of the fatal illnesses of the dance which should be the art of creating beautiful forms in motion in time and space by means of the human body. We would not dream of forbidding those who love acrobatics not to take delight in them; we are merely inviting them not to mistake as dance this legitimate object of their taste.

At the other extreme of the art the dance is beset by the temptation that threatens all the plastic arts: expression. In a time like ours in which architecture itself lays claim to the expression of feelings, how could the dance avoid being gnawed by the same ambition? This desire necessarily leads it to imitation. To imitate for the sake of expression can become the principal object of the dance, but in that case it ceases to be itself and is metamorphosed into another art. Mimicry, according to Littré, is the art of expressing thoughts through gestures, and he adds: "mimicry is a language all its own." Some mimes have other ambitions. They want merely to show the

7. See Alain, *Système des beaux-arts,* book II, ch. 3, "Des acrobates." In it we will find a wholly different approach to the same problem, but one that is justified in its order.

beauty of natural movements through the perfection with which they execute them and, if necessary, by disclosing their structure through a sort of motor analysis of the elements that make up such movements. There is in that case a return to natural beauty which, as we have already said, often is undeniably superior to that of art which, we repeat here, is something else entirely. Through its most ancient origins mimicry, as the very meaning of the word indicates, has always been an imitative art which belongs to that of the theatre. What results from it in that case is pantomime, to which the silent film in the recent past gave an unexpected development. A Charlie Chaplin, for example, has demonstrated how creatively inventive the language of a great mime can be. The fact remains, however, that being a mime is not the same as being a dancer.[8]

The evidence of the facts seems to favor the opposite thesis but it is only because the arts and the philosophy of art do not have the same end. The latter analyzes, defines and distinguishes in order not to confuse, whereas artists making use of a sovereign freedom—at their risk and peril, to be sure—join, combine, and arrange the resources of the most disparate arts with no other consideration save that

8. If usage, king of common language, made law in philosophy, we could easily maintain the opposite. The art which the Greeks called *mimos,* and the Latins *mimus,* was held by the latter to be a *saltatio.* See in this connection the remarkable chapter in Abbé du Bos, *Réflexions critiques* . . . vol. III, section 13: "De la saltation, ou de l'art du geste, appelée par quelques auteurs la musique hypocritique." Here it is not a question of the gesture of the orator, which accompanies the word, but of that of the mime which replaces it. See, p. 251, how Cicero and the actor Roscius fought over who could say the same thing better, Cicero through words, Roscius through gestures. When Cicero said the same thing with other words, Roscius repeated it with other gestures. What is at stake, obviously, is to express and to speak but no longer to dance, despite the name.

of pleasing themselves and pleasing the public. The dance is not mimicry, but insofar as a dancer is master of his attitudes, gestures and, up to a certain point, even of his expressions, he can also be a mime. The dance can be utilized as a kind of mimicry. The dancer in that case becomes an actor; he can be entrusted with the representation of a dramatic action in dance form, whereupon the dance becomes ballet. We are familiar with the extraordinary development that has been attained in our day by this charming genre—of which there are engaging hybrid types—which with the so-called "Russian" ballet ended up by forming a medley of all the genres, of which it can be said that it is the form of dance preferred by those who have no real love for the dance.

Strictly speaking, one male or female dancer suffices for a ballet. Indeed the modern development of this art tends to make of it one to be executed by soloist virtuosi. On the other hand tradition here favored performances conceived as a group composition. There was no ballet without a "corps de ballet." Today this collective body of dancers, where it still manages to survive despite the prohibitive costs of its upkeep, has been reduced to the role of a theatrical element whose patterned movements and ranks of ballerinas with their reappearance on stage in different costumes give the public a pleasure akin to that which it gets from the circus. This is the "ballet" billed as a grand spectacle which is a commercial, indeed almost an industrial, enterprise requiring a formidable outlay of funds, bankers, committees of wealthy patrons and sometimes the State for its support. This composite art pleases and this fact alone is its justification. There is always an element of the dance in ballet but it includes other arts in variable proportions. A ballet is a theatrical representation in dance form: it requires a play acted by dancers and mimes

(*Coppélia, Gisèle*); further, it requires the art of painting
for the decor and the costumes; at times, as in the opera-
ballet, it also requires poetry and spoken or declaimed
language; and, finally, music always. The dance proper,
as a distinct art having its proper end, somehow gets a
little lost in the process, but this is no reason for disparag-
ing this somewhat mixed genre. This development of the
modern dance is bound up with its history: it has provided great artists with a public which would probably
have been discouraged by the pure dance; the scenario or
the play let the dance get by, so to speak, and it is impossible to imagine how artists such as Grisi, Taglioni, Perrot,
Njinsky and so many others, now legendary, would have
been possible without the existence of ballets. It is simply
a question of not mistaking for the dance in its pure form
these spectacles which can be reproached only for being
overgenerous in welcoming all genres—extending their
hospitality even to the cinema.

Thanks to its hybrid character, however, the ballet
renders the philosopher the service of shedding light on
certain problems connected with the nature of the dance.

When we are young there are times when we feel a
desire to dance and as we grow older we long for moments
of this kind. We are thus aware of the fact that the dance
can be a personal pleasure: we can dance for ourselves,
and alone. The dancer who yields to this natural impulse
freely improvises the steps of his dance. Many professional
or semi-professional dancers do the same thing, as happens
still in many Spanish *fondas,* not, moreover, without lean-
ing on solidly established traditions which they are content
merely to interpret and vary freely. Finally, there is no
completely formed dancer and master of the resources of
his art who is not capable of improvising to any kind of
music, provided only that the rhythm is regular and the

cadences foreseeable. In all cases of this kind the dancer is at once the author and interpreter of his art, like the musician who improvises. He is still both if, like the musician who executes one of his own works, the dancer has foreseen and regulated the sequence of his movements in advance. The dance in this case is one of the arts in which the artist is at once author and executant. He conceives the idea of the work and brings it into being.

The opposite necessarily occurs as soon as the dance changes from an individual to a collective execution. Such is the case when the "executant" is a group like a *corps de ballet*. The executant in this case is subjected to the directives of personages new to him, namely the choreographer and the ballet master. The choreographer is a composer of the dance, similar in his art to the composer of music. His is a work of creative imagination in that he foresees the sequence of the plastic forms unfolding in the dance which upon being joined will constitute the ballet. His directions can run the gamut of extreme vagueness to minute specification according to the nature of the imagined spectacle and the personality of the dancers who are to carry out his project. The modern development of ballet has progressively led to the fusion of different systems of notations which make it possible to compose a dance almost as one composes a piece of music. The positions of the body and the movement of transition do not have the precision of a tone scale nor the exactness of musical duration, they cannot be "written" with the strictness achieved by musical scores. Nor has an agreement yet been reached on a system of notation common to all choreographers. We can, however, already reconstitute with sufficient exactness certain choreographies which in some way bear the name of their creator, such as Petipa, Fokine, Massine and several others. Thus we can also "revive" a ballet in the choreography of this or that author. This development perhaps heralds a time in which the plastic forms of the dance will funish the material of definite works, stabilized through the resources of an appropriate score and as easily transmittible as are musical compositions today. In relation to the age when this choreographic repertoire will have been constituted, as regards the dance, the present epoch will be what the music of ancient Greece is for us: only names will be known, but not a single work which could be put together as an organic whole.

The ballet master seems to play a more modest role but one that is no less necessary. Anyway, it is a different role. He ensures the execution and the technical pinpointing of the dance scores invented by the choreographers. He can be both ballet master and choreographer but not necessarily, and he does not always have the qualities required to perform these two tasks successfully. If the choreographer can be compared to the composer of music, the ballet master is comparable to the orchestra conductor. He must have an exact knowledge of the technical resources placed at his disposal by the particular troupe that he is to direct, and the intelligence and plastic imagination necessary to foresee what the forms desired by the choreographer will be once they are realized. Often, moreover, he will need sufficient personal inventiveness to make these forms realizable, the talent for assigning the right role to the performers along with the tact necessary to have them accept them, and finally exceptional pedagogical gifts so that each performer, and the troupe itself, thoroughly understands what is expected of each and every one of them. These are the many qualities that a choreographer does not necessarily possess, even if he is a genius, but which the ballet master must unquestionably possess so that the work may come into being. Without him it would remain simply a potentiality.

Among all the arts with which the dance can be associated, only one is its constant companion, music. This is not necessary however. Dance without music is possible. Indeed an adventurous attempt has been made, not without success, to create a silent ballet (Jerome Robbins, *Moves*, 1961). Moreover it is not necessary to have seen a spectacle of this kind for us to imagine its possibility. The spectacle of a machine in operation whose movements are accomplished silently with impeccable measure and rhythm, at times so fascinating to observe, is enough to convince us that a dance can be performed without music and without loss of its characteristic beauty. The kinship of the two arts explains the frequency of their association. Just as music is made of sonorous forms succeeding each other in time, so is the dance made up of human forms in motion in space also succeeding each other in time. We have already noted that the division and structuration of time through sounds is easier to achieve and more precise than that which is achieved with the aid of forms such as bodily movements. It is therefore natural for the dancer to demand from sound the temporal structure within which his dance will be inscribed. It seems to the spectator in this case that the dancer's movements participate in the strictness of the measure and of the rhythm defined by the sounds. In fact Spanish castanets, rattles, and even the clapping of hands with which the spectators spontaneously accompany the dancers attest to the common feeling of this formal convenience. But when we see a dancer work in silence, we know that it is an art which is sufficient unto itself and can create its proper beauty by itself.

No general rule can be cited for the propriety of this

association. First of all it can be considered from the point of view of the dance or of music. The dance profits from music to the degree in which the latter has been conceived with the former in view. This is the case with real dance music from the primitive tam-tam to jazz and to the orchestras of opera houses. The musician in that case conceives his musical forms according to the model of the plastic forms of a certain type of dance, or, if a ballet is in question, with an eye to accompanying the execution of classic and classified dance forms. Listening to a music thus conceived the choreographer, and even the solo dancer, know which patterned bodily movements it is inviting them to execute, which step it is calling forth from them. In such cases music profits from the dance as much as the dance profits from music. Since all that is being demanded of it are measures and rhythms, music is simply being invited to be itself and to display its own resources by putting them at the service of another art. The proof of this is that a great number of musical forms were dance forms at first: the *branle, bourrée, passacaglia, gavotte, minuet, polonaise, waltz,* and so many others, including the *round* and the *gallopade.* These have become for the musicians as many rhythmic frameworks capable of receiving and sustaining the most varied sonorous forms. There is nothing that we cannot expect from a *tempo di minuetto,* indeed almost anything rather than a minuet!

This is not at all so when the dance, becoming theatre, acrobatics or mimicry, strays from its proper essence and by so doing assigns music tasks that are alien to rhythm, tasks for which it was never made. Only special cases exist in this respect, too. The only concern of the old comedy-ballets was to find pretexts for their dancers to dance. In them the dance had no other reason for being save itself, and since the spectators often came to the spectacle only to see the dance, it was enough for them. Campra has defined the ballet as a dramatic action which is represented through the dance with the aid of music; but in fact the steps of the dance were always the same and therefore represented practically nothing.[9] The terms of the problem changed when the dramatic action, losing sight of the exigencies proper to music, burdened the dance with tasks beyond its means. There was no harm in trying this, and, besides, the judgments regarding its results exhibit the infinite variety characteristic of all esthetic judgments. It seems reasonable, nevertheless, to assert that it is not *a priori* certain that any sonorous form can be translated in visual space into a corresponding plastic form. The terms of the problem change from the moment when dramatic action, losing sight of the prerequisites of music, imposes on the dance tasks beyond its means. There is no harm in such experimentation and the judgments to be pronounced on the results will vary to infinity, like all esthetic judgments.

9. Pierre Michaut, *Histoire du ballet* (Paris: Presses Universitaires de France, 1945). Campra's definition is quoted (moreover, as requiring to be broadened today), p. 6.—The following remark (p. 5) is well wrought to fix the philosopher's reflection: "An interpreter of music (the ballet) offers itself, moreover, as being its physical *content,* this content which is not at all lacking in painting, sculpture or architecture, but of which the art of sounds is destitute." We clearly see what the author means; but sounds need no other physical content save themselves. When the mighty chords of an organ fill a cathedral with sounds that cause the stained-glass windows to shake, music is not lacking in physical reality. But we will agree that the building material of the dance is more corporeal than that of music; it is a solid. Consequently, it adds nothing to it, except in the mind of those for whom pure music is not quite complete—that is the great majority. The observation added by the same author is a very engaging one: "Finally, as an art of allusions and transpositions, (the ballet) has only a slight support in reality: it supports itself on music" (Ibid.).

Nevertheless it seems reasonable to assert that it is not *a priori* certain that any sonorous form can be translated in visual space through a corresponding plastic form. The arabesques performable by the human body do not correspond to sonorous arabesques either in suppleness, rapidity or in the number of possible variations. It is to be feared, therefore, that by wanting to dance to any music one may end up by spelling the melomane's pleasure in listening to the Sixth Symphony, for example, at the same time that one obliges the dancer to create plastic inventions whose meaning is not in the dance itself but outside it.

The complexity of the problem shows up when it involves music expressly written for a ballet whose subject is frankly mimed theatre. We have seen musicians in various times bend their art to the requirements of representing a dramatic action. We can understand why they agree to do so. In order to justify writing so many operas Camille Saint-Saëns pointed out that a musician has to earn a living! The ballet has provisionally replaced the opera as a recipient of benefices; it likewise involves commissions from wealthy patrons, sometimes rich ladies tormented by the desire to dance themselves, or to mime, which seems less difficult to them. In collaborations of this kind the dance loses all that music gains. The less the composer is a slave to this kind of dance, the more the music he writes for it can be beautiful: to risk a personal impression, Ravel's *Daphnis and Chloë* gains in being heard rather than being seen. On the other hand, the more the musician forces himself to model his music on different episodes of a theatrical representation, the less does he preserve his internal creative compulsions and that "golden thread" which Schumann called one of the surest signs of genius. Some music-lovers feel that Stravinsky's *Petrouchka,* captivating and

rich as it is in musical substance, loses as much in not
being seen as would an opera in which the singers' parts
would be suppressed. For this very reason, perhaps, it is
the perfect modern ballet, that is to say a charming hybrid
of a dance that is no longer altogether dance, and of a
music that is no longer purely music. This genre has a
beauty of its own which is its justification for being, but
it is good to know what we are admiring. Concertgoers
who are fully satisfied with scores of this kind at bottom
do not truly love either music or the dance.[10] But pure
forms are not easily accessible, and no pleasure that we
take in art is proscribed.

The central problem posed by the arts therefore remains the same. By dint of trying all manners of possible
combinations, each of the arts spontaneously comes to
prefer those which favor imitation and expression to the
detriment of the formal elements which are its very substance. Present Gounod with the first prelude of the *Well-
Tempered Clavichord* and he will cap it with an *Ave
Maria;* give the same prelude to Fokine and he will find
some way of creating a choreography for it; only the real
musician will find the musical response to Bach's prelude,
which is to write another from it and we will have the

10. Ordinarily it happens that the spectacle devours the music.
On this point the chapter "Le mimodrame" in Jean Cocteau's *La
difficulté d'être,* makes interesting reading, particularly p. 258,
footnote 1. "The music chosen to accompany the action was Bach's
Passacaglia; it was thus moreover that I saw the work. The actors
got tired of it and asked for a change; the poet decided to alternate
Bach's *Passacaglia* and Mozart's *The Magic Flute.* By that he intended to prove 'how the eye excels the ear in the theatre.' It will
be noted, moreover, that here it was not a question of a ballet
properly so-called, but of a mimodrame even with a touch of acrobatics. Both actors, who were equally excellent, did not really dance."

intellectual *Doctor Gradus ad Parnassum*.[11] Thus for the dance it cannot be a question either of interpreting a musical work, which is content to signify itself, or of imparting to it the physical consistence which some may think it lacks in comparison to the plastic arts whose material can be seen, touched and weighed. Thanks to the dance, music in this way shares in the facilities that the arts of space offer to the imagination. It is difficult to approve these ingenious observations except in the way they make music endurable to those who do not like to listen to it.[12] But we cannot see what the dance gains thereby. Its proper nature is not to give a physical content to music which

11. The first piece in Debussy's *Children's Corner* suite for piano. It is a musical portrait of a child bored with practicing who lets his mind wander from the exercise.

12. There are very noble impediments to the experience of the beautiful, notably thought. Those who philosophize on art enjoy it less purely than those who simply surrender themselves to it completely: "Music bores me after a little while, and all the more quickly the more it acts upon me. The fact is that it disturbs what it has just engendered in me, thoughts, illuminations, types and premises" (P. Valéry, "Choses tues," in *Oeuvres*, Pléiade, tome II, p. 476). Music makes some people talk, and it makes others think; in both cases it's good-bye to music! The same is true of the dance and Valéry knew this well. When he shows him a woman dancer, his Socrates asks: "O my friends, what is the dance truly?" Valéry is amused by the question but his Socrates continues to talk about it no less unpityingly, until the dancer Athikté collapses as though dead. She is then restored to her senses and utters the words with which the dialogue ends: "I was in thee, o movement, outside of all things . . ." It is the dancer who faints, but it is Valéry who is restored to his senses. ("L'âme et la danse," in *Oeuvres*, II, pp. 161–162 and 176).—On the philosopher and the dance, see our *Introduction aux arts du beau*, Paris: Librarie Philosophique, J. Vrin, 1963), Appendix. Cf. Susanne K. Langer, Problems of Art; I, the Dynamic Image: Some philosophical reflections on Dance (New York: Charles Scribner's Sons, 1957), pp. 1–12.

finds that of sounds sufficient. It is no mediocre dignity to be an art of the forms of the eminently intelligent human body in motion. The true source of the dignity of the dance is to remain faithful to its proper essence, regardless of the multiple alliances into which it may be obliged to enter.

SEVEN

Poetry

AMONG THE ARTS of which man is the material, that which comes after the art of the body is the art of the mind, poetry. Thought can become the material of art only because it itself has its own body, namely language, the embodiment of the word. It is here that we see how all human art is necessarily carnal. Purely spiritual beings, who could communicate directly without the means of audible words in the form of sounds, would perhaps possess an art of the mind, but we cannot imagine what it would be like. Poetry is a human art like the rest only because it first of all addresses itself to the ear. Words, spoken, heard and understood, constitute its material.

Poetry is a plastic art, like all the others, at least if by these words we still understand an art of form. However, we must make an effort similar to that required by the notion of musical plastic form. First of all the term evokes in the imagination the genre of the most obvious forms, that composed of visible and tangible lines and of volumes arranged in space, solids in short. A plastic material is one that can be modelled; in the same sense a plastic art is the art of modelling this or that material, clay, plaster and others of this kind; by extension, drawing is added to the plastic arts, for even though it does not produce volumes, it traces their contours and suggests them. We went even further in speaking of musical plastic form because music in fact seeks beauty in sonorous forms in motion. A final extension remains as a possibility, not by taking the word in a still more figurative sense, but rather by returning to the most material meaning to which it is here susceptible.

Poetry is a plastic art because the material of which it consists is suitably receptive to different, numerous forms, and even infinitely varied forms like those of musical sounds. We will have to distinguish the principal elements which make up these forms, but we can be assured in advance, as in all the cases until now in which it has been in question, of finding therein a plurality of quantitative and qualitative elements whose relations are apprehended by the senses as a unity. Here more than ever we shall be reminded that this formal unity is perceived by the sensory apparatus of a rational being whose intellect always reaches down into the sensibility. The senses of the man who perceives a plastic form always constructs it, more or less. This occurs with all the more certainty when language is the material of the form in question. The fact remains, however, that poetry is the particular case of poietics in which the material of the works to be produced consists of the sounds of an articulated language, taken together with the ensemble of the quantitative and qualitative relationships that make it up. Each word, each group of words, each sentence or element of the sentence in consequence is perceived as a sonorous form. When forms of this kind are combined in such a way as to constitute a unity whose aperception pleases and is desirable for its own sake, the person arranging and producing them achieves the genre of beauty that we may expect from language. We call him a "poet" because he has just "made" these verbal forms endowed with beauty; indeed, without him they would not exist.

What new element does poetry add to the given reality? To go back to an ancient formula, hackneyed but always in order, what is it here that art adds to nature? The poet in no way creates the substance of his art any more than does the musician, this other artist of the incorporeal. He finds his material ready-made in the language, whose words, structural forms and essential rules he accepts. There are as many poetries as there are languages. In this respect, the poet is less master of his material than is the musician. The latter is largely free to fashion new sounds and to combine them in accordance with rules that he himself has posited. If his work is not pleasing he has failed, but his failure is always relative, for his own ear, at least, may delight in sonorities that do not yet satisfy the acoustic sensibility of others. In any case, nothing prohibits him from trying. On the other hand the poet is caught on all sides by the restraints of language with its conventions and its traditional forms provisionally accepted by those who speak it. He works therefore on a material that is forced upon him; no matter how he makes use of it, he will work only on "the words of the tribe."

What is a word? According to Littré, it is a monosyllabic or polysyllabic sound, composed of several articulations, which has a meaning. Let us accept this definition. What strikes us immediately is the word meaning. In fact the essence of the word is to signify, and we immediately think of the most obvious meaning that is attached to it: the ensemble of intelligible notions that it suggests to the mind. Ordinary intellectual activity, such as that which we exercise every time we speak, consists in developing the intelligible content of the meaning of words, in formu-

lating it into definitions and in structuring these definitions into judgments, into reasonings destined to explain or
justify the thought. Language presupposes that these operations have already been accomplished or assumes their accomplishment as a possibility. Actually, this is often a gra-
tuitous assumption; whereupon comes Socrates and his
polite question: What are you talking about? The fact is
that the ordinary ends of language are practical, and that
the desire to make it express definite intelligible knowledge
is already tantamount to making a disinterested use of it,
hence not natural. Correctly speaking, this is to philosophize. But the philosopher makes no less use of language
so that he can signify himself; as with the ordinary man,
which he is at times, as with the orator, physician, biologist or sociologist, the kernel of what the word signifies for
him is an actual or virtual cognition which is called its
meaning. The usage of words in the service of intelligible
meaning, regardless of their arrangement, defines the domain of prose. Since it is a natural usage of words, it is not
necessary to know what prose is in order to know how to
make use of it. If there was a touch of the ludicrous in
M. Jourdain's astonishment, let us share it with him.

But the word has a meaning other than its intelligible
signification. Being a physical fact, perceived by the ear,
it has a sound: there is a considerable variety of language
sounds within a given language, indeed it goes to infinity
if we consider the ensemble of spoken languages. Roughly
speaking, each language has its own sonority within which
innumerable variations are possible. The sound of a word
has affective resonances similar to these accompanying
musical sounds. At the heart of the concept lies the image,
or rather images, flitting about each word mistily like
summer insects around lights. These images can combine
among themselves with an almost total freedom and, at

least, *independently of any intelligible necessity.* Images
have a life that is not subject to logic, which some minds
allow themselves full freedom to develop for its own sake
without subjecting its play to any extrinsic end. When
words are used for their sound, for the emotional effects of
which they are the cause, for the images to which they give
rise in the present or which they evoke of the past, and
when these images are combined with the emotions that
bring them into being or which they bring into being, they
are like blocks charged with diverse energies, each one of
which can release unforeseeable reactions in the mind.
Thus understood, the word is the material of poetry. The
poet uses it before all else in order to achieve all those
harmonics on which the sensibility and the imagination
are nourished. Persons who are not sensitive to them live
and die without ever knowing what poetry is. They can be
very great minds, or even very great writers. If such persons are forced to take pleasure in poetry—a most ingen-
uous form of coercion—they turn against it and define it,
quite naturally, in terms of an objection that indeed can
be levelled at poetry: its lack of what it would have to
possess if it were prose, namely meaning. This hostile
reaction on their part is natural. As Claudel says: "Order
is reason's pleasure, but disorder is the imagination's delight."

The essential ambiguity proper to the word explains
the complexity of poetry and the difficulty of defining its
nature. If he uses it as a poet, the artist of language constructs the poem, as Mallarmé said, with words, that is to
say with the word taken in the totality of its possible
meanings. Thus employed, each word strikes home and
resonances of all kinds radiate into the mind from around
its point of impact without our being able to foresee which
of these harmonics will go to seek, among those of another

word, the elected one which will let this very word spring up along with the whole retinue of its different resonances. To use words in this way is to make a poetic use of them; for, this usage not being natural, the person who applies himself thereto must himself *fashion* the verbal structure in which the words will take their place. This structure is not dictated to him by the rules of logic, no matter how flexible one might make them; the poet alone can discover them while producing them. This sensitiveness to the word as such is the very condition of the poetic experience; those on whom the word has no resonant effects are not only incapable of creating poetry, but of feeling it. The poietic experience is extremely rare, and the esthetic apprehension of the poetical is less frequent than is believed. Its absence is practically irremediable, the more so since it is of its essence to be ignorant of its self. For the conceptual meaning of the word is included in its harmonics, and since it is the first meaning which its natural usage imposes it can never be completely eliminated. Essentially a word conveys meaning, and where any meaning disappears, the word itself disappears and any art of language disappears with it. If poetry is made with words, it is made with all that which they signify, including their meaning. The very building material of poetry therefore involves the coessential temptation to use it with its meaning in view. If the writer yields to the temptation, he becomes a prose writer again; if he victoriously defends himself against it, he will be censured for it as though it were a fault. The non-poet in that case reiterates what for him is a first principle, closely related to the very essence of language: when we speak we do so in order to be understood. Now, rightly, it is not primarily for this reason that the poet speaks, but rather in order to create a verbal structure whose real meaning is the beauty proper to it.

The history of poetry in all countries, but particularly in France, registers a kind of oscillation between two poles, being diluted into prose at one extreme or distilled into an essence unapprehendable by the mind on the other. Two names will make this clearer. Voltaire represents the first pole; his formula (which Sainte-Beuve quotes several times) for ensuring himself of the quality of French verses, was to put them into prose. Sainte-Beuve added that this explains the dearth of lyric poetry from which French classic poetry suffered until the birth of romanticism.[1] Although he pushed the mastery of versification to the point where this art secretes its own beauty, fashioned of propriety, justness and polished elegance of language, Voltaire himself never reached the level of poetry.[2] Mallarmé represents the other pole. Upon being criticized for his obscurity he replied, paradoxically but in all truth, that he was really perfectly lucid. Indeed, since his poetry did not propose "to be understood" it could not be obscure, and since it offered itself to the taste of the reader, such as it desired

1. "Voltaire gave his famous recipe for determining whether French verse was good or bad: *put it in prose!* French poetry followed this path since Malherbe up to the end of the eighteenth century. Instead of having, as elsewhere, what one would call *sacred balconies,* it had only a pavement, if we may speak in this manner, very ably constructed indeed, but only slightly above prose." Sainte-Beuve, *Chroniques parisiennes,* LXXXII, June 6, 1845; pp. 329–330. See *Les grands écrivains français, XVIII siècle,* "Voltaire," ed. Maurice Allem (Paris: Garnier), footnote 5.

2. Voltaire himself understood it, since he understood nearly everything that can be understood without much ado. One day when someone placed him on an equal footing with Boileau he protested modestly—and I am sure sincerely—stating that this was not so but that he did hope that he was not too much below him. Indeed, but no matter how little below one may be to Boileau, poetry is no more.

to be, it could rightly consider itself lucid exactly as it was.[3] In short, it is true poetry because the problem of its rational intelligibility has no meaning.

Like music, poetry is an art of time. This does not mean only that it requires time to perceive a poem, for the same holds true with respect to an edifice, a statue or a picture; music and poetry are arts of time in the wholly particular sense that their works do not have a total simultaneous existence, like that of the arts of space. A poem exists materially only in the form of written or writable signs, juxtaposed in space like the notes of a musical score but which are not words any more than musical notes are sounds. Saint Augustine's justly famous analyses have demonstrated this. If the genuine poem is made of words actually heard, no poem ever exists in its material totality; only one line of poetry at a time can exist and of this line only one word, and of this word only one syllable or vocal emission, the whole being structured in the memory which absorbs its elements to the degree that the ear perceives them. What is true of the total form of the poem is first of all true of the elementary sonorous forms of which it is composed. It is therefore proper to classify

3. Nothing can replace Mallarmé's very text here, a perfect prose in which every word is just right, and signifies: "I am not quibbling with you save about obscurity; no, my dear poet, except through awkwardness or bungling, I am not obscure from the instant that one reads me in order to look for what I have stated above (see footnote 10), or for the manifestation of an art which avails itself of language—granted that it does this incidentally, the profound reason for which I know." Letter to Edmund Gosse, quoted in Henri Mondor, *Autres précisions sur Mallarmé* (Paris: Gallimard, 1961), p. 115. Poetry avails itself of language *incidentally* because it does not use words with the natural ends of speech in view.

poetry, along with music, the dance and all the arts whose works depend for their actual existence on the existence of man himself, among the arts of movement and of time.

In order to construct relationships in the temporal sequences of poetry whose structures are perceived as forms, words must first of all be divided and arranged into measurable units. Therefore the notion of measure, or "meter," is common to poetry and to music, as is seen in Saint Augustine's *De musica*. Hence the invention of verse which divides discourse into unities of duration of comparable length. This comparison is possible only within the same language. In a language obeying the rules of "quantity," like Latin, the duration of the verse is measured by the number of feet it contains; these feet themselves are made up of short or long syllables, variable in number and diverse in arrangement, the length of the verses varying in accordance with the poet's choice (hexameter, pentameter, etc.). In French, where the tonic accent replaces quantity, the number of syllables, or feet, will play the same role (Alexandrine, verse of eleven, ten feet, etc.). In any case, a unit of measure is required if only to permit the licenses that a poet will be able to take with it. The poetry of every language contains its own metric system as can be seen simply by leafing through a book, regardless of its contents. If it claims to be poetry, it is written in measured phrases of comparable length, in short, in "verse."

Rhythm, which consists in defining groups of sounds within the measure whose different durations and speeds of succession constitute unities apprehended as such, comes into play, based on the meter.[4] Rhythm does not exist in the

4. The specificity of the two modes of expression explains why they combine so badly. From ancient times masters of prose have advised against the surreptitious introduction of formed verses into

signs of language. Belonging only to actual verse, that is to say verse that is uttered and sonorous, it rests upon a duration which can be variable for the same number of syllables and differently measured through the relationships of its parts. The variety of poetic rhythm matches that of musical rhythm, and since it depends upon the person reading the verse aloud it escapes the poet to a certain degree in order to bend itself to the will of the narrator. Like the executant of a musical composition, the narrator of a poem can regulate at will the speed of delivery, by slowing down some verses and groups of verses or, conversely, by reciting at a rapid tempo without emphasizing the unimportant

---

ordinary prose. While reading the *Dialogue de l'arbre* by Paul Valéry, there came a moment when I felt a dull malaise come over me, the cause of which escaped me, when suddenly two rhymes burst forth:

> Tandis qu'à tes chansons mon oreille se fie
> Je crains d'être sans gout pour ta philosophie

(While my ear trusts your songs, I fear I have no taste for your philosophy).
The charm was broken; I thought I heard Bélise, one of Molière's learned ladies:

> Et les moindres défauts de ce grossier génie
> Sont ou le pléonasme ou la cacophonie.

(And the least faults of this gross genius, are either pleonasms or cacophony).
Thereupon, when I resumed my reading, I noticed that blank verse had been introduced already for some time in this dialogue between Lucrèce and Tityre (the philosopher and the poet). It is troublesome, and Valéry knew it because it is precisely this that he has Tityre say: "I like your verses indeed, but not your philosophy: My voice pursues only a shadow of thought. But for you, great Lucretius, and your secret thirst, what is the word once it sings? It loses therein its power to pursue the true . . ." Nothing could be more correct. One day I asked him why he had shifted from prose to verse without warning. Valéry replied simply: "It's much easier than prose!" I felt I had been graciously dismissed.

parts. Sarah Bernhardt was famous for swiftly dispatching a block of verses, delimited at her convenience but which she could endow with a sonorous structure ensuring its unity. She was also sovereign in the art of arranging silences at will which would not only affect the total duration of a line of verse but modify its structure and at times affect its meaning. How did Racine hear his own line of verse? "Me voici donc tremblante et seule devant toi?" * Probably as do all his readers, with a light caesura in the hemistich. How did Mme. de Caylus recite it? No doubt in the same way. But Sarah Bernhardt imagined a different pause, the effect of which was extraordinary: "Me voici donc/ tremblante et seule/ devant toi." In this case, the silence which the mute sound of "seule" imposes dominates the whole verse, provided that we hear it rather than just see it. All of us can easily bring to mind many examples of this power of rhythm, the sovereign creator of sonorous verbal forms. In a language like French, where the least shift of the accent of intensity is enough to transform the constitution of verbal groups and to modify the ensemble of their equilibrium, there is no limit to the possibilities of the invention of forms and rhythm. This can be seen in La Fontaine and Hugo.

Poetry is not the opposite of prose. As we all know since M. Jourdain, its opposite is verse. Poetry can creep in everywhere in the form of fleeting intuitions and as isolated flashes. There is even a poetic prose. The latter consists in using prose for the ends of poetry, that is to say to write a prose whose exclusive or principal end is beauty. Fénelon, Maurice de Guérin, Rimbaud and others have given remarkable examples of this. They are, however, relatively rare, the most frequent case being that of the prose writer whose mind is traversed by poetic images and

* Here I am, trembling and alone before you.

who yields to the pleasure of expressing them. Poetry, in
that case, fulfills an ancillary function in the service of
prose and its ends. There is more poetry in the first chapter
of Chateaubriand's *Mémoires d'outre-tombe,* written in
prose, than in all of Voltaire's *La Pucelle* and *La Henriade,*
which are in verse. More modestly, but often with a wholly
charming effect, Sainte-Beuve embellished his literary
analyses with images, thereby giving French romanticism
entry into criticism. There is poetry every time the prose
writer, having said what he wanted to say, gratuitously
adds words which are there not to make us better understand what he is saying, or even to express it better, but
for the sake of their beauty alone. It is noteworthy, moreover, that whereas so many great poets are also excellent
prose writers, the practitioners of poetic prose run aground
when they try their hand at verse. Chateaubriand, an incomparable master of French prose, was no great shakes
as a poet; as for Sainte-Beuve's pedestrian muse, careful
as he was to limit her flights to modest altitudes, she
rarely succeeded in getting off the ground. Actually, the
very nature of the instrument compromises the chances of
success. To want to write poetry in prose is a sure way of
courting disaster.

It would be wrong therefore to claim that there is no
necessary relation between verse and poetry. The restrictions of verse, the established rules which the poet himself
often contrives to make even more rigorous than those
which have been handed down by his predecessors, aim at
the creation of a mode of expression which is not that of
the ordinary word whose end is expression, information
and the communication of ideas or feelings. Verse reminds
the poet of his real function. "Verse," says Littré, "is the
arrangement of words measured and cadenced in accordance with certain fixed and determined rules." Why these

rules and this verbal arithmetic? Are they not impediments
to discourse? Indeed, but this is versification's very reason
for being. Verse is there to prevent the poet from speaking.
Some persons are afflicted with a natural gift for versification. To a degree this was the case with Ovid:

*quidquid tentaban dicere, versus erat.**

Others, Voltaire for example, go to infinite pains to acquire
this gift or to bring it to its peak of perfection. Since their
ideal, at bottom, remains that of prose, the great versifiers
imagine they have arrived at poetry when they succeed in
expressing themselves in verse as well as they would express themselves in prose. In that case they judge the
writings of others in accordance with this certitude. It's
hard to believe that Voltaire should have preferred Saint-
Lambert's *Saisons* to James Thomson's treatment of the
same theme. He was sure of his judgment and we cannot
imagine how he could have been disabused of it. Prose has
its characteristic beauty; it can even have incomparable
varieties of beauty, but all of them are directly or indirectly
related to the art of expressing thought, which is an art of
the true, not of the beautiful. Verse and its rules, all the
literary forms of which it is the substance, are the sole
language invented by poetry having its proper end in view.
Verse itself is not poetry, but it is the verbal material
created by man with an eye to poetic form and fashioned
to receive it. It was proper to have an artificial language in
order to offer a material suitable to the forms of the art.

Poets themselves are not in agreement on the importance that ought to be accorded to the rules of versification. The fact is they do not all have the same gifts. The
formal restrictions which aid some, hamper others. Lamar-
tine, Musset, Claudel on the one hand, Gautier, Baudelaire

* Whatever I tried to say, ended up in verse.

and Mallarmé on the other represent two groups, the first
of which, above all, includes orators hoping for opportunities to create poetry out of an ornate eloquence. Words
come easily to them, even in verse; they gladly talk about
themselves, the restrictions of verse throttle their creative
drive and at times they express their impatience with it.
The price paid for this freedom is the lack of solid workmanship which explains the caducity of the building material and the diminution of their work. The other group
is made up of technicians. They embrace the restrictions
rather than submit to them, being wholly convinced of
their beneficent character, and they look upon the most
arbitrary of formal requirements as useful challenges.[5]

Since art in essence remains the same under all the
forms answering to the different materials which it uses,
it was inevitable that poetry, like painting and music,
should waver between its potential two-fold vocation of
being either a plastic art or an art of expression. But
poetry finds itself in a particular situation, owing to the
fact that its material is language. When we ask whether it
is possible to have an art of painting which neither imitates, represents nor "signifies" something, or anything at
all, an affirmative answer is perforce in order. No doubt,
many would protest that painting of this kind does not
interest them at all; all that can be said in reply is that
what they like in pictures is perhaps not painting. Like-

5. The author of *Emaux et Camées* advised the use of hard
matter in all the arts of the beautiful, even poetry:
> Oui, l'oeuvre sort plus belle
> D'une forme au travail
> Rebelle,
> Vers, marbre, onyx, émail.

(Yes, the work emerges more beautifully from a form, rebel to
work, verse, marble, onyx, enamel).
He was joining example to the precept.

wise in music. Those who would like a musical composition to suggest precise images to them and, if possible, to recount an intelligible story, are entirely within their rights and no objections can be raised. The symphonic poem and all kinds of "program music" are there to grant them satisfaction. Yet, if they can say that program music does not interest them, these same listeners cannot claim that a musical composition that would not mean anything is outside the realm of possibility. Innumerable sonatas, quartets, symphonies and musical pieces of all kinds abundantly attest to the fact that there is music which tells no story whatsoever and speaks not. Sounds, colors, and forms have no definite meaning in themselves. Inasmuch as it is not in their nature to signify, they can be combined with ends in view other than signification, to the point where they will actually have no meaning at all without the result ceasing to be a work of art.

Does the same hold true for poetry? At bottom this was the issue at stake in the dispute over pure poetry. Fought over a formula, the dispute was bound to be endless and come to no conclusive results, yet it bore the mark of its time. Pure painting, pure music, pure poetry are typical phenomena of epochs in which, as a rule, decadence is tormented by a strange thirst for purity.

The three cases, however, are not entirely comparable, and it can be easily seen why if we refer to the considerations on poetry which served as our point of departure. Lines, colors, forms and sounds can signify, but their signification is not bound up with their nature: it is not born of necessity. The professor of cosmography draws two circles on the blackboard: one can represent or signify the earth, the other the moon. If they are drawn by the professor of geometry, they signify "circle," the ideal object of its definition. Giotto passes by and draws a circle, his famous O, and it signifies *Giotto me fecit*. Anyone can amuse himself by drawing nearly perfect circles on a sheet of paper. They *are* circles, they *signify* nothing. Likewise with sounds. The blast of a whistle can signify: Come here! or Stop!, but it can also signify nothing and be nothing else but the fact of a child amusing himself by making noise. On the other hand we said that a word signifying nothing would not be a word; the very notion of it is contradictory and impossible. If it is the essence of poetry to be fashioned out of words as its proper material, an element of signification necessarily enters into the composition of any poetry.

It does not follow that poetry's object is to signify anything whatever: concepts, images or feelings. Poetry always does this, more or less, but this is not its proper end; nor is poetry authorized to do so except to the degree that it can do this without making it impossible for it to achieve its proper end which is to create beauty with words, including their meaning, but without linking them together with their intelligible meaning in view which is their truth, granted admittance here with a view to beauty. Truth is the handmaiden of beauty in poetry and nowhere else. For the love of truth, we ask the friends of truth for permission to assert a truth. If at first sight it troubles them, a little attention will suffice to familiarize themselves with it. Beauty is not superior to truth; the very opposite is true, for truth is being itself present in cognition. The true always partakes of the intelligible, but artistic beauty partakes of the intelligible perceived in sensible experience. In it beauty is linked to the material in the object and to the body in the percipient. Rather than deploring this, it should be a matter of rejoicing that man, made of body and soul, can come into contact even with sensible beauty, particularly in the objects which he produces expressly for beauty's sake. It might be objected perhaps that if this is the whole story, the beautiful and the art which produces it are without importance. There have always been philosophers to assert this proposition and many more still who think it. This is their prerogative, provided they are not scandalized by the assertion that art taken in itself and in the pursuit of its proper end is free to make use of everything in order to attain it—even of truth itself if necessary. Poetry makes abundant use of error, for which it should not be condemned.

We shall halt on the threshold of arguments which obviously might be interminable. The cause for such argumentation is inherent in the nature of poetry, for its material is language which is by far the most spiritualized of all the materials used by the major arts. A language is at once a spiritual and corporeal reality in which the word is a sound informed by a meaning. We do not think without images, but neither do we imagine without thinking. The psychosomatic complex which is the signifying word, understood and felt in affective harmonics along with the accompanying remembrances, is so totally imbued with spirituality that it offers poetry a material whose formal vocation would seem to be the true rather than the beautiful. But we are not asking philosophers to sacrifice truth to beauty; nor do we forbid them to press beauty into the service of truth; rather, we would praise them for doing so, provided only that in the process they do not kill the beauty whose services they require. In order at the same time not to wound truth, it is no doubt fitting to define each transcendental, not in its relation to others but as it is by itself.

Two sorts of reflections may help us to familiarize ourselves with this truth which many find paradoxical, and some almost sacrilegious. First of all, let us mentally pass in review the ensemble of profound thoughts, or even rare feelings, that we can find in poets of the first rank. Lyric poetry contents itself with artful variations on the classic platitudes about life and death, heaven and earth, the mutability of seasons and of the human heart. The more ambitious poets have recourse to ideas, using them solely as pretexts for literary developments whose banality would be difficult to deny if they had to be judged by themselves. If we put back again in the ensemble of the poem the loftiest thoughts of poets, instead of extracting them from it in order to provide material for lectures on the philosophy of Vigny or Hugo, for example, it will become obvious that these are not thoughts in the speculative and cognitive sense of the word, but ideological elements chosen and retained by the writer because they appropriately lend themselves to integration with his work and to the nourishment or the substance of the poem.

No one has expressed this more aptly than John Middleton Murry: "We speak, for instance, of thought in poetry; but if poetry is pure and uncontaminated the thought it contains is of a different *kind* from what is ordinarily called thought: it is perception, not a cogitation, and in the finest kind of poetry it is a perception of the general in the particular. But there again, and quite inevitably, by dragging in these words 'general' and 'particular,' as we are forced to do, we are doing violence to the unique thing. We are, in spite of ourselves, assimilating poetic thought to ordinary thought. We cannot do otherwise: exposition in such a case is necessarily transposition from one order of reality into another. How then can one convey the truth that poetic apprehension and comprehension are of a totally different kind from the processes we ordinarily understand by those names? Yet this is a vital point, and unless we have some grasp of it, a real penetration of poetry is impossible; and we shall fall into the error of imagining that poetry which contains the greatest amount of explicit and recognizable thought is the profoundest poetry." [6]

The distinguished English critic's difficulty is understandable. It is that of any writer who undertakes to talk about beauty in any one of its forms, for we cannot talk about beauty except to say the truth in regard to it whereas its reality is not of the order of truth. The philosophers, of whose company I am, who place being itself at the summit of all, followed by the truth of being and the goodness of being, fall easy prey to the illusion that by refusing to identify beauty with truth, or to subordinate beauty to truth, one sets them over against each other. This is not necessarily so, for the only thing at stake is to distinguish them; at the level of abstractions where transcendentals are in question, we can do no more than achieve the object completely or miss it completely. Truth being the object of knowledge, beauty is barely perceptible except in small dosages and mixed with a strong proportion of truth, hence of cognition and intelligibility. This is the very reason why classic French poetry is the favorite haunt of the platitude. The more platitudinous it is, the more it feels at home. Désiré Nisard exhibited no hesitancy on this point. He even extended this notion to art in general: "What, then, is art in the most simple acceptation of the word," he asked, "if it is not the expression of general truths in a perfect language, that is to say in perfect conformity with the genius of the country which speaks it and with the human mind?" [7] France has her art when "she expresses in her turn general truths in a

6. J. M. Murry, *Keats and Shakespeare* (New York: Oxford University Press, 1925), p. 22.

7. Désiré Nisard, *Histoire de la littérature française,* vol. I (Paris: Firmin-Didot, 16th ed., 1889), p. 4.

definitive language." [8] Cut to measure for Boileau, the poet destined to formulate the following notion of poetic beauty:

"Rien n'est beau que le vrai, le vrai seul est aimable." *

After that, it will come as no surprise that many minds find it difficult to accept the notion of beauty desired for its own sake, and not as a vehicle of truth. It is not that they are insensitive to works of beauty but that their beauty seduces them only in the species of truth that it serves. Theirs is a desperate plight; they will never love beauty, for they believe they already love it.

A. E. Housman, who had a deep insight into the essence of poetry, expressed himself with perfect lucidity on this point: "If a man is insensible to poetry, it does not follow that he gets no pleasure from poems. Poems very seldom consist of poetry and nothing else; and pleasure can be derived also from their other ingredients. I am convinced that most readers, when they think that they are admiring poetry, are deceived by their inability to analyze their sensations, and that they are admiring not the poetry of the passage before them but something else in it, which they like better than poetry." [9] This observation is of an absolute general character, true of poetry but also of all other arts without exception. Most people who think they admire sculpture, painting or music actually admire in these arts something altogether different which is indeed found in them and which they prefer to painting, poetry or music. To determine whether this is a good thing is an altogether different problem. The great

* Naught save the true is beautiful, the truth alone is lovable.
8. Op. cit., p. 6.
9. A. E. Housman, "The Name and Nature of Poetry," in *Selected Prose,* Cambridge University Press, p. 185.

tradition of philosophers and moralists wholly approves this attitude which relegates the arts of the beautiful to their true place, namely that of amusement and games. Saint Thomas saw the hallmark of poetry in its "lack of truth (*defectum veritatis*), and we know what Pascal thought about painting and Kant about music. This is not here in question. Our concern is merely to ascertain whether such is actually the case, and of this there can be no doubt.

In a sense nothing is more simple to assert. Perhaps the good Abbé du Bos who thought that the origin of the fine arts is traceable to the need to escape from boredom— and there is much truth in this—said what is essential on this matter in the most simple terms: "We do not read a poem for self-instruction, but for the pleasure of it; and we stop when it no longer has a charm capable of holding us." But the professors scarcely admit that we read a poem for the pleasure that we may find in it. From ancient times to our day poems have been delivered up as victims to philology, history, philosophy, and even science. Ethics is no longer in fashion, but it has been replaced by psycho-analysis. In short everything about a poem is of interest, save the poetry. True enough one cannot venture a recall to order without incurring the question: "What is poetry?" And if the answer is that poetry is experienced but cannot be defined let us acknowledge that there are good excuses for not talking about it.

If we simply grant first of all that the failure of any attempt of this kind is inscribed in the nature of things, we will no doubt recognize one of the most courageous, lucid and penetrating attempts to wrestle successfully with a problem in the pages of a poet who most assuredly has the right to speak on this subject, Stéphane Mallarmé. For him what was undoubtedly at stake was to say what poetry *is*, if he could.

"That's the gist of it. I make music and I call this not that which can be drawn from the euphonic proximity of words, this first condition is self-evident, but what lies beyond this and is magically produced by certain arrangements of the words in which the latter remain only in the state of material communication with the reader like the keys of a piano. Truly this transpires in absolute purity, between the lines and beyond the glance, without the intervention of strings and horns as with the orchestra which is already mechanical; but it is the same thing as the orchestra, except in a literary relation or silently. Poets of all times have never done otherwise, and today it is amusing to be aware of it, that's all. Use music in the Greek sense, at bottom signifying idea or rhythm among relationships; there it is more divine than in public or symphonic expression." [10]

"Very poorly put," concluded the poet. The opposite is true. He put it marvelously by defining poetry as something produced by "certain arrangements of the words" when the latter act upon the reader as though materially, in the manner of the keys of a piano, for this is precisely how poetry, even the most classic, acts upon us. Every word acts upon the reader without requiring him to contribute anything of his own save his openness to it. This is the place to recall that the word is not a mere sound and that the music of words is a music of signs taken with the various harmonics they awaken in us, including their meaning.[11] The poet arranges these poetic unities into poetic

10. Letter to Edmund Gosse, January 10, 1893, published by Alain Lhombréaud and quoted in Henri Mondor, *Autres précisions sur Mallarmé*, p. 115.

11. I find the same idea, loaded with so much gold and precious stone by the flood of Claudel's prose: "Words have more than the strictly limited meaning assigned to them by the dictionary. In addition to their power, which is, let us say, useful to the profit of our personal expression, they wield a charm of evocation around

sentences whose unity is not necessarily that of meaning,
or it goes beyond it and includes it. As much intelligence
is required to create poetry as to create music, but in
poetry intelligence is employed for a reason other than to
understand or to make others understand. It is employed,
literally, *to charm.*

To achieve this effect poetry must be in the words
before being in the sentences, and the words must be
poetic in themselves, so that to say poetry is made with
words amounts to saying that it is made with poetry. At
the same time it follows therefrom that poetry can be made
only with words that are already poetic. The poet creates
the poem with the poetry latent in the language, which he
finds and does not create. The awareness of this truth has
led many poets to make use of a special vocabulary, as
though poetic language could not be the same as that of
prose. We rightfully poke fun at this language whose least
fault is that it quickly wears out. The French classics made
abundant use of it and this is why their poetic language
has often aged. Yet it must be understood that this artifice
betrays a kind of necessity, or expresses a wish, to avoid

---

us, they yield an attraction, they call beyond logic to the vast resources of our sensibility and our memory. The word FLOWER
'this absentee from every bouquet,' as Mallarmé calls it, in reality
rises from countless necessities, and not only from an actual garden,
but from a prodigious flower-bed of analogies, and, far from paus-
ing at the frontiers of horticulture, there and then it touches on
the most diverse resemblances and contrasts." Paul Claudel,
L'oeil écoute (Paris: Gallimard, 6th ed., 1946), pp. 191–192. We
must look for the observation in an essay of 1943 entitled "Les
psaumes et la photographie." It is interesting to observe that Claudel
could not express this idea without recalling Mallarmé. For it is
between these harmonics of words that the specific poetic meaning
is knit, and this is what Mallarmé never ceased to repeat: poetry
is between the lines, in the white of the pages and in the space
between the lines.

a-poetical or anti-poetical words as much as possible because it is always difficult to make poetry out of them and
sometimes altogether impossible. The poet's first gift seems
to be a particularly broad and keen sensitiveness to the
poetic potential with which some words of the common
language are charged. They think of words which we
would never think of summoning into being so as to create
the charm which puts the reader in a state of poetic re-
ceptivity. They know that words are like the keys of a
piano which if properly struck will produce the sound
waves of which music is made. Poetic genius certainly is
attributable to this innate gift, a kind of co-naturality between a sensibility and the forms of a certain language
which enables the writer to demonstrate the incantatory
power of words by choosing them and by arranging them
in such a way that their action is brought to bear in all
its force and which no sin against their musicality prevents
from coming into being, or destroys. Those who are totally
bereft of this gift cannot even have a feeling for poetry; if
they write verse it is but prose, or else we see something
that frequently happens with many great poets: the most
soaring flights of the imagination collapsing into the
flattest kind of prose of which they themselves seem to be
unaware.

The philosophy of art arrives here at the threshold of
a domain that goes beyond it. Mallarmé clearly perceived
the essential nature of poetic being and of the central place
which the word occupies in it as a living complex whose
reverberation in the consciousness creates innumerable and
unforeseeable relations between notions and images that no
logic would ever connect. Gaston Bachelard's impressive
works, especially perhaps his *Poétique de l'espace,* suggest
the manner in which this world of poetical relationships
could be subjected to an objective analysis. The poetic

world is not answerable to the methods of scientific expli-
cation: it does not lend itself to demonstration but it certainly can be explored. This exploration can even be
fruitful in that it will help poets to acquire a better knowledge of the substance worked by their art, to avoid some
possible errors on the object of poetry, and to dare to run
intelligently calculated risks.

We can already see the limits that such an inquiry
may expect to encounter. First of all, it must always agree
to come *after* poetry. It presupposes the latter for it is the
poet who invents, the philosopher being able to do no
more than to observe. It will agree, moreover, not to limit
the poetic substance of the word to the single images that
it evokes in the consciousness, even by charging them with
all the affective resonances that one would like. A unique,
organic, vital, intimate entological relationship exists between the word and man that will always defy analysis.
Except in the case of singing, which is language, music
itself utilizes a material that is less humanized than poetry
which is fashioned out of human ingredients. It is in this
sense that the poet is the most creative of artists in the
cases, very rare to be sure, in which what he creates is
truly poetry. He creates, in that he extracts the substance
of his work only from himself and in that he does so without for an instant ceasing to remain free toward it as
toward himself. This is the realm in which Bergsonian
freedom is truly at home: namely that of a freedom anterior to causality.

Thus linked to the word, poetry is not completely
perceptible except to those whom a vital relationship unites
to the language it uses and who not only understand the
meaning of words and sentences but hear their sound when
they read it. There is something awesome in the thought
of the immense contingency that prevails in the world of

poetic reality. If the beauty of the poems of Theocritus and Virgil is closely related to the particular musicality of their respective languages, what would we understand of it today inasmuch as we do not know how to speak it as they spoke it, nor hear it as they heard it? The pronunciation, elocution and diction within every language change with time. Do we today hear Corneille and Racine as they heard themselves? Speaking more generally, if we may push this problem to its extreme, what is the meaning of this agreed upon admiration for the world's classical literature whose language we have never heard and which we pronounce, as is said, in the modern way? The problem would be different if it concerned prose whose proper function is information and the transmission of knowledge. But when it is a question of poetry, whose formal beauty is inseparable from the music of language, what remains of it where this language is missing?

Merely to glimpse a response to this question makes us dizzy, for Virgil would be able to recognize nothing in the poetry of the *Georgics,* deprived of its hard "c," of its diphthongs, of its tonal accents and of its syllabic quantity as we, however, loved it in our distant student days. Hence the teaching of the classical poets, as well as that of modern poets using foreign languages which those who teach them at times speak in a comic way, is in reality a misunderstanding and bears on something other than poetry. The poets in that case become mere pretexts to push further the study of their language, a function which their abnormal grammatical constructions predestine them to fulfill. As for works in translation that are assigned for study, obviously nothing of their poetic content remains. What is *The Tempest* translated into French, if not *The Tempest* translated into prose? What is most remarkable is that the translators scarcely perceive this and that the spectators feel no discomfort. The French acting companies who pushed innocence so far as to perform a translation of *Hamlet* in England really believed they were playing *Hamlet*, and the French who see this translation played in France really believe they are hearing Hamlet. Indeed, they do hear all of it, except the poetry. It is an impressive sign of the richness of his dramatic art that even when it is stripped of its poetry, what remains of Shakespeare can pass for it.

There is a general contingency which comes before these particular ones which affects poetry in all languages, in its very substance. Up to now for the convenience of exposition we have talked equally about poetry read aloud and actually heard or about poetry simply read in the silence of a mind that speaks to itself. Is the same thing at stake both times? Is the substance of the poetry the same in both cases?

This problem is born of the conditions of existence proper to the poem. Since everybody knows how to speak some language, everybody early in life possesses the natural building material of poetry. The technique of versification—which Abbé du Bos called the "mechanics" of poetry—is a relatively easy apprenticeship in most civilized languages. In French it is ridiculously easy. All that is required is the ability to count syllables up to twelve and to amuse oneself by looking in a rhyming dictionary for words that end in similar sounds. Thus the number of rhymers is considerable. True enough, the rules, assonances, alliterations, interior rhymes and all the subtleties of the ear or of the meaning of words and of their nuances can be refined to infinity, but in that case we are embarking on the dangerous path of pure and simple fabrication in which this or that modern poet has all too often lost his way, and the danger of imitating Jean Baptiste Rousseau is all the more serious because it is not necessary to step out of the common usage of language to expose oneself to it. At most one adds to it the skills of the grammarian, which smell of midnight oil.

In this respect the poet resembles the musician who would be able to execute all his own works for the reason that from early youth he had a good voice, and knew the art of singing and of playing an instrument. In fact the musician can imagine more or less perfectly the effect that his music will produce; he can hum some fragments of it with the "voice of a composer" but he does not by nature have the means to impart to his music the actual existence that only a good execution can do. On the other hand the poet can be his own executant. He himself can talk his poetry and, as is said, "recite his verses," but the passage from thought verse to verse recited in a loud voice, or even in a low voice, profoundly modifies its nature. Spoken verse is a physical reality; it is composed of sounds, hence first of all of sonorous vibrations which can be measured with the aid of specially built instruments and whose relationships can be calculated. Phoneticians have shown a great interest in verse as vocal emissions. Verse read silently is also answerable to the word, but to what is called "the interior word," whose substance is not made up of sounds but of images of sounds; this material distinction affects the respective modes of existence of these two kinds of poetry. Psychology and psycho-psychology alone are competent exactly to define these two modes of existence, all the philosopher need know is that they are different. The image of a sound is not a sound; if he wants to change the sonorous image into a real sound, the poet himself will have to choose between several possibilities each one of which excludes the others. If the poet is replaced by a narrator, he is at the mercy of interpreters as much as are composers. The same verses will be recited by different interpreters; they can even be recited in many different ways by the same interpreter "by varying the tone," without it being possible to ensure that one of them is good to the point of excluding the others.[12] Everything alters in the physical substance of the line of verse in keeping with each of these alterations; the pitch of the sound and the timbre, the speed of the delivery which is the very movement of poetry, the arabesque of the verses which varies in accordance with the different pauses imposed on the same verses by those reciting them. And more still. When we hear the verses of the same poet read by two different interpreters, especially if they are professionals, we note that each one of them has his personal conception of the art of reciting verse, being either cadenced, musical and almost sung or, in contrast, broken, closer to prose, and full of surprises and turnings. We would be led to believe

12. The ancient custom of public recitations, not to go as far back as the sung and recited poetry of the bards of the high Middle Ages and their successors, produced a poetry which, having been made through the word, naturally returns to the word. But it would be quite interesting to hear a record of several pages of the *Aeneid* read by Virgil himself. In our day, overlooking the individual differences in pronunciation and of voice (Claudel with his Tardenois accent reads his own poems admirably), the problem of passing from the poem to the interior word to that of the external word is still with us. Many excellent actors read poetry badly, they believe they must *act* it, which is quite natural since acting is their trade. Among those who *read* (Jacques Copeau did not act his poets, not even Péguy) there is no one, so to speak, who does not feel the necessity of adopting for this purpose a particular tone of voice and delivery, somewhere between speech and song. They are right, but they themselves know what a monotony ensues if the reading is prolonged. The result of this situation is that the purer the poetry, the more difficult it is to read it aloud. The reality of the problem is confirmed by a curious passage in Montaigne, *Essais,* book II, ch. XII, ed. A. Thibaudet, Pléiade, p. 577: "And Zeno was right to say that the voice was the flower of beauty. . . ." etc.

in that case that the same poet wrote two kinds of poetry, that both bear his name and nothing about either of them, moreover, guarantees that the poet himself would recognize them as his own.

But when we think a line of verse, what is it? Actually, most of the time we don't know. The interior word is quicker than the exterior word; we never read as slowly silently as when we read aloud. Compared to thought, speech is slower and longer. Interior sounds lack the vigorous articulations of the actual word, but on the other hand they have a more flexible, more subtle, more delicate musicality which permits the mental combinations of sonorous images difficult to materialize in the form of real and actually perceived sounds. By virtue of examples, leaving each one free to find his own, we can ask whether there may not exist at least two types of poets, one whose poetry is made to be heard like that of Malherbe or of Hugo, and others whose poetry often seems to lose something when recited, like that of Racan in his best moments and, almost always, La Fontaine or Racine. We are so accustomed to hearing it so wonderfully in ourselves that it becomes practically impossible to find a voice that would impart an actual existence to it without robbing it of some element of its perfection. Such statements infuriate some of the admirers of these poets. Immediately they quote: "Le jour n'est pas plus pur que le fond de mon coeur," * which according to Valéry is "the most beautiful line of verse." But it is precisely this line of verse, so delightful as a thought, that is so difficult to recite. The actor instinctively lowers his voice in order to attenuate the triple shock that the hammering of the three successive *p's* inflict upon the ear. These accidents are rare, but it is when he is perfect that Racine floats in the memory above any possible diction.

* "The day is not more pure than the bottom of my heart."

The material music of the voice puts to flight the imaginary music of the simple verbal images, ever more etherealized thanks to their very unreality. In that case the
same verses are no longer in question. No actress, not even
Julia Bartet, has ever been able to recite "Que le jour recommence et que le jour finisse . . ." * as well as we recite
it to ourselves, simply because we do not say it at all.[13] All
we have to do is to try it in order to be convinced that we
ourselves do not know how we would like to hear this or
that line of verse or this or that sentence from Chateaubriand or Sénancour because the sounds that we expect
have no possible existence in reality. All poetry is not of
this nature. On the contrary, Shakespeare never loses when

* "May the day start again, and may the day end."
13. How often have we not had public readings of the fables
of La Fontaine? They are perfectly rendered insofar as they can
be *acted:* as regards the specific poetical element (Les alouettes font
leur nid . . .) the more it dominates, the less is the success complete. Each one of us can try the following on ourselves:
Volupté, Volupté, qui fus jadis maîtresse
    Du plus bel esprit de la Grèce,
    Ne me dédaigne pas; viens-t'en loger chez moi;
    Tu n'y sera pas sans emploi.
    J'aime le jeu, l'amour, les livres, la musique,
    La ville et la campagne, enfin tout: il n'est rien
        Qui ne me soit souverain bien,
        Jusqu'au sombre plaisir d'un coeur mélancolique.
(Pleasure, Pleasure, in olden times the mistress of the finest mind
of Greece, Disdain me not; come live with me; You will not be
idle. I love games, love, books, music, the city and the country,
in short, everything; there is naught that would not be a sovereign
good to me, including the sombre delight of a melancholy heart).
These verses are found in *The Loves of Psyche and Cupid.* Not a
trace of hermeticism. It is not even necessary to name "this finest
mind of Greece." Everything is simple; we would think it is everybody's language, but the voice puts to flight this victory w'nged
with leaden sandals.

his lines are spoken and Corneille's verse always gains when it is recited.

Philosophical reflection must limit itself to a definition of the general postulates of the problem with respect to so contingent a matter in which judgment ultimately depends upon the personal and ever mutable dispositions of the judge. Let us once more recall, since this opportunity is afforded us by a subject which unleashed the interminable controversies over "pure poetry," that poietics does not pronounce any esthetic judgment upon any kind of poetry or poetic work. Rather it would invite us to the reflection that no monopoly is justified in this regard. If there is one point on which the most resolute defenders have agreed with their opponents, it is that which holds that *"pure poetry* is an abstraction." As A. C. Bradley says in his Oxford Lectures on Poetry, which Henri Bremond quotes in this connection, "something which would be nothing else but poetry" does not exist in nature.[14] In contrast to what the heralds of pure poetry since Poe

14. After finishing the revision of this chapter, I wanted to re-read Henri Bremond, *Prière et poésie.* The experience was discouraging, because he has said everything, and the spirit of gladness that animates the book makes one doubt that a philosopher would be wise to touch upon the subject. But perhaps a little philosophy may be necessary in order to prevent poetry from evaporating once more, even if this time it would be at the side of prayer. Poetry is not prayer either in actuality or by analogy. In order to convince ourselves it suffices to re-read in the last page of the book (p. 221) what a spiritual author, M. Hamar, says about prayer: "The concern to find words greatly harms the movement of the heart." But this concern is the greatest one the poet has. His poietic activity is totally different from the mystic passivity of the saint: *pati divina.* This said, *La poésie pure,* a lecture delivered to a public meeting of five Academies, on October 24, 1925, will mark a date in the history of French letters. Or at least we would like to hope so.

think, it is not didacticism which puts it to flight. There is
no didacticism, no matter how abstract, from which a poet
cannot make the purest poetry gush forth: *De rerum
natura, Georgicon liber, la Divina Commedia*. Didacticism
can become poetry, nonsense can become poetry:

> "L'air est plein d'une haleine de roses,
> Tous les vents tiennent leurs bouches closes,
> Et le soleil semble sortir de l'onde
> Pour quelque amour plus que pour luire au monde." *

All we have to do is to surrender to the charm, without
thinking about it.

It is with difficulty that we resign ourselves to ad-
mitting a failure to distinguish the poetry from the poem,
as A. E. Housman so pertinently recommends. For it is
quite true that many love everything about a poem except
its poetry, but the fact is that the rest can merit being
loved. How manifold the beauties in *The Divine Comedy!*
The grandeur of the subject, the loftiness of the feelings,
the moral nobility of the passion for justice which animates the whole work, the creative power that resuscitates
so many personages, illustrious or not, but all restored to
life by the poet's imagination; let us not forget the universal history seen in the history of Rome, nor the philosophy, nor the theology expounded in the work, each of
which has its characteristic beauty. Never was the rule of
the cumulative act of different kinds of beauty confirmed
more strikingly than in the *sacro poema*. But its poetic
beauty is attributable to another thing, to that element
of pure poetry which flows and circulates throughout this

* The air is full of the fragrance of roses,
  All the winds keep their mouths closed,
  And the sun seems to rise from the wave
  More for some love than to shine on the world.

grandiose epic, now offering itself openly as a lyrical out-
burst, now informing privately so many erudite exposi-
tions—we know not how many—over which it throws a
poetic mantle. Dante's poem is doubtlessly a greater work
than Petrarch's collection of sonnets, but to ascertain
whether there is more poetry in the one or the other work
is a meaningless undertaking. More particular kinds of
beauty, yes, but more poetic beauty? Boileau himself had
doubts on this score: "A flawless sonnet . . ." The fact is
that the notion of *more*, or of *greater*, is not really applicable to the quality that is poetry. Poetry is, or is not. It is
an absolute: Rien, cette écume, vierge vers à ne désigner
que la coupe . . . Once we begin to make comparisons,
the poem has already taken flight.

EIGHT

The Theatre

POETRY CAN HARDLY BE discussed without bringing up the subject of the theatre, for which many poets, including the greatest, have labored, but it is possible to discuss the theatre without including poetry in a descriptive analysis. There is poetic drama, just as there is musical drama, and dance theatre. Like architecture, the theatre is receptive to all the other arts, indeed it could hardly exist without recourse to several among them, but it does not consist of any of them in particular. Richard Wagner was a dramatist of the first rank, a fact confirmed by the precise directions regarding décor and changes of scenery contained in his librettos. Here music dominates everything, but it is so far from being pure music that, as music, it suffers an obvious loss when it is stripped of dramatic action and of the elaborate staging that accompanies it in the theatre. Wagner was a man of the theatre to his fingertips, and pure music is not to be found with him. Neither do we come upon pure poetry in the theatre. Keats or Shelley, rather than Shakespeare, represent poetry desired for its own sake, with no other end in view. As the poet A. E. Housman tried to put it: "I call William Blake more *poetic* than Shakespeare, although Shakespeare contains so much more poetry . . . !" [1] The names of famous dramatists are the first to come to mind, precisely because they are less purely poets than the writers of lyric poetry and because poetry has only relatively few faithful followers. Poetry compromises itself with the theatre, as do music and dance with the ballet, at times out of a liking for the theatre, often simply to earn a living for its practitioners.[2]

In Chapter IV of his *Poetics*, Aristotle asserts that tragedy and comedy emerged from the epic through a spontaneous evolution. This provides food for thought. In the beginning was Homer and others who like Homer

1. A. E. Housman, op. cit., p. 57.

2. Camille Saint-Saëns was not afraid to recognize that the reason why he wrote so many operas was that music for the theatre was the only kind which at times enabled a composer to earn enough money to live on. Nothing could be more legitimate, but he was jealous of Wagner's success and stubbornly contended that his music was as good as that of the German composer. Perhaps it is, but this is not the question. Wagner's music was essentially theatrical; this is precisely why Saint-Saëns' music is closer to pure music, that is to say, it never succeeded in animating his operas. Too many musicians have paid dearly for disdaining this distinction. A good libretto is essential for an opera to be a theatrical work. *The Marriage of Figaro, The Barber of Seville, Faust, Carmen, Pelléas and Mélisande* have good librettos, and they are played; *Fidelio* has a bad libretto, and it is played rarely, and only out of deference to Beethoven; *Ariadne and Bluebeard* by Paul Dukas has an execrable libretto and despite its admirable music, the work has been a fiasco every time that a theatre has been found to revive it. On one occasion, someone in my presence was criticising a French novelist, commenting on the dryness of his character. I defended him by pointing to his love of music, especially Mozart. "No," replied the speaker, "he does not love Mozart, he loves *Don Juan*." Let us acknowledge, at least, that Molière's *Don Juan* is a good libretto, but its failure proves that the subject is not everything, even in the theatre.

were animated by a powerful imitative instinct. Those with noble-minded souls imitated noble actions by portraying them in their poems; those with souls made of more common stuff imitated common actions and held them up to censure in their satires. Thus the distinction between tragedy and comedy made itself manifest from the start. In this historical perspective, Homer's noble works (the *Iliad* and the *Odyssey*) and his common works (the *Margites* and other similar creations) were already tragedies and comedies because they were dramatic accounts imitating human events. They were plays with one or more characters impersonated by the author alone.

It is not certain that Aristotle has an altogether clear view of this problem.[3] The transition from epic to tragedy

3. I would not dare to affirm it outright, not because it was Aristotle, but because he was very intelligent. Naturally, he noted that "tragedy . . . is an imitation of action that is serious and also, having magnitude complete in itself, in language with pleasurable accessories, each kind brought in separately in the parts of the work, in a dramatic, not in a narrative form . . ." in the *Poetics*, VI, 1449b 25–26, *Introduction to Aristotle*, ed. by Richard McKeon (New York: Random House, The Modern Library, 1941), p. 631. This is precise to the point of perfection; it is merely a question of determining whether tragedy is still poetry. Racine believed it was: *Principes de la tragédie*, the text of Racine's notes on the margin of Aristotle's *Poetics*, established by Eugène Vinaver (Paris: Librairie Nizet, 1951). See the author's cogent observations on p. 45. "That Racine interpreted his task as poet in this way is attested to by his theatre, which lends itself so little to definition and which escapes any attempt at reduction to the tragic type" (p. 45). For Racine, in fact, tragedy is an epic in dialogue form, something generically different from a play. Seemingly Sainte-Beuve—hardly a naive person!—did not perceive this when he criticised Racine for not placing the most tragic events on the stage, as Shakespeare does. With Racine the "narrative" always dispenses with the representation. Sainte-Beuve does not distinguish between the "poets" of the theatre and the others (Homer, Pindar, Aeschylus, Dante and Shake-

implies a change of genre; they differ, as we said formerly, *toto genere,* because it is the genre of poetry carried over to the theatre, hence from one major art to another. This event occurred when "Aeschylus first introduced a second actor," as Aristotle himself says. In fact, Aristotle is describing here an impossible operation, for if only one character is involved, he is not yet an actor. Theatre begins with dialogue which, by definition, requires two persons.

Reading is the normal form for the presentation of the epic. Whether it is a public or a private reading makes no difference as regards the genre of the work. Public reading was the usual way for spreading poetry before the invention of the printing press. It is still practiced in our day. The reader may be a professional actor and in most cases he frequently is. In his public reading of a play he can even imitate several different actors by varying the tone and timbres of his voice and make us believe that we are listening to a man or a woman, a young man, an old man or a child speaking. The Japanese have developed the art of public reading to the peak of perfection, inasmuch

speare are for him in the same class, Horace, Virgil, Corneille, Molière, Boileau and Racine being in the second rank); he distinguishes them, but as poets of genius "independently of the genres," "XVII siècle," *Les poètes dramatiques,* ed. M. Allem, p. 193. See his criticism of Racine ("We can rightfully criticise Racine, above all, for having described rather than staged the banquet scene . . . ," pp. 210–211). Assuredly, but any stage manager can mount a banquet scene. It is not poetry. Sainte-Beuve criticizes Racine for not being Shakespeare, and he certainly is not, but the reason why he steers clear of spectacle is that he remains faithful to the epic. When, today, a director desires to add the dimension of spectacle to *Bérénice,* he has a perfect right to do so because the theatre exists for our amusement, but it is a mistake from the point of view of the Racinian ideal itself. To add the dimension of spectacle to *Bérénice* is like removing it from Wagner's *Die Meistersinger.*

as they have developed specialists who themselves speak all the parts of the same play, while all the actors do is mime them. Yet the public reader, as such, is not an actor. As we know, he is alone and instead of seeing several characters we see a man by himself who vainly tries to talk as if he were several men at once.[4] The first one to introduce a second actor, again according to Aristotle, created the actor and the character at the same time, for the public reader is himself and not an actor since he speaks for others without claiming to impersonate them.

The difference was manifest to anyone who entered the tiny auditorium of the Vieux Colombier where Jacques Copeau used to give his public readings. The only décor was a table behind which a man sat reading. Obviously his self-assigned function was not to give a performance in the formal sense; he himself made no effort to make the audience believe, even temporarily, that he was any personage other than the one who was holding the

4. This is what distinguishes the theatre, as a major art, from all its derivatives, such as the marionette show, or the cinema; the images that are projected on a screen exist, but the persons they represent do not. They have existed, but their images survive them; no real actor continues to act after his death. We can consider cinema as the image of a theatre that has ceased to exist, but the film has never existed as theatre. There is never a "general rehearsal" of the film as there always is with a play; it is only after the montage and on the screen that a film attains its unity, that of an image whose reality already is no longer there. It seems, therefore, that cinema has an interest in seeking its paths outside those of the theatre, even of a faked theatre. Perhaps it is one more case of a new material in search of its form. On this score Henri Gouhier, "Théâtre et cinéma," in *L'essence du théâtre* (Paris: Plon, 1943), pp. 8–14, makes profitable reading. We quote a sentence relating to the core of the question, italics ours: "These five *acts* are *actions* in search of *actors* who *actualize* them" (p. 4). And a few lines further: "Hence it is the actor who is the dramatic fact."

public reading; if he was reading Péguy, Péguy's work alone occupied the whole stage, it alone had the floor and Copeau acted neither Joan of Arc, nor Madame Gervaise, nor God. He did not even impersonate Péguy. In fact he did not act at all, and his auditors sensed the tact with which he guarded himself against acting. For him to have done so would have been a transgression against art, for his function at that time was not to simulate the presence of any character but to ensure the presence of poetry. The moment there are two readers, they become actors. The actor is born the moment when, instead of speaking for the author by presenting his work, he speaks for any one of the characters imagined by the author as though he himself were this character, temporarily endowed with a borrowed reality and life which we agree fictitiously to consider as real by virtue of a convention tacitly accepted in advance. Indeed this is the spectator's personal contribution to dramatic art: to help to defray expenses by paying for his seat and to become himself an actor by accepting the role of the spectator who plays at believing in the reality of what he sees. He does not go to the theatre to see Corneille, not even to see Talma, but to see the actor Talma playing the part of Augustus as conceived by Corneille. The theatre truly begins when, the narrator having withdrawn into the background, the parts of the story are *acted* by *actors* whose very name clearly states what they do.

What is true of the actor is also true of the play in all its constitutive parts. Just as the narrator makes way for the actor, the descriptions in the play become décors, its lines are actually pronounced, its portraits are replaced by rouged and made-up faces as well as by bodies dressed in disguises that are as easy to see as it would be difficult to imagine them. The transition from reading to theatre is

effected every year in Christian churches each time that at
the hour of the Passion, while the celebrant is reading the
Gospel for himself at the altar, several celebrants chant it
publicly and transform into real characters what before
were only the parts of a story. One becomes the Witness,
who is the evangelist Matthew or John, another becomes
Jesus, a third plays the role of episodic characters; the only
necessary convention as far as the latter is concerned is
that he represent only one person at a time. The choir
naturally is the multitude but alternately it also represents
the Christian people in prayer. The celebrant who plays
Christ no longer reads the Gospel, but impersonates Christ
in the grave voice and the lofty and slow diction that is
chosen as apparently befitting the Man-God. It would be
easy to note what distinguishes this liturgy from a play
proper, but here we can observe the spontaneous transition
from narration to dramatic action, from reading to representation. A theatre is not a church; everything in it is
fiction and willed as such, but the fiction is embodied there
in a very real matter. When theatre people are told that
their art is illusion, the authors, actors, stage designers,
costumers, accessorists, stage directors and financial backers
know all too well what a heavy, burdensome, and costly
mass this illusion requires for its embodiment. The physical substance of this embodiment is the material of the
theatre; the proper function of the author is to inform it
with the ends of beauty.

The actor stands in the foreground of this material
and altogether apart from the rest, for if the theatre is
representation of human events and, as is said, of life, in
this regard it surpasses all the other arts in that this representation of life is made with living persons and that of
human events with human beings. Everything in the
theatre is a portion of the real charged with a fictitious

signification, but those who signify fictitious persons are themselves real persons. When an actor is assigned to impersonate a certain character it is said that the actor has a "part" or a "role." According to Littré a part, or role, is "that which an actor must recite in a play. Thus called because it is written on a role, on a sheet of paper. When Molière in *L'Impromptu de Versailles* tells his troupe: "But pray, let us set about our rehearsals," Mlle. Béjart replies: "How do you expect us to do this if we do not know our parts?"

Assuredly that is what a part is, but it is more than that. When an actor looks for the first time at the lines that he is to recite, he grasps them as a unity. They are the words of one and the same character whose utterances follow one upon each other and, moreover, they meet up with the utterances made by different characters; they are like the substance of the fictitious being whom the actor will be charged to impersonate in his countenance, his attitudes, his bearing, his gestures, his tone of voice, his inflections, in short in his whole body. A part, good or bad, is more than a sequence of lines written on paper; it is a virtual theatrical being whose actualization is at stake. Furthermore, this is the distinguishing trait between acting and reading. If I read *Le Cid* in public, I am simply a professor or a lecturer who is reading the play, but if I take it upon myself to play the part of Rodrigue, the words that I utter in his name become a part forming a continuity beyond the interruptions imposed by the dialogue; they assume a unity and become reality by borrowing the reality of the actor who pronounces them. His person becomes that of the fictitious character who speaks the words; the real action of the actor is like the embodiment of the action he is charged to portray.

The actor, in some way, is the executant of the theatre

without whom the dramatic work would remain in the planning state, or at best in a state of potentiality, waiting to be brought to fruition. The only musical executant whose situation is comparable to his is the singer. Actually, a singer is an actor who sings rather than speaks his role; this is why music in that case becomes theatre because the musician really draws from himself the music that he is performing. Ordinarily, the musician's role is limited to playing a musical instrument well, whereas the actor's role, whether he is speaking or singing, consists in playing himself well, as it were. His instrument is the man he is, his very person, body, mind, his natural gifts and acquired talents, in short his total self. There is no theatre without this real presence of actors engaged in their roles. Alceste in the theatre is the role of Alceste literally "personified."

Therefore, the actor's specific contribution to the dramatic work is to commit his very person to the service of its realization on stage. This extraordinary vocation exists. It is not even rare, but all those who are called do not have the means to respond successfully to the call. This is first of all decided by the physique: build, carriage, voice, which pre-determine the career of the future actor by fixing the uses to which his artistry will be put. Molière, an excellent comic actor, was never exactly brilliant in tragic roles. The actor does not play the role he wants, but the role he can. It requires an arduous apprenticeship and long hard work to cultivate these gifts. Finally, assuming full mastery of his trade, the actor must make a special effort every time he approaches a new part. He must re-form himself so as to become the character whom he is to personify. It is essential that he enter into the meaning of his lines, but his object is not to grasp their meaning as such but to imagine himself already on stage and under the skin, as the saying goes, of the character he is to play unless, conversely, the character has gotten under his.[5] This is not all. A role stands in relation to other roles. Therefore the actor must think of himself as one of the beings making up the microcosm imagined by the dramatist. Thus the actor will conceive his manner of acting, his place and his role in terms of the ensemble and of the "cast." In this sense, he is not a negligible factor. Even if it is only a supporting role, a role can be acted well or badly. There are, moreover, major or minor supporting roles, and often the weight of a play rests on the actor or actress with the supporting role. An excellent actor of the *Comédie Française* once told me that besides the role of the star in whom the public is primarily interested and who walks off with the laurels, there is often a role less dazzling but of a kind which will cause the play to "flop" if it is not perfectly carried off. Orgon alongside Tartuffe, Bartholo next to Figaro. Lengthy collective efforts, nowadays often regulated by a stage director, finally culminate in the play acted on the boards. But the play is not truly acted except on the night of the "premiere," that is to say with the indispensable collaboration of the public. When at the curtain call the artists come on stage as a group to receive the applause, they can rightly feel that they have deserved it, for even if the play has failed and

5. It happens that a role is played by an actor who does not have the physique for it. Since beautiful voices are rare and powerful voices require a rather large chest, the disparity between the actor's physique and the role is almost the rule in opera, at least as far as concerns a certain genre of roles. But we have seen many comedians tormented by the desire to play high tragedy, and many tragedians work at parts that simply were not for them. If he has the wisdom to resist such temptations, the great actor commissions one of his pupils to play the role for him. "I am working on Silvain's Harpagon," a young actor told me one day, "he's the one who wants it."

dragged them along with its failure, the actors at least "defended" it well. Why should not a theatrical company, why should not an actor or an actress be proud of the part they have just taken in the extraordinary event which is the production of a work of art willed only for the sake of its beauty?

Here a problem arises, however, which the speculative philosopher would prefer to avoid because it relates to morality. But its roots dig so deeply into the ontology of dramatic art that he can hardly avoid it.

The actor is the only creative artist who fashions the building material of the beauty that he creates out of his own person. This is true, of course, only insofar as he is actor. Speaking absolutely, the actor remains wholly himself while he is on stage. He is like other mortals, with his own character, thoughts and feelings. If he does not become God while playing the part of Jesus Christ, neither does he become a devil playing Mephistopheles. The problem is of a more hidden character; it requires some effort to meet it on its own ground.

First of all there is a moral problem, real and supremely important in its order, which is not that of pure speculative philosophy treating of the essence of the arts of the beautiful. This must at least be recognized, because it is one of the constants of the problem, and it merits this recognition if it serves merely to situate our own problem exactly.

There must have been a meaning behind the Church's repeated condemnations of minstrels, mountebanks and actors of all kinds. One specific point ordinarily held the attention of theologians. There were no actresses in ancient comedy or in ancient tragedy, and this custom lasted for a long time in some modern countries, for example England. But in Bossuet's time women already tread the boards, posing a serious problem in the minds of theologians for whom decorum, modesty and decency were the distinctive attributes of the Christian woman. How could a woman exhibit herself in public and in full view of everybody, and mimic the language, gestures, and attitudes of the most violent or tender emotions without spreading a feeling of disquiet in the hearts of the spectators? How could she do this without exposing herself to these same feelings? This is the question which Bossuet posed in terms that clearly reflect his ideas on the subject.[6] On this point all we have to do is to refer to what he said about it.

The problem in all its aspects goes beyond the personal situation of the actor or the actress. Even assuming that an actress is completely insensible to the emotions which she inspires, which is not only possible but in a sense useful to her artistry, she is not without responsibility for the emotions she arouses in others. In this other sense, she is a being professionally dedicated to the function of kindling these emotions, feelings and passions in the hearts of others. To expose a woman on the stage in this

6. "What mother, I do not say one who is Christian but who has a modicum of respectability, would not rather see her daughter in the grave than on the stage? Did she raise her so tenderly and with so much wariness for this shame? Did she keep her night and day, so to speak under her wings, with so much care, in order to deliver her to the public and to make of her a peril to youth? Who does not regard these unhappy Christians, if they are still in a profession so contrary to the vows of their baptism, who, I say, does not regard them as slaves on display, in whom modesty is extinguished, except for the kind of glances they attract, they whom their sex had consecrated to modesty, and whose natural frailty demanded the sure refuge of a well-regulated household? And here they are spreading themselves out right in the middle of the stage . . ." etc. Ch. VIII, Bossuet, *Maximes et réflexions sur la comédie,* ed. A. Gazier (Paris: Belin, 1881), pp. 39–40.

way, offered to the desires of men, a woman whose talent
consists in exciting them by making believe that she feels
them herself, in Bossuet's words "is to sacrifice them to
public incontinence in a more dangerous manner than
would be the case in places that we dare not call by name."
A perusal of Chapter VIII of *Maximés et reflections sur la
comédie* would show how deeply Bossuet pursued the
examination of this problem. He knew all the answers of
those who defended plays. "When plays are criticised as
dangerous, the fashionable folk . . . repeat daily that they
do not perceive this danger at all. Press them further and
they will tell you the same about nudity, and not only
about nudity in painting, but that even of persons . . ." [7]
Bossuet, moreover, does not speak only in the name of religion. The aforementioned chapter of the *Maximés* expressly cites the authority of Plato and it is on this occasion
that he pronounces the word suggested by the developments that we have just seen. Despite the licentiousness of
their theatre, the pagans never showed women on the stage.
They believed that a sex dedicated to modesty "should not
be exposed to the public in this way, and that it was a kind
of prostitution." [8]

7. Op. cit. . . . p. 43, and the further development of the
argument which is Bossuet at his best. It is very strange that such
a subject of literary history has not yet found the historian it de-
serves, especially in a time when whole theses are dedicated to the
life and work of some "stage managers" whose importance, real as
it may be, nevertheless interests only one of the least literary "parts
of the theatre."

8. Bossuet, op. cit., p. 56. Bossuet does not quote Plato merely
as a decorative authority. Plato does not countenance the theatre,
as he does music and poetry, except in the service of morality. The
actor follows the fate of the theatre. Plato cannot allow that a future
political leader imitate a woman, a slave, a beggar or coward, a
debauchee, etc. Why? For fear that by imitating their baseness and

This is not the core of the problem, if not for the moralist at least for the speculative philosopher. Even if we do not attach any moral connotation to the word, the fact remains that the actor is a professional "simulator." To imitate feelings that one does not feel, to say things that one does not think and to do it as perfectly as possible to the point where the spectator, though unbelieving, is gripped by the performance, is truly to simulate. No intention to deceive is involved in this game; the public knows that the actor is imitating and it lends itself to the game to increase the pleasure which it derives from the spectacle. But this is not the question. What is solely at stake here is that the actor, whatever his intention, assumes the appearance of an imaginary personality and creates the illusion of a nonexisting reality. In Aristotle the art of the actor was called *è hypokritik*.[9] Later, the appellation actor *hypokritès*, was to designate a "knave," a "hypocrite." The meaning which links these two different usages of the word is that of "the simulation of an imaginary person by a real person." While he is playing a role the actor assumes a "borrowed personality." What is his own in that case? This is the core of the question.

No doubt we shall be tempted to dismiss Bossuet's testimony. After all, it will be said, his attitude was predictable because he was merely plying his trade. But there is also the testimony offered by Diderot, the permissive moralist of the *Supplément au Voyage de Bougainville, ou Dialogue entre A. et B. sur l'inconvénient d'attacher des idées Morales à certaines actions physiques que ne'en com-*

---

vices, he may contract them in reality: *Republic,* III, 8, 395 c-d. In citing this passage in Chapter XIV of his *Maximes,* Bossuet rightly asserts "it is a sapping of the foundations of the theatre, removing from it even its actors . . ."

9. Aristotle, *Poetics,* ch. 20, 1456b. 10 (op. cit.).

portent pas.[10] On the other hand, it seems that their imitation involves very precise moral ideas when we read the famous *Paradox sur le comédien.* Here Diderot discusses the "degradation of actors," of those people who "are debased to the condition of the lowest mountebanks," and if his testimony differs from Bossuet's the reason for his contempt of the actor's calling is expressed no less forcibly by Diderot: "Where is the poet who would dare suggest to wellborn gentlemen to repeat in public talk of a vapid or gross character, or to women, more or less sage as our own, to recite brazenly before a large audience words that they would blush to hear in the privacy of their homes?" In fact Diderot points out that actors are excommunicated by the Church and rejected by public opinion. "This public, which cannot be without them, despises them. They are slaves ever under the whip of another slave. Do you believe that the marks of a constant degradation can remain without effect, and that under the burden of this ignominy a soul is strong enough to be a match for Corneille?" Save for the difference in language, the views are identical.

Diderot introduces a new point of view here. All we have to do is to follow it to its end to arrive at conclusions of great importance. Pushing beyond Bossuet, his merit is that he posed the question of what might be called the soul of the actor, and perhaps, above all, he sensed that by proceeding along these lines one might find the answer to the

10. *Supplément au voyage de Bougainville,* in *Oeuvres* (Paris: La Pléiade), definition of modesty: "Man does not wish to be disturbed or distracted in his pleasures. Those of love are followed by a weakness which would surrender him to the mercy of his enemy. This is all that there can be of a natural element in modesty: the rest is institutionalization." p. 1025, and the subsequent passages in which the almoner learns many things obviously new to him.

problem of the social condition of the actors of his time, as well as of the times anterior to his own.

Distinguishing between two temperaments of different dramatic artists, Diderot formed a first group of those who, acting by some kind of instinct, are dominated by their sensibility. Such actors are wholly in the grip of their roles and become as one with the character being portrayed. If they have this gift, they experience sublime moments followed by painful letdowns. The others have no sensibility whatsoever. By calculating in advance the manner in which they are to act down to its least detail until they achieve perfection, they succeed admirably in imitating all the gestures and all the expressions of a person like the one whose role they are to play. They will make the most regular and the most perfect actors, provided only that they never are carried away by the stirrings of their sensibility. Herein lies the "paradox of acting": the less the actor himself is stirred, the more he stirs his audience. Now in both cases he is never himself, that is to say whether he renounces his real being to become the personage of his part or whether, having no definite self-identity, he deliberately fashions the soul of his character. It is when he has nothing of his own selfhood to sacrifice that he identifies himself most perfectly with his character; therefore this is also when the actor is at his greatest.

It is not necessary to share Diderot's contempt for the actor but we must be aware of it because it is an essential factor of the celebrated paradox. To make clear that the sensibility of actors is not the root of their art, Diderot vigorously asserts that true actors have no sensibility to sacrifice, nor much of anything else for that matter. "What leads to their infatuation with the stage? The lack of education, poverty and libertinage. The theatre is an expedient, never a choice." In short, "one never becomes an actor for the love of virtue." If this is so, whence do actors get these admirable feelings which they express so forcefully? In point of fact they do not have such feelings at all, they mimic them and their imitation of these feelings is all the more perfect the more they themselves are completely devoid of them.

The core of the problem posed by the actor's art appears here in all its fullness. Is it possible for the actor to practice this art without sacrificing his own personality, provided he has one, or must he be without one at all so that he can always be ready to assume what Diderot so aptly called "a borrowed soul?" Here is his awesome judgment: "It has been said that actors have no character whatsoever, because by acting all of them they lose the one which nature gave them, that they become false just as the doctor, the surgeon and the butcher become callous. I believe that one has taken the cause for the effect and they are fitted to play all the characters because they have none." [11]

The interpretation of these testimonies is no easy task because they are compounded of disparate elements. Some are religious, others are moral, others social and related to living conditions that are no longer the same today or that have ceased to exist. Nowadays actors and actresses are in no sense recruited as they seem to have been in Diderot's time, if we are to believe his testimony. Moreover, there were always exceptions at all times, even in the hostile judgments pronounced upon the theatrical profession: Roscius, Garrick and other famous names can be cited in protest against summary condemnations which are contradicted by some cases of a striking character.

11. Diderot, *Paradox sur le comédien* (Paris: Pléiade), pp. 1065–1067, 1068, 1070, 1071–1072.

Finally, it must not be forgotten that plays have been performed by other than professional actors. The desire to
appear on stage is extraordinarily widespread. All, or
nearly all, children love to do so. Religious schools, especially those of the Society of Jesus, include theatrical performances in their educational programs. The fashionable
theatre flourished in the seventeenth and eighteenth centuries. Plays were staged at Cirey, Ferney, and Coppet, and
not only Molière and Voltaire but also Louis XIV and
Frederick II walked the boards. Consequently, it seems
impossible that the judgment upon the art of the actor,
and above all of the actress, could have been as summary as
we have just seen.

Upon closer examination it will be noticed that these
testimonies converge toward a kind of focus located
beyond religion, social convention and even morality. The
scandals described by Bossuet, assuming they were real,
were also found outside the world of the theatre. The
court and the Church itself had their share of them, and
the "good society" of the eighteenth century was not
exempt from those described by Diderot. But we see a
wholly different idea gradually emerge by way of censures
of this kind, that of the alienation from his personality to
which the actor must acquiesce, at least in part, if he
makes the theatre his calling. Diderot had in mind the professional actor who cannot choose his parts when he described him as a marvelous puppet whose strings are pulled
by the poet.[12] If we disregard what is exasperating and,
moreover, inexact about the comparison because an actor
is not a marionette, the fact remains that the actor views
himself as one on whom different forms of being are
imposed from without and which he must successively

12. Op. cit., p. 1065.

assume. Let us ponder Goethe's reply to Eckermann when the latter asked him how to choose a new member of the company for the theatre at Weimar. If he's a young beginner, Goethe observed, he should be chosen if he has, among other things, enough self-control to appear in the most favorable light, that is to say, to act in a play for his personal benefit. Thereupon he added, "The profession requires continual self-denial and a continued existence in a foreign mask." [13] Is the mark of the genuine actor, therefore, the fact that he never stops play-acting? Surely not, but what Goethe meant to say is that he is unceasingly called upon to insert a fictional self of his own creation between himself and his spectator. Perhaps Baudelaire got closer to the truth by pointing out that the actor's art can be compared to the world's oldest profession only

13. Goethe's *Conversations with Eckermann,* tr. by John Oxenford (New York: E. P. Dutton & Company, Everyman's Library, New York, 1930), p. 100. An observation made in the conversation of April 14, 1825. Charles Dullin forcefully declared: *"The playwright is the master of the theatre.* All the actor can do is to bring his inventions to life, the stage manager cannot animate any other ensemble save the one foreseen by the author. Let us repeat, all the substance is given by the playwright." Charles Dullin's remarks in H. Gouhier, *L'essence du théâtre,* pp. IV–V. This temporary and willed abdication of his personality for the sake of a simulacrum is the enduring substance of the problem.

All roles are not equally heavy to bear; there are even some light ones, but some are such that the actors or actresses who tax themselves to embody them nightly for months, sometimes for years, end up by feeling the need of liberating themselves of it like an obsession. On the psychological problem, see the remarks commented on by H. Gouhier, *L'oeuvre théâtrale* (Paris: Flammarion, 1958), p. 23, footnote 14. This note refers in addition to André Villiers, *La psychologie du comédien* (Paris: O. Lieutier, 1946). The moral conclusion is obvious: can one, without danger, accept feigning to be (sometimes, or often, for a long time) a being whom he is not and whose substance is made of the person that one really is?

with reservations, for it does not involve either the same act or the same end.[14]

The feature common to all these observations is that they were made by writers who adopted the public's point of view and who were even on the side of that public for whom the theatre is primarily an erotic spectacle. Such a view forgets that the art of the actress, about which nothing is said, could not be wholly different from that of the actor, and above all that the actor by definition sees things from the "other side of the footlights," so different in all respects from that of the orchestra pit. For the actor, acting is work. Furthermore, it is arduous, long and painstaking work during which a show must be staged. The show, if the efforts of the cast are crowned with success, is accomplished only after numerous, wearisome rehearsals. Failure is discouraging, but success means that the actor must rehearse the same part every day, when not twice on the same day, for weeks, for months, sometimes for years. Certainly the objections raised against the actor's art are not without foundation, but they are one-sided. They

14. "The considerations relative to the courtesan, up to a certain point, can be applied to the actress. For she too is a creature of display, an object of public pleasure. But here the conquest, the prey, is of a more noble, more spiritual nature. It is a question of obtaining general approval not only through pure physical beauty, but also through the talents of the rarest order. If on the one hand the actress is akin to the courtesan, on the other she borders upon the poet. Let us not forget that apart from natural and even artificial beauty, there is in all beings an idiom of the trade, a characteristic that can be translated physically into ugliness, but also into a kind of professional beauty." Charles Baudelaire, "Le peintre de la vie moderne," in *Curiosités esthétiques, Oeuvres* (Paris: Pléiade), p. 916. Here we deliberately avoid engaging in an exegesis of the famous texts of Fusées (op. cit., p. 1189): "What is art? Prostitution." Is there a single trade which the writer does not think he can practice, by writing it?

overlook the actor's curious vocation—of which very few of the audience have any personal experience—which is born from an innate desire to create out of his substance another human being, imaginary no doubt but offering all the appearance of a real human being. They overlook the correlative desire to contribute one's share to the production of the collective reality which is the play, composed of men and women who consecrate part of their lives to the effort required to produce it. The moralist does not know what it is to feel the elements of the play falling neatly into place, the parts finding their right tone and gradually harmonizing with each other until the day when, although the outcome is almost totally uncertain, the director feels in his bones that the play is ready for public performance. The ultimate meaning of the vocation of actor and actress is this final moment at the end of the performance when the whole "cast" comes on the stage to receive the hoped-for applause from the public. And why should the public applaud if not because it feels that all this effort has been extended for its benefit and that now it behooves the audience to thank the actors for the pleasure they have just given.

Please the public. Corneille, Molière, Racine vied with each other in quoting this Golden Rule which so many others put into practice after them. Please the public, indeed, but by giving it what sort of pleasure? If it is a question of eroticism, the lowest forms of the music hall (which is much better than this suggests, if it wants to be) and the indescribable commerce of sexual excitation, to which a notable part of films are dedicated nowadays, are able to purvey cheaply to millions of spectators all the merchandise of this kind that they can desire. It is art for *voyeurs.* But the theatre as art is something quite different. Its object is to present to the public serious drama or comedies, operas or ballets which offer the eye, ear and mind the spectacle of works conceived and executed with beauty alone as the end in view. The public is quite aware of this. If upon leaving the theatre the spectator must make an effort to re-enter the real world from which the play, comedy or opera have temporarily liberated him, it is proof that for a few hours art has succeeded in imparting the illusion of an imaginary life. This temporary removal from his selfhood and his environment has pleased the spectator, and by applauding he is expressing to the cast his appreciation for this pleasure. Thus we have shifted the problem but, even if the reasons for doing so were serious, we have not in the least changed its nature thereby. The profession of the actor depends upon the manner in which he can and wishes to exercise it.[15] It is not surprising that its exercise poses problems; they arise every time that the human being is in question. We can recall in this connection that the human being ought to be treated as an end, never as a means, but how many times does he not voluntarily sacrifice himself to ends that tran-

15. In his engaging preface to *Tartuffe,* Molière quite appropriately recalls the religious origins of drama from the Ancients up to the "holy plays of Monsieur de Corneille, which have been the admiration of all France." The need to defend himself leads him to consider "the Comedy in itself, to see if it is condemnable." He defines it as "an ingenious poem which, through pleasurable lessons, reproves the faults of men." Everything which follows which begins with: "I confess that there have been times when Comedy has been corrupt. And what is there in this world that one does not corrupt every day?" is at once very forcefully and cogently expressed and, if we pay attention to it, with an extreme wariness. For in the end when he says "even the holiest things are not sheltered from the corruption of men," Cardinal de Retz, the archbishop of Paris, would have shown bad grace to deny it. And as regards the private life of the Very Christian King, Bossuet himself assuredly was informed.

scend him? The public's applause expresses the grateful admiration it feels for those who have let it share in the creative joys of art.

The play is a "well-contrived poem" said Molière; and Pierre Corneille wrote a *Discours sur le poème dramatique.* Indeed a play is a *poiema,* something that is made, the result of a *poiesis,* or fabrication, which is the work of an artisan, the *poietes.* In short, a play is the product of a poietic activity. Yet it is not a poem, for a poem is made with words, whereas a play is made with actors who are human beings impersonating characters. The characters themselves speak and act, but they say only what the author makes them say and do only what he prescribes they are to do. Hence the author is here the first cause of the dramatic work. Is it possible to define this work in terms of its essence? [16]

The words of ordinary language are not intended to express philosophical notions, even when the object of these notions is the work of art. Since we must make a detour here, let us start out from a distinction for which our language has no words either but which are happily found in German: *Geschichte,* history as event, that happens (*geschiet*), and *Historie,* history as narration, that is told. If we had a recording apparatus that could note all events as they were taking place, the result of this notation would be chaotic. To render it intelligible it would have to be cut up into a number of fragments, as in narrative history. Hegel's *Philosophy of History* is an excellent example of

16. The problem is approached from all sides in the excellent work by Henri Gouhier, *L'essence du théâtre* (op. cit.) to which we also add his *L'oeuvre théâtrale* (op. cit.). Both books, written by a philosopher who is well informed about the theatrical production of his time and familiar with the world of the theatre, in every respect go beyond the restricted frame of my own reflections. I cannot restrain my envy for the richness of their insights, but it is a satisfaction to think that they are the work of a friend.

this reconstruction of events that have occurred since the beginning of the world, as they have affected man and to the extent in which some documents have preserved a memory of them. In Hegel's works events are arranged in groups roughly corresponding to the major peoples known to us and intelligibly linked to one another within these groupings in terms of a principle of causality. We see peoples form, grow and perish, and within these peoples the social classes, the leaders of men in all orders, sometimes even vast unities created by the Spirit expressly for the purpose of assembling the greatest number of particular events possible under a single category. History in that case fashions its myths, such as the Middle Ages, the Renaissance, the century of Louis XIV and other fictions of the same kind which are universally accepted because of their convenience. The feature common to all these groups is that they obey a scheme: they have a beginning, a middle and an end. Beginnings or birth, maturity or perfection, decadence and death, thus does narrative history view the intelligible elements that it cuts up as events in the continuity of history in order to find a meaning in it or to confer a meaning upon it, if it has none.

The event is the intelligible unit of real history. Generally speaking, an event is anything that happens, but history retains only a minuscule part of what does happen; what it retains of it, that is to say the historical event, is a privileged event. For a great variety of reasons, such as its greatness, nobility, beauty, but most often because the event in itself summarizes the meaning of a determined historical situation, the historian sets it aside from the others for closer scrutiny. Whatever it may be, the historical event is never a brute fact; history takes possession of it so that it may not remain in the raw state, and what it does with it is already a history, with a beginning, a middle and an end.

Invented narratives obey the same law. Anecdotes which we polish for a long time to achieve a perfection of form, tales, stories, novels in prose or verse, all these imaginary histories individually form a complete whole; we know where each one begins, how it develops and also how it ends. The story-teller assumes the responsibility for arousing our curiosity, and he must satisfy it. The dramatist also invents a human event similar to those that history relates, but instead of telling the story like the novelist, he lets it transpire on a stage by having it acted out by actors before an audience. The author himself may or may not play a part in it. Shakespeare and Molière were both authors and actors, but this is not necessary. The author as such invents the human event which he intends to bring on the stage; if he draws his inspiration from history, he chooses the event and decides what elements of it to retain, the essential thing always being that actors will undertake to portray it. If, for example, the event in question is the assassination of Julius Caesar, the dramatist will reconstruct the series of events leading to the crime. The play is an event that happens on stage according to the dramatist's decision and the order that he has freely decided upon in advance.

Like any event, the one which the play portrays has a beginning, a middle and an end, whose reciprocal relationships impart being to the play by imparting unity to it. Since its unity is that of a whole, it can consist only in the relationship between the parts which allows them to be conceived as a discrete and distinct grouping. This is why the author, actors and spectators agree on the need for an exposition which describes the situation from which one starts. It is the point of departure for the event. The great dramatic enterprises confirm this concern to the point where the work itself is preceded by a prologue

which serves to situate, so to speak, the play's absolute
point of departure: the *Prologue in Heaven* of the first
Faust, *Das Rheingold* for Wagner's Ring Cycle, or that
other prologue in heaven which forms the first scene of
Claudel's *The Satin Slipper,* in which the Jesuit Father
takes his leave from the world so that he can entrust his
brother to God. This grand play begins with a death,
which is an absolute, in itself the reason why death ends so
many plays. Comedy often ends with a marriage because
it too marks the end of a life and the absolute beginning
of another. This does not constitute "a slice of life," as
some have called it, in the first place because life is not cut
up into slices which have only two ends but neither
a beginning or end, and in the second place because the theatre is not life, but the appearance of life. The living
being, says Aristotle, has its cause in itself, whereas the
product of art has its cause outside itself. This is what permits the dramatist, who is the cause of his play, to freely
assign it an absolute beginning and end. The actors and
the stagehands interrupt their real lives so as to be at hand
at the moment when the three traditional knocks, which
also have a beginning, a middle and an end, mark the
beginning of the acts which are to simulate life on the
stage. *Faust* begins in heaven, *Don Juan* ends in hell; the
whole intermediate period is made up of words and gestures regulated by the dramatist and which are the very
substance of the work. We will concede all the possible
derogations of these general rules, but the authors do not
abuse them, for if the play is to come to life the public's
curiosity must be satisfied. At bottom this curiosity is only
a requirement of the mind which always wants to grasp an
event through its cause and demands that it be carried out
to its end in order that it may be, and be intelligible. Thus
we are back to the observation made long ago by Aristotle,

and which was taken up again by Corneille: a play must represent a whole action and that to be whole means "to have a beginning, a middle, and an end." [17]

The proper work of a playwright therefore is the invention of this action performed on stage before a public. It is the actual performance of the play that constitutes its reality. This is the end to which all the rest is ordered and subordinated: the work of the actors, staging, décor, costumes, hair-does, make-up, lighting, music and dance if called for. Whether or not he takes part in the performance, the author is a kind of creative demiurge, in the Platonic sense, of a cosmos that owes its existence to him. He knows it, and doubtlessly this demiurgic aspiration is hidden in the background of the dramatist's vocation. If he could, the author would like to engender the play solely through his will and thought, the way God created the world. At least, he would like to be able to be all the characters at once. Molière in the *Impromptu de Versailles* has Mlle. Molière say to him: "May I tell you that you ought to have written a comedy where you would have played all alone." All that Molière can come up with as a rejoinder is: "Hold your tongue, wife, you're an ass!" But since the remark actually originated with him, Molière knew that it was eminently fitting. Hence this characteristic that so clearly marks the dramatist, and which distinguishes him from the immateriality of the poet whose creation is accomplished entirely in the mind; namely his

17. Aristotle, *Poetics*, Ch. 7, 1450b, (op. cit.), p. 634. See also preceding passages, which are of a definitive character, on the primacy of action in tragedy, in which the personages do not act to imitate their character, but in which their character results from the action, VI, 1450a, 27, p. 631. On tragedy as the representation of an action, 1450b, 3, p. 633. The unity is not that of a personage, but of "one action, a complete whole," containing only elements that it would be impossible to transpose or withdraw without affecting the whole: VIII, 1451a, 30–35, p. 635.

love for the orchestra, above all for the stage and for everything that transpires on it. He is dedicated to this *mundus scaenicus* where reigns a semblance that deceives nobody, with its décors and painted cardboard cities, its actors and actresses, fashioners of illusion, its invented action without concern for the true and all the ingenious fakery which contributes to create the illusion desired, willed and acquiesced to by all.[18] Only one thing matters to the author for as long as he is engaged in writing his play, namely that the world which the theatre accepts is his own work. The public demands only that this invented world captivate its attention and hold its interest so completely that it will temporarily forget the real life which the spectacle has suspended. To achieve such an effect this world must possess a feigned reality sufficient unto itself. The form, of which all the rest is like matter, consists of this infinitely subtle, fragile relationship of the parts of the work to the whole and which mere nothing can destroy.

18. To cite an example among a hundred, Goethe was a man of the theatre to his fingertips. He knew that a theatre had to make money in order to exist and said that "Shakespeare and Molière did not think differently." Everything interested him from the recruitment and training of actors and actresses up to the architecture of the building. Goethe's *Conversations with Eckermann* abound with observations on this subject, notably the entry of March 22, 1825: "Anyone who is sufficiently young, and who is not quite spoiled, could not easily find any place that would suit him so well as a theatre . . ." etc. (op. cit., p. 92); his remembrances of the time he directed the theatre at Weimar (pp. 93–94) (Schiller and their common concern to gain entry into the best circles for actors and actresses), above all, perhaps, the entry of January 29, 1926: "I was really interested in the theatre only so long as I could have a practical influence upon it. It was my delight to bring the establishment to a high degree of perfection; and when there was a performance, my interest was not so much in the pieces as in observing whether the actors played as they ought. . . ." etc. (op. cit., p. 127).

The necessity for unity explains the classic rule of the three unities, for as preposterous as it is the rule had a reason for being and, moreover, nothing prohibits the dramatist from subjecting himself to it if he pleases. Actually, only one law seems necessary: the unity of action without which the play would not exist since the event that the action represents is the very substance of the work. It can be the unity of a fable or even of several fables woven together into one, but the more deeply the unity of action is rooted in the characters the more coherent it is and the more does the play take on substantiality.

The simplest way of obtaining the maximum unity is to let it emerge from that of one or two of the main characters, moved from within by some ordinary passion or from without by some fatality. This is why so many tragic or comic plays bear the name of a hero or of a type, whose role is the *title role. Hamlet, The Misanthrope, The Miser, Faust* dominate the plays in which they appear and which are ordered mainly around them. Therefore, the invention of the play necessarily implies that of characters who will accomplish the human acts which make up the event. The creation of types like Alceste, Harpagon or others like them is often considered as the triumph of genius in an author. In any case, it offers a chance for the success and duration of his work because there will always be actors who will want to revive such composite roles which can give greater scope to their talents. But at the heart of the concern which animates him, the dramatist finds the desire to obtain to a certainty the maximum ontological density for his work by ensuring it the maximum of unity. The actor who "revives" a role of this kind occupies in relation to him a situation like the individual-species relationship in Aristotle's philosophy. Actors resemble each other as being possible Hamlets, Phèdres or Tartuffes, but all are different from each other and this clearly shows that the role has no existence of its own, it exists only in that it is played.

This strict unity, closely related to that of a character or a situation, is not necessary. The unity of a fable suffices, for it is enough that the public watching the play perceives and understands the action as being of one piece.[19] The unities of time and place are scarcely important and, in fact, they have never been observed. It would be really absurd to impose them for the sake of plausibility, for in the theatre nothing is plausible beginning with the place itself, the actors and the public. In what sense is it more plausible to compress into three hours an action that ought to last twenty-four hours, or for that matter twenty-four years? The unity of place is even more arbitrary. Corneille, on whom these restrictions weighed heavily, noted the price that the observance of this rule entails.[20] Moreover, do we not go to the theatre to enjoy the improbable and to find in it relief from what is all too commonplace in reality? Corneille perceived this too,[21] but he lacked the boldness to free himself.

In an absolute sense the creation of the dramatic form does not require writing, but most often it is through this form that it is fixed and transmitted. In any case, the fable itself is the only part of the dramatic work that must necessarily be invented and executed by the author. In the

19. P. Corneille, *Discours sur le poème dramatique,* beginning of the second discourse: "the unity of action in comedy consists in the unity of plot, or of obstacles to the plans of the principal actors, and in the tragedy in the unity of danger, whether the hero succumbs to it or whether he escapes it."

20. *Discours sur le poème dramatique,* second discourse: "As regards the unity of place . . . ," particularly "The same does not apply in *Rodogune* . . ."

21. *Discours sur le poème dramatique,* beginning of the first discourse, where Corneille declares "very wrong" the maxim that "the subject of a tragedy must be plausible."

dance theatre, or ballet, the action is invented by the author of the scenario and the choreographer; in the opera by the author of the libretto and the musician; in comedy or tragedy, in which the events are the actions of persons as talking animals, language is the natural means of expression. This is not absolutely necessary, however, since action can be mimed. At all events the gestures, attitudes, and facial movements will play their role, but in the theatre, as in reality, these accessory means of expression will be ordered around the principal one, namely the human voice. Not only will the characters talk but they will talk much more than real persons do, for the latter think, reflect and spend much more time in silently preparing the acts that they intend to carry out. In short, they are silent for a longer time than a character in a play being performed in a theatre is allowed to be. The author views the creation of the character, through whom the action will take place, essentially as the invention of the lines that he will have to speak before the audience. He can indicate some stage business, if he desires, but essentially Molière's *Don Juan* consists only of words which he puts into his hero's mouth. Therein lies its whole substance, and it is up to the actor to do the rest. Hence the dramatist will inevitably be a writer.[22]

22. Since the work of art has its cause outside itself it is not answerable, like the works of nature, to the principle of the unity of substantial form in the structure. On the contrary, it is a remarkable example of the case in which the doctrine of the plurality of forms is applicable. This is particularly true in the theatrical work. The author imagines a sequence of possible events presenting a certain unity of action. In order to impart existence to it, the writer must have recourse to other persons, none of whom is the author of the play but each one of whom practices a particular art, or represents a particular technique, all of whom, however, contribute to imparting to the theatrical work the actual existence to which it aspires. Each of them acts as a subordinate form to the principal form, which arranges them into an hierarchical order.

To say that a play is a written work before being spoken is a confirmation of this obvious fact. But from this it does not follow that a play is at one and the same time a written work by virtue of its essence and its destination. It is possible that the performance adds nothing to the literary beauty of the great dramatic works, especially if the reader is himself a writer who reads them as a writer, but a play is first of all written with a view to being heard and it is not well-written unless the text grips the imagination of the public when it is spoken on the stage by actors. This quality distinguishes what is "well-written" from what is "well-written for the theatre." A man of the theatre no doubt can form an opinion merely by reading the play, but the performance is the crucial test. Racine was an incomparably better writer than Corneille and Molière, but they were better writers for the stage than Racine because with them language itself was always action. Real dramatic dialogue, that which is well-written for the stage, is that which the writer creates as a language that is spoken and even acted. One of the major difficulties which a dramatist must overcome is to refrain from writing except when under the command of imaginary voices already "on stage" in his own being in those parts which real actors some day will play on the boards. The eighteenth century bequeathed us a quantity of very well-written plays whose language, however, is devoid of theatrical virtue. A critic in the nineteenth century would have occasioned surprise by declaring Victor Hugo's language, as theatrical dia-

From the banker and the theatre director, by way of the stage manager, the actors, including the costume designer, the hairdresser, the dressmaker, in short all those whose names must be listed at the beginning of a film or on the program, each one of whom is commissioned to do well what he can do and pursues the particular end that the structure of the play imposes upon him. Here the highest form does not dispense with the lower forms; without them, indeed, it could do nothing.

logue, to be inferior to that of Alfred de Musset. If necessary we can "explain" a play by Racine as we would
explain a canto of the *Aeneid,* but the authoritative commentary of a great work that is essentially dramatic is
beyond the competence of a purely literary culture.
"Rodriguez, do you have a heart?" "Allow me to say two
words, Count! . . . . Sire, Sire, justice. Ah! Sire, listen to
us!" What have such utterances to do with the art of "writing well?" Here the beauty of language in itself is not the
aim of the work as it would be in poetry; what is aimed
at here is the beauty of the play performed on stage to
which the beauty of language must be subordinated in
order to serve it. Theatrical styles are infinitely varied; but
all of them as a whole differ from the other styles which
narrate only for the sake of narration and sing only for the
sake of singing. The best theatrical style is that which finds
the perfection proper to it by coinciding with the action.
No doubt it would be better to reverse the proposition
and say that action creates style. This is the deep root of
Shakespeare's supremacy as a playwright: his poetry is the
very substance of theatre. It would be difficult to go beyond *The Tempest* in this direction. If ever there was a
"prodigious magician" it was certainly he who made theatre out of dreams. For Prospero is a dream, but Shakespeare commissions a real man to tell us that dreams are
the stuff of which man is made.

Here reflection reaches the point where it would be
wise to pause if we wish to avoid the charge of engaging
in useless subtlety. But perhaps we should risk taking one
or two more steps so that the profound nature of the theatrical work will not escape our apprehension now that
we have come to the end of our effort.

We have sufficiently stressed, perhaps too much, that
the theatre is essentially dedicated to the presentation of
all events embodied in persons who actually exist. This is

true, but perhaps it is necessary to determine exactly whether the theatrical work does not create any other existence save that of an illusion without any reality of its own. The actors exist, but the characters do not. When Mounet-Sully appeared at the curtain-call with his beautiful blood-stained head, the audience was not applauding Oedipus but him, the actor, the real intercessor between the beauty conceived by the poet and us who had seen it through him. Oedipus does not exist, even when he is being played on the stage; he does not exist either as an individual or as an event. It is only his representation that exists, and if we want to speak of the existential vocation of the theatre, the existence of the representation alone can be the object of discussion. This is the reason, moreover, why the actor is a creator of beauty and it is the artist in him whom we applaud.

We know that the reality of the theatre is in truth but appearance and if we examine the feelings of the spectator closely we will probably see that he never completely loses his awareness that he is watching theatre. Nor do any of us wish him to do so, for it is as a work of art that the semblance which the theatre creates enchants us. We see young children brought too early to the theatre, for it is not as an art that it interests them. They believe in the reality of what they see and are afraid. Fortunately, no book of etiquette exists on how to enjoy oneself at the theatre; the only practically certain rule to go by as we enter is to leave philosophy at the door. But once we have experienced this, there is no law against thinking that one of the best ways of enjoying ourselves in the theatre is to surrender naively to what it can give us, provided only that we know how to receive it as the pure pleasure of art.

It is not necessarily the pleasure of a pure art. It is useful to recall this now that we have arrived at the last of the major arts, with our discussion of the theatre. Let us recall here that all the arts are rightfully connected with each other since all have the creation of beauty as their aim. Moreover, they remain free to pool the resources which are proper to each one and which each art has at its disposal, provided only that they observe an architectonic order among themselves and, so to speak, a hierarchy among the forms of the arts with which one of them enters into partnership and subjects to its own end. Of no other major art is this as true as it is of the theatre. It could almost be said that the notion of pure art is never posed with respect to the theatre. Since it is capable of representing virtually any event whatsoever, *a priori* we can see no reason why the cooperation of any other art ought to be forbidden in the theatre if it helps it attain its proper end. Greek art combined architecture, the dance, music and poetry in the drama. Perhaps the art of the theatre secretly aspires to subsume under its own form the greatest number of elements possible in the other arts. Racine himself admitted that when he received the invitation to write for the theatre of Saint-Cyr it awakened in him the plan to which he had often given thought, namely "to combine as in the ancient Greek tragedies the chorus and the singing with the action, and to use that section of the chorus which the pagans used to sing the praises of their false divinities to sing the praises of the true God." Here religion itself is once again associated with the theatre as it seems to have been in its beginnings. But neither comedy nor tragedy is necessary to the theatre. Reduced to the role of pretext in the ballet comedy, they are absorbed by music in the opera or in the musical comedy, both of which, however, belong to the theatre. Everything can legitimately be tried, given up, revived, varied, adorned or stripped of its adornments, for in contrast to knowledge which takes cognizance of its object, the function of art is to create its own object in freedom and for beauty's sake.

INDEX

Liszt, Franz, 149, 180n, 196
Literary Comedy (Sainte-Beuve), 14
Littré, 3, 212, 251
L'oeil écoute (Claudel), 232n
Louis XIV, 108, 261

Madame Bovary (Flaubert), 34, 35
Madame Pasta, *see* Negri, Judith
Magnus, Albert, 10
Mallarmé, Stéphane, 38, 90, 214, 216,
    223, 230, 231n, 232n, 233
Malherbe, de, François, 216n, 239
Mariolini, Marietta, 100
Marquis-Sébie, Daniel, 81n
Massine, Léonide, 201
Melanotte, Adelaide, 150
Mengs, Anton Raphael, 95n
Michaut, Pierre, 205n
Michelangelo, 30, 80, 84, 87, 91, 95,
    104
Molière, 170, 219n, 245n, 247n, 251,
    252, 261, 264, 265n, 266, 268, 270,
    271n, 274, 275
Mondor, Henri, 38n, 176n, 231n
Montaigne, de, M. E., 14, 238n
Monteverdi, Claudio, 72
Moses (Church of St. Peter-in-
    Chains, Venice), 103
Mozart, W. A., 153, 153n, 155, 176n,
    183, 207n, 245n
Murray, John Middleton, 227
Musset, de, Alfred, 222

Name and Nature of Poetry, The
    (Housman), 229n
Negri, Judith, 150
Nisard, Désiré, 228, 228n
Njinsky, 190n, 200
*Notice sur la vie et les oeuvres de
    Charles Girault* (Widor) 42n
Notre-Dame de Paris, 74
Notre-Dame-du-Port (Clermont), 65

Odyssey (Homer), 246
Ortensio, Mauro 173n
Ovid, 222
Ozenfant, Amédée, 140n

Paganini, Nicolò, 196
Printing and Reality (Gilson), 12

Parthenon, 73
Pascal, Blaise, 12, 230
Perrot, Georges, 200
Petrarch, Francesco, 243
Phidias, 87
Philosophy of History (Hegel), 267
Piccini, Niccolò, 151
Pietà (Michelangelo), 91, 103, 104
Pirro, André, 173n
Plato, 120n, 192, 256, 256n, 270
Praxiteles, 87
Poétique de l'espace (Bachelard), 233
Poussin, Gaspard, 109, 125, 176n
Préludes (Chopin), 11
Profils des Conquérants (Carcopino),
    102n
Puget, Pierre, 87
Pyramids (Egypt), 48

Quintillian, 108

Racine, Jean Baptiste, 35n, 90, 129,
    220, 235, 239, 246n, 247n, 264, 275,
    276, 278
Radio City Music Hall Rockettes
    (New York), 189
Rameau, Jean Philippe, 164
Raphael, 131
Ravaisson-Mollien, Jean, 8, 67
Ravel, Maurice Joseph, 206
Read, Herbert, 100n
Rimbaud, Arthur, 220
Rodin, Auguste, 91, 93
Roland-Manuel, 175n, 176n
*Une leçon d'Antoine Bourdelle à
    la Grande Chaumière* (Marquis-
    Sébie), 81n
*Réflexions critiques sur la poésie et
    sur la peinture* (du Bos, Abbé), 107
Rossini, G. A., 150
Rousseau, Jean Baptiste, 236
Rubens, Peter-Paul, 25, 131
Ruskin, John, 72n

Sacchini, Antonio, 151
Sainte-Beuve, C. A., 14, 15, 37, 216,
    216n, 221, 246n, 247n
Sainte-Chapelle, 74
Sainte-Foy de Conques, 65